INDIRA GANDHI'S EMERGENCE AND STYLE

BY THE SAME AUTHOR

Prison and Chocolate Cake, 1954
From Fear Set Free, 1962

NOVELS

A Time to be Happy, 1958
This Time of Morning, 1965
Storm in Chandigarh, 1969
The Day in Shadow, 1971
A Situation in New Delhi, 1977

HISTORY

The Freedom Movement in India, 1970

POLITICS

A Voice for Freedom, 1977

Indira Gandhi's Emergence and Style

NAYANTARA SAHGAL

CAROLINA ACADEMIC PRESS
Durham, North Carolina

Published in the United States by
CAROLINA ACADEMIC PRESS
2206 Chapel Hill Road
Box 8791 Forest Hills Station
Durham, N.C. 27707

in arrangement with
Vikas Publishing House Pvt Ltd, New Delhi

ISBN 0-89089-090-0

Library of Congress Catalog Card No. 78-54439

Printed in India

To
John Kenneth Galbraith
in Gratitude

INTRODUCTION

This book originated with a paper I contributed in March 1974 to a conference on Leadership in South Asia at the School of Oriental and African Studies at the University of London.

As I worked on this paper during 1973 I discovered Mrs Gandhi's style was not only different from that of her two pre-decessors—something to be expected since style depends on a national situation as well as individual personality—but that it represented a clear departure in political values and behaviour since independence. It was a basic difference, a repudiation of India's assimilative, absorptive tradition. India has survived as an entity, in spite of its checkered political history, because of this cultural capacity for containing and cradling its contradictions. In Mrs Gandhi, it seemed to me, we had an unfamiliar element on our leadership scene whose style arose out of fundamentally different values. The essence of Indian politics before her time had been diversity of opinion, institutions and channels for its expression, and a wholehearted acceptance of the nurture of these diverse strands as essential to the democratic faith and system. But not only a system needed their nurture. It was regarded as necessary for the growth and blossoming of a people, who had for centuries lived under all kinds of disabilities—social, economic, political, and psychological. With Mrs Gandhi, this atmosphere, along with the political structures it involved, the climate of debate and dissent it had encouraged, and the human give-and-take it had engendered, both within the ruling party, and between the ruling party and the opposition, began to be eroded. A simple formula of for-and-against, either-or replaced it. A stage throbbing with vibrant life began to narrow; the lights playing upon it became fewer; the characters began to vanish; until one person occupied the spotlight. Long before my paper was written, this development was already taking place. I came to the conclusion we were moving inexorably towards an authoritarian order, not because the Indian situation demanded it, but because of the particular character in charge of us, driven by needs of her own nature which had very little to do with the reason and rhyme of the Indian situation. The paper ended at 1973, and I said at the time I devoutly hoped to be proved wrong. The following year, however, Mrs Gandhi's style, had reduced politics to a state of confrontation from which nothing but dictatorship could emerge.

I decided to expand my paper into a book, but before I could begin, Mrs Gandhi had declared an emergency. The doors to impartial knowledge, information, and inquiry were closed. Many people whose opinions I would have sought were in prison. Some had gone underground to escape arrest. All known critics of the establishment were under vigilance or some form of harassment. And there was censorship. I decided to write the book in spite of these difficulties, to contribute my own knowledge and interpretation of the Indian Prime Minister, and of Indian events, to an understanding of recent developments in India. I felt this was of great importance at a time when no view but the official one could be expressed in India. For me it had a symbolic importance, too, as an act of freedom on behalf of the voices the emergency had silenced in my country. Above all, I was moved to write in memory of my uncle, Jawaharlal Nehru, whose life was given to India's struggle for freedom and to the building of a free society.

I could not have written this book without an invitation from the Radcliffe Institute, giving me the opportunity, from June to December 1976, to work in peace and privacy, surrounded by friendliness and warmth, and with help always at hand if I needed it. My project and pronouncements were noted and reported home by our diplomatic mission. The Indian embassy in Washington and the Indian Consulate General in New York paid me an unintended compliment when they sent senior representatives to report on my Colloquium at the Radcliffe Institute in November 1976 and my speech to the international affairs department at Columbia University in December.

I was relieved of the burden of domestic chores during these six months by E.N. Mangat Rai, with whom it has been my good fortune to share the last nine years of my life, and who, long before Women's Lib was heard of, had accepted both men and women as emancipated enough to tackle whatever responsibilities came there way.

Principally I owe this opportunity to Professor John Kenneth Galbraith. I have no words to thank him for his exceeding kindness, interest, and support. My gratitude extends to the hospitable home at 30 Francis Avenue, Cambridge, Massachusetts, of which I now feel a part.

Cambridge, Massachusetts   NAYANTARA SAHGAL
USA

CONTENTS

CONTENTS

CHAPTER ONE

INDIA'S THIRD PRIME MINISTER IS CHOSEN

Indira Gandhi was forty-six years old when her father, Jawaharlal Nehru, died on 27 May 1964. Though she was not a major political personality, she had shown signs of temperament and preference in political matters. Since independence she had been her father's companion and hostess at New Delhi, and had accompanied him on official visits abroad. In 1955 she had been appointed to the Congress Working Committee, the party's executive, with charge of the women's and youth wings, and become a member of its two subsidiaries, the Central Parliamentary Board and the Central Election Committee, soon afterwards. These responsibilities placed her at the heart of election preparations for the second general election of 1957. Her emergence onto the scene of political and public endeavour took place during a period of marital strain and difficulty, and Nehru welcomed her increasing involvement in the party, both as the natural outcome of her background and as therapy for her troubled domestic life. The Congress Party's and his own championship of women's rights had been instrumental in creating a climate of pride in women's opportunities and achievements. It was a special satisfaction to him that his daughter, whose health and unhappy marriage had been a continuing anxiety to him, should now find a way to fulfil herself through national activity. He wrote to his sister, Vijayalakshmi Pandit, on 12 March 1957, from the family home at Anand Bhawan, Allahabad, where he had gone to cast his vote:

When voting finished today, large numbers of our Congress workers turned up at Anand Bhawan, including many women. Indu has specially shaken up the women, and even Muslim women came out. Indu has indeed grown and matured very greatly during the last year, and especially during these elections. She worked with effect all over India, but her special field was Allahabad City and District which she organised like a general preparing for battle. She is quite a heroine in Allahabad now and particularly with the women. Hardly eating and often carrying on with a handful of peanuts and a banana, she has been constantly on the move, returning at midnight, flushed, slightly gaunt but full of spirit and with flashing eyes.

In 1959, at the suggestion of its outgoing President, U.N. Dhebar, the Congress Party accepted her as his successor. Nehru did not think it was time for this distinction. His reservations were rooted deep in his respect for the process—personal, political, social, or economic—that lays sound foundations. Work was the crucible of human personality or political strength, and there were no shortcuts to excellence, a philosophy reflected in seventeen years of power that rejected the dramatic and the extreme, and relied on the building of institutions. He was averse to hustle and haste. Part of a generation well and truly tried through the struggle for freedom and the years of nation-building afterwards, he believed in time and trial. He was also concerned about his daughter's health, and the inappropriateness of her holding the party's highest office while he was Prime Minister. These considerations had to be balanced against his conviction that he should not stand in her way, a point of view pressed by Govind Ballabh Pant, Home Minister and close colleague. He decided not to intervene.

> I gave a good deal of thought to this matter and I came to the conclusion that I should firmly keep apart from this business and try not to influence it in any way, except rather generally and broadly to say that it had disadvantages...normally speaking, it is not a good thing for my daughter to come in as Congress President when I am Prime Minister.[1]

Mrs Gandhi accepted the office with tears in her eyes, and it was an emotional occasion for many present at the party meeting. Her father and grandfather were among the illustrious names in Congress annals who had held the distinction before her. Her elevation to the party's most prestigious post was its tribute to her

[1]*Times of India*, New Delhi, 8 February 1959.

family. After independence, the Congress President was almost invariably chosen on the basis of his previous experience in government. All party presidents between 1951 and 1969 were chief
ministers. Mrs Gandhi was the exception. Her earnestness was
looked upon with favour and her inexperience with indulgence.

She occupied the office, normally a two-year term, for barely a
year, though during this period she took two initiatives. She advised the division of Bomby state, convulsed at the time by agitations demanding its separation into Marathi and Gujarati-speaking states. Bombay was divided, bringing Maharashtra and Gujarat
into being on 1 May 1960. She also urged the Union government's
interference in Kerala, where the communist government formed
in 1957 was locked in a confrontation with the Roman Catholic
and Nair communities over the issue of state control of schools
and colleges. President's rule was established in Kerala, and fresh
elections held in 1960, when an alliance of parties led by the Congress won a majority. The outcome vindicated Mrs Gandhi's advice as immediately beneficial to the Congress. It also demonstrated her approach to "action" as the surgical gesture to forestal
possible developments. In contrast, Nehru's temperament made
use of the tentative in decision-making as an area of positive value
in arriving at action. The overthrow of communist rule took note
of the immediate situation, not of the meaning of the communist
phenomenon in Kerala. Chief Minister E.M.S. Namboodaripad
later remarked on Nehru's reluctance to declare President's rule.
The formation of a communist government in Kerala had seemed
to him "an intriguing development" and he had written to his sister,
Mrs Pandit, on 12 March 1957:

In another three or four days' time we shall have ninety percent
of the results, and this will give a clear picture of the States as
well as of Parliament . . . Kerala is heading for a Communist
majority. If so, there would presumably be a Communist government there. This will be the first occasion anywhere in the
world when a Communist Party wins an election through democratic means. . . . They have toned down very much, and the programme they have issued is quite moderate. Nevertheless, this
is an intriguing development.

Mrs Gandhi was not, as her father knew, well enough at the

time to carry an arduous responsibility and had been under a strain
for a long time. Writing to his sister in London from New Delhi,
on 11 January 1955, Nehru had said: "Indira has been unwell for
the last three weeks or so and mostly in bed. She has had rather
a bad attack of anaemia brought on partly by too much work and
rushing about. Behind that, of course, is worry and unhappiness."
She gave up the Congress presidentship and, without defining her
dissatisfaction, made it known she was not being allowed to do as
she wished in the party. She was operated for a kidney stone on
17 February 1960.

In 1964 she was still comparatively unnoticed in her own right,
and not seriously considered as a candidate for the succession to
Nehru. She had had no training in a profession and no experience
in government. Though her presence on the Working Committee
indicated high status in the party, she had worked for the organization behind the scenes, and of choice remained in the background. A
mother, occupied with caring for her two sons, she was devoted
and imaginative about their upbringing, always torn between domestic and public responsibilities. She correctly described herself
as a "private" person, so private indeed, that no one knew her
intimately. Her griefs were well-sheltered, her joys restrained.
There was almost a pathos about her personality for those who
tried to break through to it. It was a personality that would not
step out. Inevitably involved in politics, she had hung back from
the ultimate political trial—an election—declining at her father's
death to stand for the by-election to the Lok Sabha from his constituency, Phulpur, in Uttar Pradesh. It seemed right and proper,
an act of rededication to the values he had represented, for a
member of the family to contest Nehru's seat for the Congress in
November 1964. Mrs Gandhi's aunt, Vijayalakshmi Pandit, resigned as Governor of Maharashtra to contest and retain the constituency for her party, though not before she had made certain that
her niece did not want the seat.

A year later, on 6 December 1965, she had occasion to write to
her niece, now Minister for Information and Broadcasting in Lal
Bahadur Shastri's cabinet:

I have a feeling that you are not happy about my being in Phulpur. I am conscious of the fact that this seat should have been
yours by right. It is your today should you wish to have it.

Nothing would give me greater pleasure now or in 1967 to retire from this particular constituency for you and work elsewhere. You have only to say so and it will be done and, believe
me, done willingly. There are rumours that you do not wholly
approve of my political views. I have never made any declaration of where I stand because to me it seemed that adherence
to Congress implied loyal acceptance of its basic policies and
principles. I believe it is better in a country like our own to try
and live according to one's beliefs rather than talk about them.
This I try to do. I have during the sixteen years when I had
the privilege to serve India abroad tried to explain and implement India's policies to the best of my ability and understanding.
Since my return to public life here I have done what little I
could to sustain the ideas and ideals which Bhai gave to this
country. It is true I have not joined any groups but this is because all groups today are founded on expediency and I do not
approve of this.

I am a whole generation older than you are. I am at the end of
my career and in the evening of my life. There is no desire in
my mind to attempt to compete with the younger generation,
least of all with you. Indeed this would be rather ridiculous.

I had hoped that my presence in the political field would give
you strength and support. If the contrary is the case, then obviously there is something wrong and it must be remedied in the
larger interest which both you and I have at heart.

With love,
Puphi

Mrs Gandhi herself had been elected unopposed to the Rajya
Sabha after her cabinet appointment. Though she had taken part
in election campaigns, she had never faced the electorate herself,
and did not do so until 1967, more than a year after she became
Prime Minister, when the trial could no longer be postponed. She
expressed a positive distaste for politics, replying to her aunt's
letter on 7 December 1965:

I do not know who has been talking to you but there is absolutely no foundation in the remark that I am not happy at your
being in Phulpur. . . . It may seem strange that a person in politics should be wholly without political ambition but I am afraid

that I am that sort of a freak . . . . I did not want to come either to Parliament or to be in Government. However, there were certain compelling reasons at the time for my acceptance of this portfolio. Now there are so many crises one after another that every time seems to be the wrong time for getting out. . . .

She had been an observer, albeit close to the fount of power, during her father's lifetime. The party presidentship, like her earlier appointment to the Working Committee and its subsidiary bodies, had been bestowed on "Nehru's daughter," not positions she had earned through the rough apprenticeship of state politics with their numerous considerations of region, faction, and caste. She had not had to work her way up through the vast amorphous organization, or show outstanding talent, in order to be singled out. And she had shown no desire to stand out as a political or public personality. Her predominant image was one of retreat and extreme reserve. The country knew her as her father's companion and the mother of two boys. If her father was grooming her for prime ministership, there was not enough evidence of it in events, or in his own avowed aversion to undemocratic procedure, to make his colleagues unduly suspicious or jealous of the possibility, though some believed, nevertheless, that her presidentship of the party indicated he was doing so. Above all, her own personality had given them no cause for alarm. She did not have the recognizable ingredients of public appeal or charisma. She was expected to play a greater role in national affairs, and her political involvement had grown to the gradual exclusion of her personal and private life, but front-rank leadership was not an idea easily connected with her. The imposing will and determination she later displayed in public life had as yet left their mark only on the family circle. At her father's death, grieved and undecided about her immediate future, she made no move to enter the leadership fray. Nor did the party's High Command dwell on as a possibility.

In order to avoid a contest for leadership that would present a picture of discord at Nehru's death, senior leaders headed by Kamaraj, Congress President, worked to bring about a unanimous choice. The principle of consensus, not new to Congress politics, was used this way and defined as such for the first time, and Lal Bahadur Shastri was chosen Prime Minister as the neutral and most generally acceptable candidate.

Morarji Desai, cut out by this procedure, saw the situation differently. His standing in the party hierarchy was high and his ability proven during his chief ministership of Bombay state and his experience in Nehru's cabinet as Commerce and later Finance Minister. With a right based on his record to lead the country, he wanted an open contest that would set a healthy precedent for the post-Nehru Congress, enabling the party to throw up its own choice rather than one arranged behind the scenes by those who controlled votes and patronage. A man of definite views and stern character, he did not have the pliability the bosses considered an important qualification for the job. He accepted their verdict as a matter of party discipline, and Shastri became the leader. The consensus was welcomed in India and abroad as an impressive exercise in mature political functioning, along with the fact that the parliamentary system had been upheld during this critical transition period and thus strengthened. It had, however, acted as a brake on the "natural" process of political selection.

Mrs Gandhi, who had declared no personal stake in the succession, was a potent, if passive, presence on the scene. Even after the consensus she remained, as daughter of the charismatic Nehru, a figure whom his party could not comfortably ignore in the emotional aftermath of his death. Shastri gave her the portfolio of Information and Broadcasting in his cabinet, but her relations with him were cool and distant, and she made no secret of her disdain for a man she considered a minor character whom chance had made a leader. Interviewed on 11 November 1965[2] she said India had "swerved from the right path" after Nehru's death, and that socialism and non-alignment were being forgotten. Though she had described herself as "wholly without political ambition" she became a determined contestant for the succession when Shastri died suddenly at Tashkent in the Soviet Union on 12 January 1966.

Nehru's daughter would be an important asset in the coming election of 1967, but her eligibility was linked chiefly to her party's insistence on uncontroversial leadership in the void left so soon again by Shastri's death. Shastri's nineteen-month tenure had been dominated by two wars with Pakistan. There had scarcely been time to survey the post-Nehru scene and assess its priorities. And the party needed a period of reconstruction to rebuild its declin-

[2]Interviewed by Kuldip Nayar of the United News of India (UNI).

ing reputation. Indira Gandhi had what mattered greatly to the
group of leaders who masterminded her rise—a reticence apparently content to stay in the background of events. She had never
been embroiled in controversy or ambition, and her subdued public manner ensured respect for the principle of collective leadership.
As between her and Morarji Desai, the other contestant, she looked colourless and manageable, the safer choice for a party whose
political fortunes had suffered a severe setback with the Chinese
attack in 1962, and needed to pull together. On her part Mrs
Gandhi knew she needed the party bosses, who did not favour her
so much as oppose Desai. She tactfully refrained from canvassing
for votes or formally declaring her candidacy and said she would
abide by Congress President Kamaraj's wishes. Her reticence was
noted and approved. After hearing from Kamaraj, she made her
own moves to enlist support. There was less visible hurry and
strain in New Delhi than there had been on Nehru's death. The
Congress ruling clique felt its main crisis, the succession to Nehru,
safely over, no other succession would present a critical problem.
Desai's insistence this time on a vote was conceded, but the "open
contest" proved, in effect, to be a trial of strength between him
and the party bosses. There was little doubt that with the party
machine behind Mrs Gandhi, with the general election just a year
away, and most MPs anxious for tickets and support, they would
follow their chief ministers' orders to vote for her. The Congress
Parliamentary Party elected its leader by secret ballot on 19 January 1965. Mrs Gandhi, with the bosses and a coalition of chief
ministers solidly behind her, won 355 votes to Desai's 169 and became Prime Minister on 24 January. There were other reasons for
her election. Desai belonged to the Old Guard. Mrs Gandhi was
young. Desai represented the Congress past, Mrs Gandhi its future.
A man of ascetic habits and implacable opinions, Desai had a
"grey eminence" aura that could be forbidding. Mrs Gandhi would
be modern and flexible. Through her, Congress radicals believed,
the party would be regenerated.

The selection of a parliamentary constituency for Mrs Gandhi
could no longer be postponed. Mrs Gandhi declined her aunt's
offer to vacate Phulpur, and refused an invitation from Shastri's
constituency, Jumnapar, also near Allahabad, to represent it. She
said she had offers from all over the country and would decide
later. On 28 August 1966 Mrs Pandit (the author's mother) wrote

to me from Allahabad:

> I have filed my application for the Phulpur constituency after a
> talk with Indi[3] and her *written* consent . . . [she] is still hesitat-
> ing. Two safe but inconspicuous seats are being prepared, but
> it is the general desire which I share that she should stand from
> Allahabad City and face any challenge that is offered.

The Phulpur question remained open. Mrs Pandit wrote to me
from New Delhi on 18 September, though by now her application
had been approved and filed:

> You must have seen from the papers that I offered Phulpur to
> the P.M. and she refused . . . I did this because I knew she has
> wanted it and because inspired rumours were being circulated
> that "the people" want her there. . . . Before the meeting I
> spoke to Indi. She seemed pleased but said she would not permit
> me to make "this sacrifice." Or did I want something else? I
> said the offer was unconditional—there was no sacrifice. . . .
> When I announced my decision at the meeting, the very same
> people who had been turning around in circles carrying on a
> whispering campaign against me were a bit stunned and started
> saying I mustn't make such a "sacrifice". . . . In her speech Indi
> said I should keep Phulpur but added that "these things" were
> to be decided finally by Kamaraj. So we are held up until the
> end of October when the decision will be made.

Mrs Gandhi was reluctant to stand from Allahabad or its environs. The Samyukta Socialist Party concentrated its full fire on this
Congress stronghold, Nehru's birthplace and political base. "Dumb
doll,'' Ram Manohar Lohia's mildly derisive description of Mrs
Gandhi, signified an irreverence that refused to concede special
status to the Nehrus or to treat Allahabad as their fief. Lohia, who
could rub shoulders in camaraderie with the crowd, also had an
intellectual's appeal for the rebellious young. His language was
incisive and brilliant and Mrs Gandhi, unsure and apt to seek
refuge in her family's sacrifices for the national movement, was no
match for it. She chose eventually to stand from her late husband,

[3]Indi, like Indu, is an abbreviation of Indira.

Feroze Gandhi's constituency, Rae Bareilly, and Mrs Pandit kept the rural Phulpur seat. Congress credit was low and each known and respected party member who could win an election was needed. Mrs Pandit's political base was Uttar Pradesh, where she had twice been Minister for Health and Local Government (1937 and 1946), and twice been elected to the Lok Sabha after independence (1952 and 1964). This time the support extended to her by the party machine in Allahabad had noticeably cooled and dwindled. She wrote to me from Anand Bhawan on 31 January 1967:

> If I win this campaign it will really be something. I have to do everything on a shoestring—unpaid workers, very little transport facilities and no assistance, moral or otherwise, from the Congress elite. . . . Hardly any workers around Anand Bhawan—no noise or bustle—few flags and the rest of the trimmings. It will be fun to win, and I hope with a bigger majority.

The attitude of the "Congress elite" may be partly explained by this extract from the same letter:

> Broken roads and whirls of dust all through, but huge meetings at the end, and warm and genuine welcomes at every stop. There was only one difficult moment with a local bigwig who spoke about a ban on cow slaughter. I had decided to follow my father's line on this issue, so when the learned gentleman stopped for breath, I said very quietly, "Surely this painful subject is not a proper topic of discussion between two Brahmins." He begged my pardon and shut up immediately. Another difficult moment was when a dear old man got up and said he wanted to put a question on behalf of the village—why did I not seek election to the office of Prime Minister—the people of the constitueney wanted me in that chair and so did many others all over India. I replied that my child was in that chair, and had all my attributes plus the advantage of being so much younger!

For the Indian public Mrs Pandit's career in politics and diplomacy (at the United Nations, and as India's Ambassador to the USSR, the USA, and Britain) made her the senior and more mature Nehru presence in politics. Mrs Gandhi reacted to it with visible strain. Before the election campaign Mrs Pandit had written to me from New Delhi: "I went yesterday evening by appointment to see Indi. We sat in stony silence for fifteen minutes after which I came home. Most frustrating. I don't know what to do to make a breakthrough. God knows I've tried and tried. It makes me sad."

Her victory in the campaign did not make matters easier and the strain continued.

Two days ago Indi asked me to see her in her office. I had asked permission to leave for Manila before the Presidential election[4] and she said it would be difficult to give me permission as there was going to be a grim struggle and every vote was needed. Could I get a day's postponement of the convocation etc. She then said she wanted to say something personal. Her eyes filled with tears and she was obviously distressed. She said she knew I was being wasted. She wanted to use my talents. She kept thinking what she could do for me. But she kept hearing things which shook her trust in me. I told her there was nothing I could do to prove my real affection for her and my desire that she should succeed in the task she had undertaken. Trust, I said, was something intangible. It was there or it was not. . . . I would have been satisfied if I could have been associated in a small way with either the Government or the Congress. What was mortifying to me was to be left out in the cold year after year when so many things required to be done intelligently and honestly. I said I had been thinking of resigning my seat as I was tired of being an extra vote for an organisation which had ceased to have any use for me. This last shook her and she said, "You can't resign—I wouldn't let you. We can't keep Phulpur without you." At this point I thought it best to leave and I asked her not to worry about me as I had infinite resources within myself.

Mrs Pandit resigned her seat in the Lok Sabha in 1968.

The question of leadership became a live issue again a little over a year after Mrs Gandhi became Prime Minister, following the general election of 1967. Her year in power had jolted the High

[4]The forthcoming election of the President of India. Mrs Gandhi had proposed Dr Zakir Husain for the presidency, and had achieved his nomination by her party against some opposition.

Command. She had devalued the rupee in June 1966 on the advice of her inner circle or "kitchen cabinet." Without the advance measures needed to cushion the economy against a drastic reduction of 57.5 per cent in the value of the rupee, prices had risen, with consequent hardship to the consumer. Angry criticism assailed devaluation from all sections of opinion in Parliament. To the men who had put her in power this showed a reckless disregard for the homework hard economic decisions require. It had also been an abrupt departure from the concept of joint cabinet responsibility for decision-making, and an indication that either she did not understand parliamentary method, or had deliberately ignored it. Three days after devaluation the party registered its disapproval of the action, though accepting it as a *fait accompli*. It marked a divide in Mrs Gandhi's relations with Kamaraj. She now made it a point to distinguish between the party as represented by its bosses, and the people, whom she identified with herself. Asked about her differences with Kamaraj in an interview before the 1967 election, she replied: "You see, here is a question of whom the party wants and whom the people want. My position among the people is uncontested." The publicly stated assumption of a privileged position distinct from, and even opposed to her party, made surprisingly little impression on a party wracked by election fever.

The election was a debacle for the Congress which lost power in five states, and in three others had a slender majority that did not last. In the Lok Sabha it was reduced to a small majority of about 22, while in the states a new pattern emerged. Kerala and West Bengal formed Marxist (CPI-M)[5] led governments, while the Jan Sangh became the dominant party in the Hindi belt in the north. Some powerful Congressmen, including Kamaraj, lost their seats. Since 1963 there had been hard thinking, and at least one concrete programme (the Kamaraj Plan) to revitalize and strengthen the party at the grassroots. The election revealed how inadequate these had been. The last lustre of the national movement had worn off the Congress. In these circumstances the party clung closer to "consensus" to avoid the friction of a new leadership contest, pro-

---

[5]The Communist Party of India (Marxist) as distinct from the Communist Party of India (CPI). The CPI-M broke away from the CPI in July 1964.

posing Mrs Gandhi remain Prime Minister and take Morarji Desai into her cabinet as Deputy Prime Minister. There had been no Deputy (Number Two in the cabinet) since Sardar Patel's death in 1950. Mrs Gandhi, in a stronger bargaining position since Kamaraj, had been defeated at the polls, agreed to Desai's inclusion as Finance Minister with the label of Deputy, but not to "any duality of authority." Her authority, she said, would be "unfettered." In Nehru's time a rank had been assigned to each minister. She dispensed with this practice, instituting alphabetical order, so that cabinet positions provided no opening for conjecture about future power line-ups.

CHAPTER TWO

THE PERSON

Mrs Gandhi remained for the country at large a muted figure. A poor speaker, and instinctively swift to prevent any encroachments on her position or prestige, she gave an impression of inhibition and wariness. Her first year in office, with the general consternation over devaluation, had made a weak start. Yet her remarks revealed herself as special to the Indian scene in background, judgement, and above all in her Nehru birth. Her childhood, or other personal reference, frequently figured in her speeches, containing the nuance that she had, since her tender years, borne a heavy burden in the struggle for freedom.

She appeared to be straining to convince through the medium of her family's role and reputation:

Having lived in the midst of crisis from my earliest childhood, I am not overawed by present difficulties.[1]

I have no doubt our difficulties will mount, almost 100% each day. But I go to difficulties head on. Since I was a child I have been able to proceed only in this way.[2]

... I have not eaten any cereals for a year except when I eat out. I just cannot when I know others are not getting enough.[3]

You are all experts in your fields and I am not. ... But I am an expert at dealing with people. This is something, I think, I was either born with or I learnt from my very childhood ... I developed what may be called a "feel" of the people, and I find that

[1]Speech to Federation of Indian Chambers of Commerce and Industry (FICCI), New Delhi, 12 March 1966.
[2]Speech to Planning Commission, New Delhi, 12 July 1966.
[3]Speech to Planning Commission, New Delhi, 12 July 1966.

this intuition helps me with the ordinary people. . . .[4]

Politics rarely, if ever, produces modest, hesitant figures, doubt-ful of their own capacities, and it is not surprising that Mrs Gandhi had a high opinion of herself. It was notable only because she sought at every opportunity to convey it to her audiences, and it contrasted with the lighter, more confident tread of speech and manner her father had had. The Indian public was not familiar with her as it had been with her father when he became Prime Minister. Nehru's life, his intellectual development, and even his private anguish were part and parcel of the events and literature of the national movement. Introspection and outburst were part of his public speaking. His ideas were on record in his writings. And those who could not read knew him through personal encounter and public presence on the scene over many years more intimately than most national figures are known among their people. He was in all his strength and weakness a thoroughly familiar quantity. Mrs Gandhi was not. The heavy brooding self-portrait she now re-vealed by stages seemed curiously at odds with what was generally known about the atmosphere of her home and the spirit inspiring it.

The extended family headed by Motilal Nehru included the children of his elder brothers and sisters, some of whom he had helped to educate and set on their feet in careers. Motilal was in-ordinately proud of his clan and made much of it. To him it was the most intelligent, attractive brood imaginable, and it, in turn, admired and revolved around him. A natural leader of men, his personal magnetism and the prestige he enjoyed in politics and the legal profession made his home the meeting place of some of the most brilliant, vital, and dedicated society of his time. His resound-ing laughter and flaring temper were both legendary, as was his generosity. His zest for life carried the family with elan through an almost revolutionary change in life-style when he and his son joined Mahatma Gandhi. Incontestably a man of "family," in the great tradition of shelter and nurture, with the personality and instincts of a patriarch, Motilal lavished an extravagant affection and indulgence on the elder of his two daughters, his favourite *Nanni* or *Nan*, as she was known. But his most inviolable love was reserved for his only son. Jawaharlal, with his wife and

[4]Speech to Administrative Staff College, Hyderabad, 24 June 1966.

daughter, were thus the focus of an entire clan's attention and concern in a way that princes and heirs apparent are.

Father and son entered with passion and humour into the freedom crusade. Jawaharlal's writings reflect the magic of the time, binding the household together in an incomparable adventure over and above the hardships involved. To some extent every member of Anand Bhawan, even visitors to it, were touched by the aspiration, the glow and romance of the national movement. In Mrs Gandhi's recollections another picture emerges, sombre, tense, aggrieved. Not surprisingly, as an only child, she turned the circumstances around her to exaggerate and dramatize her own importance in a busy, fully caught-up household, and recalled her own role as one of drama. Her games, she told interviewers, had consisted of making fiery political speeches to her dolls and servants, and triumphant encounters with the police. Whatever speeches she had made recently, she once said, she had been making since she was "twelve years old."[5] Home and childhood were associated for her with dark events and crisis: "So from September 1929 a part of the house was turned into a hospital. In the beginning doctors came only at dead of night and the women of the house, including myself, aged twelve, were the nurses."[6] She told the Rajya Sabha: "As a small schoolgirl, at a time when Gandhiji undertook his historic fast in the Yeravda prison, I went to a Harijan colony to work there. This was one of my first activities in social work."[7] On the 50th anniversary of Jallianwala Bagh she said in a broadcast: "I was hardly more than a baby, but the impact of this tragedy on my elders could not but leave its mark on me."[8]

A more natural and charming glimpse of her emerges in this extract from her father's letter to his sister, Mrs Pandit, written on 23 November 1926 from Montana, Switzerland, where Kamala Nehru was being treated for tuberculosis. Indira was then nine years old:

Indu came here for her birthday and spent three days with us.[9]

[5]Lok Sabha, August 1969.
[6]In an article commemorating Motilal Nehru's birth centenary.
[7]12 August 1967.
[8]13 April 1969.
[9]Mrs Gandhi was at a children's camp in the mountains at Chesnieres.

Her English is becoming infected with her French and she talks of going jusqu' a the post office and it being presque ten o'clock! As for Hindustani, she tries to avoid talking in it. I insisted on talking to her in Hindi and I always write to her in Hindi.

As Prime Minister, Mrs Gandhi told public meetings she had often faced bullets in her life, provoking a journalist to comment tartly: "If she did face bullets, it might have been in an unchronic-led, unsung chapter of her much publicized life."[10] The publicity, however, depended almost entirely on her own statements, there being no other source for much of the material making its appearance in written accounts about her. She frequently charged the Jan Sangh with trying to kill her, an accusation she had to withdraw when Jan Sangh MPs took it up in a stormy meeting of the Parliamentary Consultative Commitee of the Home Ministry and she admitted she had no evidence for such a statement.

Of her first and only imprisonment, 11 September 1942 to 13 May 1943, in Naini Central Jail, Allahabad, she told an interviewer in 1969: "I was regarded as so dangerous that I wasn't even given normal prison facilities"—a recollection not supported by the evidence of the time. Mrs Gandhi, aged nearly 25, shared a barrack with her aunt, Mrs Pandit, her cousin, Chandralekha Pandit, aged 18, and a number of women friends and acquaintances, all subject to the same rules and regulations. Mrs Pandit writes in her preface to the prison diary[11] she kept: "The treatment given to me and to those who shared the barrack with me was, according to the prison standards, very lenient—the reader must not imagine that others were equally well treated." The diary starts on 12 August 1942 with Mrs Pandit's own arrest, and ends with an entry dated 11 June 1943, just before her release. It covers Mrs Gandhi's term of imprisonment and describes the daily lives of the inmates of the barrack. The following entries are illuminating:

August 19: The barrack in which I live is a rectangular room intended to accommodate twelve or more convicts. There are gratings at short distances along each side, one of them being

[10]Rajinder Puri, *India: The Wasted Years*, Chetana Publications, New Delhi, 1975.
[11]Vijayalakshmi Pandit, *Prison Days*, Signet Press, Calcutta, third edition, May 1946.

a door which is bolted and locked at night. One side of the
barrack is raised four steps from the ground and serves as a
latrine after lock-up. For day use a small bathroom and latrine
have been added to the barrack. . . . The whole place is in a
state of acute disrepair and the tiles on the roof are in need of
renewal. I have only been supplied with a jail cot and a small
rickety iron table. . . .

On 22 August Mrs Pandit records that books and periodicals
can come through the District Magistrate. Chandralekha's arrest
on 30 August, and Indira's on 11 September are also recorded.

Sept. 13: Indu, Lekha and I have been drawing up a plan. I am
to cook the midday meal and they will arrange the supper. . . .
The girls are planning to do a good lot of reading and Indu is
going to help Lekha with her French.

Oct. 4: Yesterday the doctor informed me that Indira, Lekha
and I had been placed in A class and that in future we would
be entitled to 12 annas per day ration money. (An earlier entry
records that Lekha has developed painful boils under her arm
and Indira has a temperature.)

Oct. 6: Ranjit[12] has sent us some seeds and cuttings. The garden
he started in his barrack last year is still flourishing and he
brought me a bunch of lovely nastertiums at our last interview.
The soil of our yard is very stony, so the matron has offered to
get us a few flower pots and boxes in which we can sow our
seeds. The girls are excited.

Oct. 15: We were weighed today. Since arrival Lekha has lost
4 lbs. and I have lost 6. Indu is steady but that means nothing,
as she is already below par and cannot afford to lose anything.

Oct. 22: The civil surgeon came to see Indira today. He has
been asked to see her and report on her health to Government.

Oct. 31: While we were having our tea this morning at about
8.30 a.m., the matron sent a note to say that Lekha and I

[12]Mrs Pandit's husband, Ranjit Sitaram Pandit, arrested and brought to
Naini Central Jail on 19 September 1942.

would have an interview with Ranjit, and Indira with Feroze[13] at 9.30.

Nov. 2: The Superintendent told me at Parade this morning that all husbands and wives in the same jail would be permitted to interview each other once a fortnight for half an hour.

Nov. 7: Purnima[14] has given the whole barrack red glass bangles. We look quite gay.

Nov. 27: The girls have been busy "decorating" our corner of the barrack. Each part has a name. Indu calls hers Chimborazo. Lekha's bit is called Bien Venue because she now has the part formerly occupied by me and which gives a view of the main gate. I am obliged to call my abode Wall View because it's so obvious. In the centre we have an old blue rug . . . which I brought along with me in my bedding. We call the entire space the Blue Drawing Room and it's here we eat our meals and sit and read at night etc. Indu and Lekha are both gifted with imagination and the evenings are seldom dull. They are planning to save up rations and have a party in the Blue Drawing Room soon. The menu is discussed daily with great enthusiasm. They can't decide whether to write it in French or not. The jail cat named by Indu — Mehitabel — has had four kittens and Indu and Lekha are quite excited. . . . The girls have a habit of giving names to everything: the lantern, table, bed, even the bottle of hair oil which has recently lost its top as the result of a fall. It is now referred to as Rupert the headless Earl. The lantern is Lucifer. After lock-up they read plays, each taking a part. I am the audience.

New Year's Day 1943: We were informed today that "the Government of India have permitted the members of the Congress Working Committee to correspond with members of their families, on personal and domestic matters only; any such letters addressed to Mrs. Pandit and Mrs. Indira Gandhi will be delivered, and they will be permitted to reply, subject to the same restrictions about subject matter."

[13]Mrs Gandhi's husband, Feroze Gandhi, arrested and brought to Naini Central Jail on the same day as herself, 11 September 1942.
[14]Fellow prisoner and old friend, Purnima Banerji.

The correspondence must soon have been established for a letter to Mrs Pandit from Jawaharlal Nehru, imprisoned in Ahmednagar Fort, is dated 21 March 1943: "My mind often travelled to you all and I was happy that you were together and could look after each other."

In two letters, dated 9 April 1943 and 29 June 1943 respectively, he wrote:

Both your letters were very welcome and to read them made me feel lighthearted and gay. Your account of life in Naini, of the energy and vitality shown by Indu and Chand, and of their continuous attempts to find humour in a depressing situation, soothed and pleased me greatly. I am worried, however, about your health . . . I have written to Betty[15] asking her to fix up with some fruiterer to send a parcel of fresh fruit weekly to Indu direct. Allahabad is very poor in fruit at this time of the year and both of you should have plenty of fruit.

I was glad to read about Indu in your letters—how she has recouped. I am pleased about this for it indicates that she has become essentially stronger and with greater powers of resistance. The experience of a hot weather in Naini after a dozen years of mountain climates and Switzerland and England was a very stiff one. Her coming through it, as she has done, is full of promise. It shows not only that she is better but that she knows how to keep well inspite of disadvantages and disabilities.

Mrs Pandit's diary contains three more entries of interest:

May. 11: On the 5th we were sent for to the office and informed that Indu and I would be released next morning and an externment order would be served on us requiring us to proceed to Almora and take up our residence at Khali . . . under the surveillance of the Deputy Commissioner of Almora. Obviously these terms could not be accepted by us and we refused.

May 13: Indu and I are being released this morning. I wonder if any order is to be served on us. If so we shall be back here before long.

[15]Krishna Hutheesing, the younger of Nehru's two sisters, nicknamed Betty.

May 27: Here I am back in Naini after an eventful week. ...
As we refused to comply with the externment order served on
us, a police officer came to the house yesterday to enquire when
I would be ready to return to jail. I said any time that suited
him and he suggested 6 p.m., which I accepted. There was no
warrant fortunately for Indu who is in no condition to return
to Naini at present as she is down with fever and a very bad
cold.

Far from being treated as dangerous, and deprived of normal
facilities, Nehru's daughter received specially courteous consideration. Yet this, and the gaiety and vitality with which she and her
young cousin made a game of grim discomfort and dreary prison
routine, did not appear to figure in her recollections.

Jawaharlal Nehru, a man bowed by many burdens as the years
of the fight for freedom took their toll, remained curiously unbow-
ed in spirit. In a conscious effort to share himself and to communicate with his child, particularly during his long absences in prison, he wrote his *Letters from a Father to His Daughter* and *Glimp-
ses of World History,* books that did more than explain the scien-
tific beginnings of the world, or the procession of men and events
constituting its history. These pages held an approach to life com-
pounded of buoyancy and optimism, a humorous tolerance towards
life's foibles and even its trials. Indira saw life in another more
solemn perspective, cast in an austere mould, shorn of lightness, as
if lightness were a weakness, a trap to be avoided. Nor apparently could the written word take the place of flesh and blood human
beings to turn to. Absent parents, though absent for well-under-
stood and admired reasons, left a void that was never quite filled,
though few parents could have given of themselves to an only
child as Indira's did. Because of her mother's invalidism, her
father was particularly involved with phases of her growth, with
the sole responsibility for major and minor decisions concerning
her, and even for periods with her daily routine normally a mother's
job, as during the long stay in Europe for his wife's treatment in
1926. He wrote to his sister in Allahabad from Geneva on 6 May
1926:

Indu has to be escorted to school and there being no servants or
other helpful persons, I have to accompany her. ...

I consulted the State enquiry department and with their advice fixed the Ecole Internationale here. This is a bilingual school and although most of the work is done in French, explanations are also given in English. I thought this would suit Indu to begin with and till she picks up a little French ... she goes to school at eight and comes back at twelve for meals. At two she goes again and all the children are then taken out in a bus to a place in the country a few miles off, which belongs to the school. The afternoon lessons often take place in the open and consist largely of games. She comes back at four. This means that I have to go backwards and forwards between our pension and the school four times a day! The distance is not inconsiderable and I get quite a lot of exercise although we take the tram for part of the way. Fortunately there are two full holidays and one half holiday a week.

A week later he wrote:

Romain Rolland has sent me a nice letter. ... He got to know from some teacher in Indu's school that a little Indian girl had joined the school. He guessed that the girl might be my daughter. He writes to say that Indu's French teacher is a great friend of his and is a highly cultured and affectionate lady who can be thoroughly trusted with children. This is very comforting as I was not at all sure that the school I had chosen was the right one.

Indu is progressing and developing in more ways than one. She now comes back from school all by herself and walks the whole distance of nearly a mile or takes the tram. Some change from the methods in vogue in Allahabad, where Khaliq and the motor were not thought sufficient and Jessie-Ma had to be constantly with her during school hours. ...

Last Sunday I took Indu up a little mountain near Geneva called the Saleve. It is two hours' journey by tram and funicular. The view from the top is magnificent, one of the best in Switzerland. One can see the whole of the Mont Blanc chain and the Jura and the lake of Geneva and the valleys all around dotted with little villages and country houses. The whole country looked like an enormous and very well kept park. At some places the fields were so neat and green that one could almost imagine that rich carpets had been spread out in various shades of green. On top of the Saleve there were the remains of some snow. This was fresh enough and, to Indu's infinite joy, we made snowballs and threw them at each other. . . .

In a postscript he adds: "I enclose two recent snapshots of Indu. Compare them to the snapshots taken in India in February and you will notice how she is growing."

The parent-child relationship has its unanalyzed loves and hostilities, but given the keen awareness Nehru had of his daughter, this relationship might have become a close mutual bond. That it did not partake of real human response and sharing, though it did of attachment, may have been because though she spent most of her adult life in her father's house, there was a point beyond which Indira could not go in simple give and take. It seemed fraught for her with hazards. The intellectual and emotional labour her father expended on her did not bring the cherished child to flower. Somewhere within her intensities locked, and the tight bud stayed closed. Her delicate health, a problem through childhood, continued into womanhood. Not disposed to study, and with no special aptitude, she was never driven to the kind of discipline that might have been expected of a sturdier child. She could not keep up with her studies at Oxford, and did not get a degree, while her earlier schooling had been uneven because of her parents' jail terms or her mother's ill health. Indu, centre of the larger family's loving concern, seldom lowered her guards. Her unresponsiveness troubled her father during her adolescence. She was fifteen when he wrote to his sister, Mrs Pandit, from his barrack in Dehra Dun District Jail:

During the last fourteen months or more I have written to Indu regularly and have hardly missed a fortnight. It has been a very one-sided correspondence as my letters have evoked practically no response. After about a couple of months of silence on her part a hasty letter would come with many apologies and excuses, and with no reference at all to my letters or the questions I had asked in them. I have sent books for her birthday and on other occasions. These are not acknowledged and I have no definite knowledge if they reached her. I gather that Kamala is treated in much the same way. Now it does not matter much if an odd

letter comes or does not come. Nor does it matter fundamentally if a joy that I might have is denied to me or to Kamala. I
can get used to that as to other things that I do not like. But I
am naturally led to think why this should be so. It is not casual;
it is persistent. And in spite of numerous efforts it continues. I
know that Indu is fond of me and of Kamala. Yet she ignores us and
others completely. Why is this so? Indu, I feel, is extraordinarily
imaginative and self-centered or subjective. Indeed, I would say
that, quite unconsciously, she has grown remarkably selfish. She
lives in a world of dreams and vagaries and floats about on imagi-
nary clouds, full probably of all manner of brave fancies. Now this
is natural in a girl of her subjective nature and especially at her
age. But there can be too much of it and I am afraid there is too
much of it in her case. . . I feel she requires a course of field or
factory work to bring her down from the clouds. . . . She will
have to come down, and if she does not do so early she will do
so late, and then the process will be painful.

Getting through to Indu was a difficulty that surfaced vividly
when she made her decision to marry, and later during the belea-
gured course of her marriage. Feroze Gandhi, a Parsi, belonged to
Allahabad, where his family owned a general store. As a student
active in the national movement, he was no stranger to the Nehru
household, in fact something of a protegé of Indira's parents. This
connection was not altogether welcome to Feroze's family who
feared it might harm him. Nehru with a characteristic regard for
propriety and family feeling went out of his way on at least one
occasion to try to set their misgivings at rest. He wrote to his sister
from Bhowali (UP) on 2 November 1935:

And now rather a delicate matter and perhaps a troublesome
job for you. It appears that Feroze Gandhi has got into hot
water with his people because of his association with us, and
especially his long stay at Bhowali. Even before this his political
activities were greatly resented by his mother and the blame for
them was cast on Kamala and me. It had almost been settled
that he was to sail for Europe with his aunt, Miss Commissariat
[the doctor], but suddenly everything has fallen through and the
poor boy is landed high and dry. Even ordinarily I would like
to help him in this quandary, but now my responsibility is all

the greater because we happen to be the cause of it.

Now my sympathy is entirely with the poor mother. I can perfectly understand and appreciate her distress and anger at us. Very probably I would have felt much the same if I had been treated in this way by my son. I think also that we have been remiss in almost ignoring the mother. But circumstances somewhat controlled the situation and what with Kamala's illness and my absence in jail, we did little . . .

. . . It is difficult to understand other people's family quarrels and even more difficult to interfere in them. Still something has to be done to save the boy from endless trouble (he is so downcast that he talks foolishly of entering some wretched ashram!) —and to put ourselves right with his family . . .

. . . I repeat that I thoroughly sympathise with the family and even quite understand their anger. We cannot presume to interfere and to tell them what to do with the boy, but I do want to tone down that anger and to remove any obstructions in the way of a reconciliation. After that a mother's love will do the trick.

So I would like you to pay a visit to the mother and sister . . . and to soothe them and apologise to them on my and Kamala's behalf and to tell them that we are extremely sorry that we should have unwittingly come in between them and their boy. That is the very last thing we would like to do. We have grown fond of the boy because he is a brave lad and has the makings of a man in him. He has our good wishes in every way and we hope that he will train himself and educate himself in accordance with his own wishes and those of his family for any work that he chooses. It is not for us to interfere. . . .

This is rather a ticklish job but yet there should be no difficulty about it as really the chief trouble is a phantom of the imagination. But phantoms are often troublesome. . . .

Nehru's reaction to Indira's decision to marry Feroze, made while she was still in her teens, rose chiefly from his regret that she had too early closed her mind and feelings to the wide world of opportunity around her. His suggestion, that she should think the matter over at home before taking a final decision, resulted in a scarring experience for him. Indira, at Oxford at the time, wanted to remain in England with Feroze for her vacation, and told her father she would not speak to him unless he agreed, an ultimatum he did not take seriously. She kept her promise. A fortnight's silence on the voyage to Bombay continued unbroken on the train journey to Allahabad. On their arrival home, Nehru—gentle and affectionate in his family relationships—was too shaken to endure the ordeal further. He asked his secretary to book Indira's passage back to England. Her marriage took place in Allahabad in March 1942. As her father's advice, and later Mahatma Gandhi's, to think again about her choice, had not prevailed, the marriage had their blessing. For Indira it was a promise to Feroze fulfilled and her own personality asserted in circumstances where another woman might have yielded to family opinion.

Indira's choice of Feroze was influenced by her mother's fondness for the young man who had nursed her devotedly at Bhowali during a phase of her illness. Indira's own shyness and stiff uncommunicativeness, mistaken in her youth for hauteur, had never made friendship or close companionship easy. Feroze represented the known, comfortable, and familiar. The relationship inevitably foundered in the role she later chose of being at her father's side at the nation's political centre. It compelled them to live substantially apart and subjected the marriage to strains and stresses from which it never recovered. Her father's house in Delhi remained Indira's priority, a setting into which Feroze, with a career and personality of his own, could not be conveniently absorbed. A journalist who became a Member of Parliament with a reputation for unearthing facts and figures, Feroze was responsible for instituting the enquiry leading to the resignation of Finance Minister T.T. Krishnamachari in 1958. He reacted bitterly and outspokenly to the unofficial separation, and it came to have untidy political and personal overtones. Those who watched this tragedy unfold, above all her father, felt their failure to work out a solution, either in complete separation or in compromise, would affect Indira in many and manifold ways, and shut a door forever to the possibilities of normal living.

Feroze was in many ways self-educated with a gift for the mechanical as well as a knowledge of classical music and fine china. He was an extrovert, generous with his help and money, popular with colleagues and subordinates. His sense of humour enlivened the Central Hall of Parliament. Short and square in build, fair-skinned, with a face that reddened with laughter, people warmed to him easily. Parliament came to have a healthy regard for his grasp and use of facts. He had green fingers, and after the death of Ranjit Pandit in January 1944, Feroze took over the supervision of Anand Bhawan's gardens. The Prime Minister's house, where his wife and sons lived, remained his domestic base, but his business was conducted from the parliamentary accommodation he rented and no slur of political advantage attached to him. One aspect of the growing chasm between him and wife was to give Indira an aura of self-sacrifice and nobility of choice, qualities people had associated with her invalid mother. These must indeed have been poignantly present in her private conflict. Apparently she saw no way out, either in final break on in final healing, for it remained with her unresolved, except for a brief reunion the summer before his death, until Feroze died in September 1960.

The shadows in Indira were in part a reflection of the mismatching of her parents. Their marriage, arranged by Motilal Nehru and Kamala's aunt, was a grievous mistake for these two profoundly dissimilar people. Kamala's problems of adaptation from her orthodox, barely educated background to the liberal, emancipated, Westernized environment of the Nehrus, built up into symptoms of illness, while the bruises of the relationship drove Nehru deeply into himself, and strenghtened his emotional and intellectual links with his sister. Since marriages in which the wife was not her husband's equal in education or opportunity were the rule rather than the exception, the flaw in this one must have resulted from more intractable problems of personality. Ten years older than his wife, Nehru tried and failed to overcome the gulf between them. The national movement, claiming them both, performed this task to some extent but could never complete it, for Kamala died of tuberculosis after a long illness in February 1936. During his last vigil over her failing health there seemed in him a foreshadowing of the event to come. Released from prison in September 1935 to join her at Badenweiler (Germany), he was shocked at the deterioration in her condition and moved into the sanitarium with her, leaving Indira and her cousin, Vidya Nehru, invited from Oxford to spend the Christmas vacation with them, at their "pension." Trying to finish his autobiography, keep an eye on Indira and Vidya, and watch over his wife, his only outlet for solace and companionship lay in writing every few days to his sister, with news intended for the whole anxious family at Allahabad, yet reaching out especially to *Nan*.

Bandenweiler
31-12-35

Nan darling—Was it yesterday I wrote or the day before? I am getting mixed up. I have sent you a fair number of letters during the last four months or less, to make up, to some extent, for the long silences of previous months and years.

I write to you again so soon because I feel like doing so. The old year is passing as I write—it is almost the stroke of midnight —and the desire to write to you on this coming of the new year became strong within me. To send you all my love.

The bells are ringing and the sound rolls up the valley in waves which seem to envelop me. There is also gun firing going on somewhere. The New Year has come. What will it be, I wonder? I have just been out on my balcony and I saw in the distance the twinkling lights on the far side of the Rhine, in France.

There was something oppressive in the air, or was it my imagination? The firing suddenly made me think of war and suffering and disaster.

But whatever terrors the New Year may hold in its womb, why should we worry about them in anticipation? It is enough that a new year is born, and somehow a feeling of growth comes with it, and a shedding away of the past year's burdens and sorrows.

All my love to mother and you and Ranjit, and Chand and Tara and little Rita. Give my greetings to Upadhyaya also, and Hari, and all others whom Anand Bhawan shelters.

Your loving brother
Jawahar

One terror was soon realized. Kamala died in February 1936. Nehru's dedication of his autobiography—published soon after her death "To Kamala Who is no More"—was his deep mourning of a discovery cut short. His later writing movingly described her wasting illness and his admiration for the burning patriotism that had become so strong a bond between them.

On the publication of her mother's biography[16] in May 1973, Mrs Gandhi said in an interview with its author that her mother

[16]Promilla Kalhan, *Kamala Nehru: An Intimate Biography*, Vikas, New Delhi, 1973.

had had the greater influence on her. In her teens she had felt her mother was being wronged by her father's family and had fought for her. "I saw her being hurt and I was determined not to be hurt." With a chronically ailing mother it may have been hard, too, for a child to forgive those in robust health around her, to feel part of an active household radiating energy and accomplishment. The effect, for Indira, was to range her parents' families, even her parents at times, on opposite sides, with a gap in understanding, sympathy, and culture between them. The distinction between the two "sides" persisted in her mind. The Nehru name was a talisman she needed and she had been deeply attached to her father. But her trust and instincts reposed in the simpler uncritical background of her mother's relations and her own preference was for them. Towards the Nehru relatives, those who had shared the family home and background at Anand Bhawan, her feelings were mixed, not often given full human play. The idea gained currency that she particularly resented the beautiful vivacious elder aunt who occupied a special place in her father's affections. Yet such simple formulas seldom tell the whole story of family relationships, where the immediate and personal often becomes blurred and mellowed by the larger cushioning of common living and common interests. Motilal Nehru's family was closely and loyally knit. If Indira resented her aunt, there was not much evidence of it during her childhood. Indira was not a letter-writer, but in the abundant correspondence between Nehru and his sister, her occasional paragraphs and postscripts are warm and spontaneous.

On 23 June 1935 she adds to her father's letter from London: "Darling Puphi—Just a very hurried line to send you my love. Just now the telephone takes all my time. I daren't budge from it. It is glorious seeing Papu again. He looks well but thin. . . . There goes the phone! Love Indu." And a postscript on her father's letter, two days later from Sir Stafford Cripps' home "Goodfellows" at Lechlade, Glocestershire: "You would have loved this very charming house and still lovelier garden. Lots of love, Indu."

If tensions were present between them, they did not affect the normal current of family life. On Ranjit Pandit's death in January 1944, not long after his release from jail, it was Indira and Feroze who gave their aunt the support she needed, with Nehru still in jail. During the years of Nehru's prime ministership the family tie was manifest in shared concern for matters affecting all their children. Any early resentment on Indira's part might have found its ordinary level in private life. The palpable difference, the cool empty distance Indira established between herself and her aunt, came with her own entry into the cabinet.

Spontaneity was not, in general, her style. Daring was. In 1962 Mrs Gandhi had gone to Jabalpur in Madhya Pradesh to investigate Hindu-Muslim riots, though she was not in the government at the time. She could show a refreshing disregard for her own safety. During the Chinese attack that year she had flown to Tezpur, headquarters of the Sector Commander, to meet soldiers and officers. She had gone to the front line at Haji Pir in Kashmir during the Indo-Pakistan war of 1965, inspiring the comment that she was the only man in the cabinet. Two years later, during an election meeting in Bhubaneshwar, Orissa, she faced stone-throwers coolly, not losing her nerve when a stone struck her, cutting her lip and displacing a bone in her nose.

Mrs Pandit's resignation of her Lok Sabha seat in 1968 closed a domestic chapter. Nehru's presence had been home for his two sisters, eleven and seventeen years younger than he, and for their children. His house in New Delhi, when he became Prime Minister, continued the hospitable tradition of Anand Bhawan, providing a sense of warmth and embrace for the larger family. Perhaps few men at the centre of power and the helm of affairs for so many years have had his talent for enduring relationships, or his intimate concern for private problems. Deeply affectionate and considerate, he had friends, not only followers, and a grace in dealing with people that did much to soften controversy and make political combat a stimulating and civilized affair. His most virulent critics in politics and the press respected him. One of the most sensitive tributes to him was written by a political adversary, Hiren Mukherji (CPI), *The Gentle Colossus*.

Mrs Pandit had been passionately devoted to her brother and they had shared an uncommon closeness. She was strongly traditional in her belief that her brother's daughter was her own, and that the family must be united after Nehru's death when Mrs Gandhi, in her new exacting position, needed support. Nehru's death, and her own entry into the cabinet, however, gave Mrs Gandhi the opportunity to dissolve the relationships that had surrounded her father. If she had indeed considered her elder aunt an obstacle to her mother's happiness in the Nehru family, this had not affected the stuff of the relationship in her father's lifetime when close family bonds had been maintained. Yet now she was more comfortable once her aunt retired from politics and moved out of the capital to Dehra Dun. The family tie was not encouraged. In 1970 when Anand Bhawan was converted by Mrs Gandhi into a memorial, Mrs Pandit was refused permission to stay at the house overnight, as Mrs Gandhi was doing, for the ceremony next day. She attended the ceremony as a guest, an incongruous situation in view of Nehru's known attachment for his sister. Bequeathing Anand Bhawan to his daughter in his will he had written:

In the course of a life which had had its share of trial and difficulty, the love and tender care for me of both my sisters, Vijaya Lakshmi Pandit and Krishna Hutheesing, has been of the greatest solace to me. I can give nothing to balance this but my own love and affection which they have in full measure. . . . This house, Anand Bhawan, has become for us and others a symbol of much that we value in life. It is far more than a structure of brick and concrete, more than a private possession. It is connected intimately with our national struggle for freedom, and within its walls great events have happened and great decisions have been reached. . . . [It] should always be open to my sisters, their children, as well as my brother-in-law, Raja Hutheesing, and they should be made to feel that it continues to be their home where they are welcome. They can stay there whenever they like and for as long as they like. I should like them to pay periodic visits to the house and to keep fresh and strong the bonds that tie them to their old home.

On the occasion of Anand Bhawan's conversion by Mrs Gandhi to a memorial, I was asked to recall my memories of my home for the *Hindustan Times*.[17] This extract conveys my own feeling for the house and the atmosphere it provided for the children and adults it sheltered:

I felt a special kinship with the house. It was as old as I was.

[17]From "Farewell to Anand Bhawan," *Hindustan Times*, 8 November 1970. For an account of the author's childhood at Anand Bhawan, read *Prison and Chocolate Cake*, Alfred Knopf, 1954, New York.

It had been built when my grandfather gave his palatial residence to the Congress Party. . . . Our love and admiration for Mamu was inextricably entwined with the soil and stones of Anand Bhawan. Both seemed enveloped in a radiance of purpose, both wide open to the world, nothing in either limited to the purely personal. Nor was there anything grim or glum about either. Even the people who came and went, villagers, town workers, university students, the little known as well as the galaxy of leaders, had a buoyancy and gaiety of spirit. There was a lot of laughter in the house. Never was history made with the joy of living so amply woven into it. . . . Even a child felt it, sitting on the verandah after dinner, the floor still warm from a day of sun, looking up at the stars.

"I'll never let it down," I promised the stars, "I'll carry it everywhere as long as I live."

And "it" was all that Anand Bhawan stood for. Without "it" I would have had a country but no passionate identification with it. "It," I discovered, made searing demands on integrity as one grew up, exacted the best of oneself in truth and endeavour, but somehow also provided the courage to give it. And to renew myself at great moments—my marriage, the birth of a child —I had to go back to Anand Bhawan. . . .

What stands out in recent memory is the journey to Allahabad with Mamu's ashes in 1964. We were weary and heavy-eyed after a long night of vigil in the train, our ears filled with the tempestuous mourning voices that had besieged the train all night. In Allahabad there was silence. Our slow motorcade took us through soundless streets where people lined the route stock still, just watching. And then we were at Anand Bhawan, servants, friends, relatives—all those for whom Anand Bhawan had also been home—gathered on the front steps. I went upstairs away from them all to the library where Munshi Kanhaiyalal[18] had lovingly laid out a panorama of old newspaper and magazine clippings and pictures. Here was Mamu at all ages, unbelievably beautiful in youth, later time-scarred as he identified himself more and more closely with the sufferings of his people and through them with suffering everywhere. Here was

---

[18] Munshi Kanhaiyalal was the Nehru family's clerk cum general supervisor in charge of household affairs.

Mamu as I had first become aware of him—a Galahad in search of the Grail—Mamu of the impassioned speeches at Allahabad University—carrying his ardour to every corner of the country. . . . He had lived in the light, submitting with equal grace to its gentle glow and its harsh glare. It became clear all over again as the chimes of the University clock tower brought me back to the present, that we must not retreat into shadows of any kind, personal or national. We belonged where he had led us, in the light, and this house had embodied it through the years, passing it in some measure to everyone who had ever come in contact with it.

I hope that aura will remain as Anand Bhawan enters a new phase, and is put to a new use. I hope the people who come and go there will sense something of that past, remember a time when in the words of the hymn "glory shone around." I wish I had been invited there when it was given to the Nehru Memorial Trust, to stand in the garden for one last look round. But perhaps it does not matter. I had said my own farewell when Mamu died—and the atmosphere of Anand Bhawan is one I will carry to the end of my days.

Mrs Pandit belonged to a generation whose traditional values are not easily discarded. She said with a poignant recollection of her brother, and the *Statesman* quoted in its "On record" column on 1 February 1970: "My tie with Mrs Indira Gandhi is, as far as I am concerned, of abiding value." Birthdays provided an opportunity to re-establish the bonds that had been abruptly severed. A typical reply from Mrs Gandhi reads:

New Delhi
November 19, 1971

Dear Puphi,

Thank you for your card of birthday greetings.

I find birthday celebrations increasingly wearisome, although touring cyclone-affected areas can hardly be considered a more cheerful way of celebrating a birthday!

With good wishes,
Indu

Mrs Pandit's gestures were not reciprocated, and she was not invited to Sanjay Gandhi's wedding in 1974. On 14 February 1977 Mrs Pandit came out of retirement to campaign for the newly formed Congress for Democracy and the Janata Party in the approaching national election to Parliament against "the authoritarian trend that has grown to vast proportions." Her strongly worded statement included the [sentence: "I cannot live at peace with myself if, by my silence, I seem to agree with the destruction of all I have been taught to hold dear." She made it clear, however, that she bore her niece no personal animus and would do nothing to hurt her personally. In reply to a question at her news conference she said she would not visit Rae Bareli, Mrs Gandhi's constituency, during the campaign "because I do not want people of ill-will to exploit my stand" and "there are some decent values and family relationship which I cherish." Mrs Gandhi made neither reference nor response to this development though a group in her party reacted vehemently against it, issuing a public statement against Mrs Pandit. After Mrs Gandhi's electoral defeat, it was Mrs Pandit who called on her.

CHAPTER THREE

EMERGENCE—1967-1969

Just before the 1967 election the Soviet journal *New Times* commented that the prestige and influence of the Congress Party had notably declined and India had lost its socialistic zeal after Nehru (a sentiment expressed by Mrs Gandhi earlier). After Shastri, the journal said, the conservatives in the party had kept the radicals out of government, while a "prominent right winger," Morarji Desai, had been installed. This analysis ignored the fact that Nehru's choice of men in the composition of his cabinets was not bound by the conventional Left-Right division. It had been based on the complexities of the parliamentary and federal system, and on his vision of India as one of the world's most complex societies, capable of generating great strength through its political and cultural hetrogeneity, once planted firmly in freedom. Morarji Desai and Lal Bahadur Shastri had both held portfolios in Nehru's cabinets. The view that India had lost its socialistic zeal after Nehru is, however, significant because it became the platform for events to come, featuring a more facile outlook and a more impetuous breed of politician than had been able to surface in Nehru's time.

Nehru's own opinion and assessment of Shastri, a man he liked and trusted, are on record. In a letter dated 27 November 1956 to his sister Vijayalakshmi Pandit, High Commissioner for India in Britain, Nehru wrote:

Over and above all this came Lal Bahadur's resignation which I decided to accept, though very reluctantly. He resigned because of the terrible Railway disaster recently which was the second of its kind in two months. Of course it was not Lal Bahadur's fault. But taking everything into consideration and more especially Lal Bahadur's extreme unhappiness, I decided to accept this resignation. It is odd and pleasing to me to find how much this resignation has affected people. There has been a cry of regret and almost of sorrow from all kinds of quarters all over the country. It shows how popular Lal Bahadur is. He has gone up in people's estimation by this resignation. So far as I am concerned, he will not be out of Government for very long. That is, if things function as expected, he will come back into Government after the general election.

A later letter written at midnight on 6/7 June 1961 to his sister in London confirms this opinion over the years:

A little while ago Lal Bahadur came to see me. He came direct from Palam where he had arrived from Assam via Calcutta. We sent him from Durgapur to Assam because of the language trouble there. He has dealt with this matter with great tact and ability and come as near to a possible settlement as we could have hoped for. Of course, there are extremists who will create trouble and I am by no means sure of the settlement yet. Anyhow, Lal Bahadur has done a first class piece of work. It pleases me to see how he has grown with additional responsibilities. This is not my opinion only, but the general impression.

Nehru's satisfaction in the accomplishments of younger colleagues, and the responsibilities he gave to men and women whose political reputations were made as a result of their exercise, produced an array of experience in the Congress, providing it with the material of leadership. His consistent refusal to name a successor showed confidence in the men who would come after him. He valued Shastri's roots in the soil and the quiet conciliatory manner distinguishing him as a successful negotiator on thorny issues. Gravely ill in 1964 from the stroke he had suffered at Bhubaneshwar, he chose Shastri to take over his work, a factor that weighed with the party leaders who made him Prime Minister on Nehru's death.

The Soviet analysis with its black-white political divisions was not yet reflected in Mrs Gandhi's utterances. Asked by a journalist what the significance of her election as the country's leader was, she replied, "Perhaps it ensures some kind of continuity—continuity of policy, and also perhaps continuity of personality."[1] The

[1]Kuldip Nayar, *Between the Lines*, Allied, New Delhi, 1969.

reply showed she believed she had stepped into her father's shoes as the imaginative rallying point for all Indians. Yet Nehru had been, of desire and discipline, a man of his party, shaped and moulded by his service of it, and profoundly conscious of his debt to it. Mrs Gandhi already saw herself as something more, a party-plus image not yet attributable to her own leadership or record, and taken for granted as a birth right. Asked if she represented the Left, there was more than a touch of impatience in her reply, "I am a representative of all India which includes all shades of opinion."[2]

The press and the public automatically identified her with her father until marked differences of political style and behaviour became obvious and finally erupted into the open in 1969. The overt likenesses were there and she cultivated them. She had adopted his mannerism of flinging back garlands she received to delighted observers, especially children, and of delving into a crowd to find out for herself what was happening. Her speech from the Red Fort on 15 August 1967 (an annual event) was patterned on Nehru's own. Mrs Gandhi, who made an awkward impression as a public speaker on formal occasions before discerning audiences, when her delivery of a written speech was flat, came into her own before a crowd, where she was fluent and emphatic. On this occasion she congratulated the people on their courage and fortitude in facing drought. Warning them of difficulties ahead, she said India was in "mid-stream" where the water is deepest and current strongest, a rural analogy of the kind her father often used, easily understood by countryfolk used to crossing monsoon-swollen streams. She gave them "a simple definition of socialism": "Poverty should be eradicated; disparities between the rich and poor should be reduced; the backward people, be they Harijans or the hill people, should have equal distribution of national resources." And she ended with a Nehru-like flourish: "Through your veins runs the blood of heroes and great men. Let diffidence give way to confidence; let despair give way to hope. . . ." In conclusion she asked, as her father had always done at public meetings since independence, that the crowd shout *Jai Hind* after her.

Her father had presided over a very different political picture from the one she now faced. Other programmes and ideas, besides those presented by the Congress, were beginning to influence

[2]Kuldip Nayar, *India After Nehru*, Vikas, New Delhi, 1975.

Indian voters. Four general elections had built an expanding and more selective political consciousness. There were choices and the voter made use of them. The chief feature of the 1967 election was the gain of the Jan Sangh in the north, and the two communist parties in West Bengal and the south. The CPI-M had broken away from the CPI after the Chinese attack as a consequence of the world-wide split in the party about that time. Contemptuous of the CPI, which it accused of being lured by power and office, the CPI-M rejected "the hoax of parliamentarianism" and believed it must "accomplish the people's democratic revolution through revolutionary people's war by uniting the fighting masses . . . on the basis of a worker-peasant alliance."

Two kinds of violence had made their appearance: the Hindu-Muslim riot Indians thought they had seen the last of after the shock of Mahatma Gandhi's assassination, and the activities of the Naxalites. So named because of their seizure of the tribal village of Naxalbari in north Bengal (an uprising put down by the Marxist government of the state), Naxalism spread and formed cells in other states, often in universities, with a powerful attraction for sections of the educated young.

This picture showed no single ideological trend, leaving the Congress, though it had lost its privileged status, with a vital central role to play in the country, once it adjusted to post-election realities. Yet with the death of the towering figure to whom its factions—always forthright in inner-party debate—had given their allegiance, its dissident voices spoke louder. The long argument over the respective importance of its organizational and governmental wings began again. And with its loss of power in five states, the Congress now entered a phase of hard bargaining with other political parties in State Assemblies. Coalitions were made and unmade by a parade of floor-crossers and defectors, as unprincipled on the part of the Congress as other parties. These gave a caustic new term to Indian politics—"Aya Ram Gaya Ram." President's rule was imposed on states where government broke down, followed by fresh elections with no firmer majorities.

Though she was still "Nehru's daughter" to the country, Mrs Gandhi's style showed differences from his, some of them fundamenal in outlook and value. In her first broadcast as Prime Minister, on 26 January 1966, she had spoken of "the disconcerting gap between intention and action." "To bridge this gap we should boldly adopt whatever far-reaching changes in administration may be found necessary." She repeated the theme during the year and developed it in her convocation address to Roorkee University on 18 November 1967:

> I have no doubt that our present administrative system uses the expert inadequately and indifferently. It gives undue weight to the generalist and persists with criteria of competence developed in times when the range of Government decision was very limited and was unrelated to the demands of economic management and growth. . . . The officer mentality is also responsible for holding up progress.

Administrative reform had been the subject of expert advice and investigations since independence. With the government engaged in an enormous expansion of its activity, and its bureaucracy, some of the ground it covered was experimental, directives not uniformly backed by political will, and the resulting performance uneven. This situation was to worsen, not improve, under Mrs Gandhi who saw a "committed" civil service as essential to remedy. "Commitment" struck at the concept of the neutral civil servant, trained to advise about the risks and practicality of schemes. It left the government (many of whose members, later handpicked by her, were inexperienced in practical matters concerning administration) free to embark on poorly assessed ventures on the platform of "ideology." The civil service found itself the scapegoat for the whims and often the failures of policy. But it was the beginning of the inner structure of personal loyalty to Mrs Gandhi that was to be the trademark of all her functioning.

"We have to ensure," said Mrs Gandhi at a meeting of the revived National Integration Council in June 1968, "that our educational processes, the books we read, the radio we hear, the films we see, do not distort the Indian mind but lead it to integration and solidarity." Her remarks were not then construed as a call for reins on the mass media, but they were the first sign that the media must be more pointedly directed by government; the first sign, too, of a policy, contrary to the principle and practice so far, that expression must be free, and it was the leadership's duty to safeguard that freedom until it became part of the people's natural expectation. India had inherited a government-controlled broadcasting system from the British regime. Mrs Gandhi, who had been Minister for Information and Broadcasting in Shastri's cabinet, was the first Prime Minister to show a recognition of its importance as an instrument of power. In April 1971 she took charge of the portfolio herself.

Though she had at first welcomed opposition governments in the states as part of the democratic process, she later said in reply to a questionnaire from *Asia Magazine* (Hong Kong): "Fanatic and parochial forces are much in evidence. Some of them have been fomented by parties or individuals. I am deeply conscious of the danger they pose to our democracy." She found it hard to accept as "Indian" any view that did not accord with her own. ". . . our intellectuals, our industrialists and businessmen do not yet feel proud of being Indians," she told an interviewer from the Spanish magazine *Revista de Occidente*,[3] voicing her suspicion of a section of her own people for foreign readers. These attitudes, perhaps because they were so unlike her father's, paradoxically went unnoticed. Nehru had regarded an ineffective and even obstructive opposition as integral to democratic growth, and had, both as philosophy and deep personal impulse, included the various elements of society as partners in progress.

Noticeably different from her father's position within the Congress and his standing with the Old Guard, hers were by no means secure or friendly. Nehru had dominated the Congress but his innate civility and courtesy had gone far in keeping diverse teams of colleagues together and had given him the personal regard of those who crossed swords with him over policy. Mrs Gandhi's determined advocacy of herself did not endear her to men who had given their lives to the struggle for freedom, been repeatedly imprisoned, and had since independence occupied important positions, some in her father's cabinets. When in 1967 she considered taking the Congress presidentship herself after Kamaraj (as her father had done for a time), the suggestion was not approved by her party, and Nijalingappa became President. At the annual session of the Congress in Hyderabad in January 1968, six of the seven elected seats on the Working Committee went to Old Guard candidates, and only one to Mrs Gandhi's choice. These circumstances, where she had the symbols but not the actuality of power, frustrating

[3]19 March 1968.

to pride and authority at home, may have led her from the start to establish wide personal contacts abroad. She went on her first foreign tour as Prime Minister in March 1966, less than two months after taking office, visiting London, Paris, Moscow, and Washington. In September 1968 she toured Latin America and the Caribbean (the first Indian Prime Minister to visit these areas) and visited the USA, Britain, and West Germany.

In sharp contrast with her father, too, she was ill at ease with the press. Nehru, whose relations with it were confident and cordial, met the capital's press corps once a month. Mrs Gandhi held her third news conference in three years on 1 January 1969. The national press was generally indulgent toward her. Men who had covered her father's speeches, activities, and policies for decades, praised or condemned him with equal fervour, were apt to tread more softly with her in her inexperience, and to be generous in their judgements. Her inhibitions were often puzzling to them. Frank Moraes, a leading editor, recalled, "Nehru talked a great deal in an interview. You started him off, and off he went. She is not forthcoming. She's rather like a convent schoolgirl, tongue-tied. Nehru didn't care what the newspapers said about him. With her, if there's an article, editorial or cartoon she doesn't like, one of her entourage lets her disapproval be known." Her disapproval was generally ignored by the editors and proprietors of leading newspapers, who had a healthy disrespect for authority, but it became noticeable enough after 1969 to be raised in Parliament, when opposition MPs objected to governmental pressure to silence dissent.

At Mrs Gandhi's news conference on 1 January 1969, Trevor Drieberg, Ceylon-born member of Delhi's press corps, noted more poise and confidence than she had shown since becoming Prime Minister. Her two flashes of temper were "whether natural or carefully stage-managed, very effective. There was more than a touch of the old Nehru fire about them. The P.M. still lives very much under the shadow of her illustrious father, as her references to him in the course of her replies showed."[4]

A critic, Rajinder Puri, later put the same view somewhat differently:

[4]Trevor Drieberg, *Indira Gandhi: A Profile in Courage*, Vikas, New Delhi, 1972.

Indira, in fact, does not have a style which she may call her own.
And because the style is phony, the words ring false, with a
jarring clatter against the manner she perhaps seeks to emulate,
that of her father. Her every gesture, every mannerism, seems
to be modelled on that of the late Jawaharlal Nehru. The hurried, almost running walk, the rambling informality, the simula-
ted anger with an uncomprehending public, it is all there, a
trifle parodied, a little grotesque, as it evokes nostalgic memories
of the original. . . .[5]

The standard people remembered was her father's, and whether
the comparison was made by supporter or critic, in kind or harsh
terms, it found her lacking. Yet the comparison persisted, no one
yet recognizing her as being differently constituted and inspired.
Her belief in her own superior knowledge and judgement dating
from her tender years displayed itself once again when on 23 August
1968 she spoke in the Rajya Sabha on the situation in Czechoslovakia. Members had objected to the government's mildly stated
stand on Soviet interference, and her Minister for Petroleum and
Chemicals, Asoka Mehta, had resigned on the issue. Mrs Gandhi
said:

I have said in the other House and I would like to repeat here,
that perhaps there is nobody in this House who has had such
close contacts with Czechoslovakia for so many years as I have had
personally, not as a member of the Government, but ever since I
was a small girl. I have known the people of the country very
well, and I have known large sections of the people in the universities and in other spheres of activity.

Yet it took another year until in the struggle for power that split
the Congress and startled the country, her typical assertiveness
finally burst through to the public, and people put her in a class
by herself, no longer in her father's shade or mould.

[5]Rajinder Puri, *India: The Wasted Years*, Chetana, New Delhi, 1975.

CHAPTER FOUR

THE CONGRESS BREAKS—1969

On 1 January 1969 Mrs Gandhi ended her news conference[1] with the reprimand, "I hope it will be a year of better reporting." It had not begun to her liking. A journalist had asked: "What are your views about the activities of the Young Turks who attack the Ministers and sometimes even the whole government, and who, at the same time, swear their loyalty to you?" Mrs Gandhi replied: "I think this is for you to judge." When he persisted, she said: "We have always given considerable latitude to our party. This is not something that is happening for the first time."

Journalist: "I would like to know when it happened except when you came to power. It did not happen when Shastriji was here, much less when your father was in office."

Prime Minister to the company: "I am sorry, he is not well-informed. It happened many times when my father was in office."

Journalist: "Could you give me one instance?"

Prime Minister: "This is not a cross-examination. I resent the tone of the question. I am not going to be spoken to like that."

This crisp rejoinder, put down to the Nehru temperament, was however different in kind from the brief flares enlivening Nehru's speeches and conferences. Mrs Gandhi did not feel the need to explain or argue. Questions she did not like could simply be cut short by a reminder of who she was. And here, she showed a flash of irritation at the unfavourable contrast drawn, by implication, between her and her father. The above exchange is interesting, too, for its light on the vocal emergent radicals in the party known as the Young Turks, whose broadsides against members of the government were attracting notice as being unusually outspoken criticism for public consumption. Mrs Gandhi's protection to this growing

[1]Press Information Bureau release, Government of India.

personal following, hostile to men in her own government, was a noticeable enough departure from the past to be taken up at a news conference.

In mid-February 1969 mid-term elections in five states showed a continuing downhill slide for the Congress. Mrs Gandhi's own equanimity at this time, a particularly bleak time for her party, may have resulted directly from this political picture. Important members of the Old Guard had been defeated in the last general election, while her own following was developing into a vigorous and distinct camp. The balance of power in the Congress was changing with the tilt in her favour.

The newspapers commented on the decline of the Congress with gloom, speculating about the new crop of fortune-hunters, the unprincipled defections encouraged by all parties, and the danger to democracy in these circumstances. On 19 March 1969 the *Indian Express* commented editorially on the uneasy relationships between the Congress Party and the government, and even within the cabinet:

> . . . if the Congress breaks up, it will be calamitous for the country. . . . Mrs. Gandhi is at times prone to ruffle her colleagues by her speech. More often she is apt to startle them by her studied silence. . . . This habit of mind and approach does not make for happy individual relations, or for the smooth conduct of public affairs. . . . Collective Cabinet responsibility is the cornerstone of our Constitution. Lapses from the principle account for much of the misunderstandings and controversies generated in recent weeks. . . . A close understanding between the Congress Party President and the Prime Minister is overdue.

A highly unusual situation had arisen out of Mrs Gandhi's "habit of mind and approach." Effective consultation and discussion with her cabinet and party were nearly at a standstill. This editorial appeal for "collective Cabinet responsibility" did not, however, take into account the personality of the leader who, confident now of a party following, saw no reason for cooperation with men she needed much less than before.

That the Congress was not one happy family had been evident for some time. Trevor Drieberg wrote of the Congress session at Faridabad in April: "The time has come when Young Turk and

Old Gandhian can no longer hang together—even if the alternative is hanging separately."[2] But the division between young and old, radical and Gandhian, Left and Right was by no means so plain or simple. Between the Young Turks, now grouped behind Mrs Gandhi for radical changes in the country, and the Old Guard, whom they accused of holding the national scene static, there was a general body of convinced moderates who preferred to proceed with caution and usually carried the day. There was now, in addition, the need for stock-taking. Congress, released from charisma, seemed about to re-examine some of the sacred texts of policy in the light of the country's new priorities and the electorate's verdict. Shastri had introduced some personal preferences in policy— small-scale projects and the completion of large ones, rather than new investments in the public sector; and attention to neighbours rather than the global involvement India had pursued in Nehru's time. This post-Nehru development, cut short with Shastri's death, was viewed with grave suspicion by Congress radicals who now projected the issue before the party as socialism or its sabotage. There were obvious fallacies in a line-up so categorical within a party whose historic position had been centrist by choice. In their bitterest ideological battles Congressmen had found scope for co-operation. Defeat had been graciously conceded and the victor had shown magnanimity. Periodically the party had shed its fringes, both radical and conservative. In 1947 the Congress Socialist Party had left its parent body to become an independent Socialist Party because the Congress programme did not go far enough in radicalism. In 1959 C. Rajagopalachari had broken away to found the conservative Swatantra Party. Reacting strongly against the co-operative farming resolution adopted by the Nagpur Congress in January that year, he had flatly rejected the idea of cooperative cultivation "except in countries where private personal property is absent and forced labour is commandeered under Communist regimes."[3]

A determined fighter for greater economic definition against the communal and conservative elements in the Congress, Nehru had been at pains to keep its frictions within bounds and prevent a

[2]Trevor Drieberg, *Indira Gandhi: A Profile in Courage*, Vikas, New Delhi, 1972.

[3]*Hindustan Times*, 26 January 1959.

schism. National integration and development both demanded a
strong unifying focus. His own domination of the party had been
accepted because, apart from the shared adventure of the national
movement and the enduring human ties it had created, the party saw
him as a national inspiration, indispensable to its own success and
significance. Nehru's unique position within it remained tempered
by inner-party criticism, by his recognition of state leadership, by
his view of Congress strength as basically a local strength, and by
the reliance others placed on his code of ethics and conduct. In
the impasse now developing between Mrs Gandhi and the Congress, no comparable cushioning existed, either of an unassailable
personal and political position to her credit, or of give-and-take,
to shield the party from the shocks it was about to receive. Distant thunder, heralding a storm, hung in the air at the Faridabad
session.

President Zakir Husain died a few days after the session and the
choice of his successor precipitated a showdown between Mrs
Gandhi and the Congress President. Zakir Husain had been Mrs
Gandhi's personal choice for President. His death removed a reliable political lever from her side. The President could, on the
Prime Minister's advice, dissolve Parliament and order a new
election. Her opponents in her party believed this had been Mrs
Gandhi's main hold on Congress MPs who did not want to face
another election so soon after the recent debacle. The situation
could go against her with a new, unsympathetic President, if enough
Congress MPs expressed a lack of confidence in their leader and
asked the President to assure himself of the extent of her support.
The choice of the country's President became crucial for both
Congress factions whose poor opinion of each other had for some
time been ill concealed. The nature of the clash that followed lifted it out of political or party confines and gave the country its
first glimpse of an intractable character.

Mrs Gandhi in consultation with colleagues considered several
names—V.V. Giri, Jagjivan Ram, Swaran Singh, and Sanjiva Reddy
—and agreed to Reddy. Soon afterwards she became convinced
Reddy was not "her" man, that the party bosses would use him to
test her strength in Parliament and remove her from the prime
ministership. She had every reason to believe this might happen.
Her performance as Prime Minister had not impressed senior leaders and her aloof imperiousness had been resented. Her removal,

in the same orderly way as she had been elevated, was entirely possible. Her opponents would manoeuvre in the manner of professional politicians through the usual politicians channels, as they had done in the past, to gain acceptance for a candidate of their choice. This was a fight she could not be sure of winning. Her technique would have to be different. It started with a campaign of rumour to establish Reddy as the bosses' choice, not hers, though individuals in her camp, urged her to declare her open support for V.V. Giri, Vice President.

Mrs Gandhi then sent a note on economic policy to precede her arrival in Bangalore where the Congress Parliamentary Board was meeting to elect its candidate for the country's President. She described it as "a few stray thoughts" on the need to "re-state our economic policy and set the direction in which we have to move to achieve our goal."

The note was indicative of the lack of cohesion in recent Congress functioning. The "stray thoughts" broadly repeated the Working Committee resolution of May 1967, known as the Ten-Point Programme. Among these were nationalization of general insurance, removal of monopolies, curbs on property, state control over exports and foodgrains, "social control" of banks, and the abolition of princely privileges. The Working Committee meeting had been poorly attended, with no detailed study beforehand of the items on its agenda. The thorough preparation characterizing policy discussions in the past was absent, as was a proper consideration of each item. The programme, superficially discussed, was adopted. During its ratification by the All India Congress Committee, the abolition of princely privileges was extended to purses, and social control of banks was changed to nationalization. Almost immediately controversy over the Ten Points began. Mrs Gandhi's cabinet did not agree to them all. In October 1967 her cabinet reverted to social control of banks, to be operated by a national credit council run by the Reserve Bank to give more aid to agriculture, small industry, and exports. Lacking the vivid gesture of outright nationalization, Morarji Desai argued it was capable of achieving more solid benefits.

The "stray thoughts" sent to Bangalore would, therefore, have been better argued exhaustively, even battled for decisively within the policy-making forum of the party rather than, as followed, taken as theatre to the streets. Mrs Gandhi's purpose was to make it clear the initative for party programmes was to be hers, at governmental level, and not to rest with the organization. Theatre, too, was intended, as publicity to illustrate this parting of the ways and establish her undisputed authority over the organization. Bank nationalization, one of the "stray thoughts," was soon to symbolize the new era of radicalism.

The party, still unclear about the Ten Points, accepted Mrs Gandhi's note in the interests of peace, and it was commended to the Union and state governments, a victory to Mrs Gandhi, but the Congress Parliamentary Board elected Sanjiva Reddy as its official candidate with five votes against two (Mrs Gandhi and Fakhruddin Ali Ahmed) for Jagjivan Ram. Mrs Gandhi told the press next day that the Board's decision was a "calculated attempt" to humiliate her and to challenge are authority as Prime Minister. She thus gave public notice that she would fight any attempt to undermine her position. Her father, twice overruled by the Board when it chose Dr Rajendra Prasad for the presidency in 1952, and again in 1957, had both times accepted its decision.

Mrs Gandhi's answer to being ignored was to retaliate with a dose of the same medicine. A week later she made the surprise announcement of the nationalization of fourteen leading banks, by passing the party to make a direct impact on the public. The manner of the measure, by ordinance, though Parliament was to open in two days, was as sensational as the measure itself. Before taking this step she relieved Morarji Desai of the Finance portfolio though she offered him another berth. Desai chose to resign, and Mrs Gandhi took over Finance herself. This lightning strike at independence from her party sent a tremor of excitement through the country. With its apparent disdain for party forum and for due processes of law, the Prime Minister's action removed some invisible restraint and decorum from public and political behaviour. Politics flared overnight into the streets. Rallies were arranged daily outside Mrs Gandhi's residence to congratulate her on bank nationalization and acclaim her leadership. The use of money and transport to bring workers to meetings, along with government's control of radio, had always given the ruling party an edge over others. But this was the first time street demonstrations had been staged by a Prime Minister. Their size and regularity, and the expertise now in evidence, had the gloss of preparation and planning, and of the commuinst genius for efficient organization. Also recognizable communist technique was Mrs Gandhi's vocabulary of class war, and the cry that all who were not with her were against her.

Mrs Gandhi and her camp did not anticipate the breakup of the Congress, nor did they desire it. But as the crisis proceeded it became evident that unity was not a concern either unless the party put her in sole command. That she would settle for nothing less, and saw the battle through to rupture, seemed to indicate her plans were not of an order acceptable to the party's broad centrist approach, and that a sharp turn in its affairs was intended. To bring this about the Old Guard had to be discredited, so that the new leadership could emerge without the taint of the old. At the same time homage to Mahatma Gandhi and Nehru—essential for a hold on the masses—had to be maintained. Both these objectives were brilliantly accomplished in a series of moves resembling a coup, leaving Mrs Gandhi's opponents confounded and confused. The rallies at her residence blazoned bank nationalization as a people's measure, pushed through against vested interests in the Congress. They marked the beginning of populist politics and a leadership cult. With its dynastic, emotional flavour the cult highlighted the theme of Mrs Gandhi's uniqueness among her contemporaries and her special claim to patriotism by virtue of her Nehru blood. A souvenir, *Re-birth of the Congress*, published in December, featured an extract from a book by Mrs Gandhi's late aunt, Krishna Hutheesing: "In her veins flows the blood of her father and grandfather . . . like the Ganga she belongs to India and India is the one passion of her life."

This sentiment was more poetic than accurate. Though she belonged imaginatively to India, Mrs Gandhi was probably less a product of the Indian environment than any contemporary in Congress circles. She had, intermittently with her Indian schooling, attended schools in Switzerland and England. Her father had never considered an Indian university for her. His own education had been British and his plans for his daughter reflected this preference. Nehru had written to Mrs Pandit from Badenweiler on 15 November 1935, when Indira was four days short of her eighteenth birthday:

The problem of Indu's further education is not an easy one to solve. Practically all the countries, excepting England, France and Switzerland are barred for some reason or other. . . . After a great deal of thought I came to the conclusion that she might go to Oxford in October 1936 and after completing her three years there, proceed to Paris for a year or so, subject to political developments on the continent. . . . The examination for October 1936 takes place in December 1935, that is, next month. Indu cannot appear for it so soon. The next examination is early in 1937 for October 1937, which means that Indu has to wait for two years before she joins Oxford. That is rather a long time. A year would have been the right period and would have suited her, for she is not quite grown up enough, intellectually or otherwise, for the university. . . . For the present I propose to send Indu, probably next week, to Mlle. Hemmelin at Bex. . . . From October 1936 onward for about a year she might be in Paris attending lectures at the Sorbonne, and if so decided, taking the Somerville entrance and scholarship exam early in 1937. . . .

V.V. Giri declared his candidature for the presidency when Mrs Gandhi failed to get Jagjivan Ram accepted by the Parliamentary Board. She had filed Reddy's nomination papers, and as Prime Minister, still ostensibly supported her party's candidate, but the campaign had become a prestige issue for her and it was an open secret that she did not intend to abide by her commitment.

This explosive change from the political style of her two predecessors lit up Mrs Gandhi's individual approach in a way that none of her statements and emphases had done till now. The dynamic for political action had earlier issued from the national movement, the multi-layered following of Mahatma Gandhi constituting a great social force, and its continuance by Nehru into the independence era. The earlier phase had been distinguished by the discipline of non-violence. After independence the Indian scene remained unusual in Asia because of the restrained, educated tone the leadership employed in seeking the cooperation of a vast, unlettered electorate for the understanding and solution of long-term problems. This atmosphere began to be rapidly dissipated. In search of support, Mrs Gandhi had found the CPI, anxious for political respectability and power, eager to cooperate. The skilful use of economic conditions and the vivid vocabulary of class war as political weapons yielded rapid initial dividends. The campaign of street arousal introduced a throbbing undercurrent of exaggeration, excess and violence waiting like electricity to be switched on.

The national newspapers expressed their downright dismay at these developments, seeing them as a virulent struggle for power carried too far for the country's good, and deplored the inflaming of uninformed sentiment by dramatic methods and catchy slogans. When the Supreme Court issued an Interim Stay Order on bank nationalization, this, together with the reservations of the national press, gave Mrs Gandhi cause to say "the people" were with her, while "vested interests" were not.

Meanwhile the quarrel over the presidential candidate raged furious. Till this election it had been a routine affair decided by mutual consultation between parties so that the highest office in the land—one above politics—should not become a matter for political bargaining. Mrs Gandhi accused Nijalingappa of "collusion" with the Right parties, Jan Sangh and Swatantra, over the choice of the presidential candidate. It had been accepted practice to solicit the votes of other parties for one's own candidate, and the Jan Sangh and Swatantra had agreed to support Reddy, though the two communist parties had declared for Giri. In the new political atmosphere the arrangement acquired the ring of betrayal and Nijalingappa the label of "reactionary" in a precision attack directed against his political integrity. The threatening mood of the party's radicals prompted him to ask Mrs Gandhi to issue a whip to Congress MPs to vote for Reddy. On 15 August, five days before the election, Mrs Gandhi called instead for a "vote of conscience" saying, "I feel that the issues go beyond the presidential poll." That morning her speech at the Red Fort had referred to the "tremendous and spontaneous reception" bank nationalization had received. "Today we have taken a new turn and a new dawn has set in. . . . I want to assure the rich and the capitalists that the step we have taken is not directed against them."

Mrs Gandhi's personal and public image—indeed her political future—were heavily dependent on the election result and it is interesting to speculate on the turn of events had Giri been defeated. He won by a narrow margin in the second count, with 420,077 votes in his favour and 405,527 against him. This was the signal for a fresh turnout of rallies and street celebrations outside the Prime Minister's house. Nijalingappa called the "personality cult a mischievous and dangerous trend in democracy" but with his candidate's defeat he and his supporters had suffered an irreparable loss of face. When the Working Committee met in New Delhi on 25 August, Y.B. Chavan[4] attempted to hold the party together by means of a "unity resolution" separating the scope and tasks of its parliamentary and organizational wings, but Mrs Gandhi did not attend the meeting and her supporters held an angry demonstration at Congress headquarters at 7 Jantar Mantar Road while the meeting was in progress, in defiance of the prohibitory orders then in force. The demonstration, organized by Shashi Bhushan, MP, consisted of more than the MPs who officially constituted it. Rajinder Puri, journalist, gives the following account:

When I approached the spot there was a great commotion going on. The demonstrators, a few hundred of them, stood in the middle of the road in front of the Congress Party office building, waiting to leap into their orgy of screams and abuse, of kicking, shoving and spitting, as each member of the Working Committee drove up to attend its meeting, Mrs. Gandhi and all her supporters having boycotted it. Most of the journalists were inside the gates on the lawn, while she stood outside it watching the spectacle. Movie cameramen from the Government Films Division and the TV men from the Ministry of Information and Broadcasting stood in strategic positions with their cameras posed to record for posterity and cinemas throughout the country the historic scenes of mass upsurge being enacted there on that otherwise quiet, mild autumn day in Delhi. . . . They were all in at last, only C.B. Gupta coming in without any mishap as his car drove into the gateway through the milling demonstrators, C.B. himself smartly rapping a cane on the knuckles of those who had the temerity to push their hands through the window of the car. . . . Poor Nijalingappa walked all the way through the yelling screeching demonstrators, barefoot, with footwear in hand, and his glasses slipping all over his face. . . . There were two aspects of it which were particularly ugly. These were for the most part old men, incapable of violence, who were being threatened in such cowardly fashion. . . . The police prevented any real violence from taking place, it is true, but they did not prevent the demonstrators

[4]Minister for Home Affairs.

from offering real provocation for a violent retaliation, which naturally could never come from Nijalingappa and company. . . . The more disturbing aspect, however, was the fact that in the capital of India this ugly demonstration with fascist overtones was not only allowed to take place but actually encouraged by the government. . . .[5]

The "unity resolution" was accepted by the party but the war between its factions, now out in the open, continued. Mrs Gandhi launched a signature drive for an early session of the AICC to elect a new President, though Nijalingappa's term was not over. Nijalingappa called this a violation of party discipline and asked her to explain her conduct. But the legalities and proprieties now looked anaemic next to Mrs Gandhi's bank nationalization coup and the election of V.V. Giri. She received the presidential seal of approval for her conduct when Mrs Giri, receiving her joyfully after her husband's victory, welcomed Mrs Gandhi as "my darling daughter." On 8 November Mrs Gandhi released a Letter to Congressmen:

What we witness today is not a mere clash of personalities, and certainly not a fight for power. It is not as simple as a conflict between the parliamentary and organisational wings. It is a conflict between two outlooks and attitudes in regard to the objectives of the Congress and the methods in which Congress itself should function.

The Letter established her personal links with the Congress past and her special claim to the Mahatma Gandhi-Nehru inheritance:

The Congress was moulded by Mahatma Gandhi and my father to be the prime instrument of social change. . . . In his last years my father was greatly concerned that there were people inside the Congress who were offering resistance to change. My own experience even before the fourth general election was that the forces of status quo, with close links with powerful economic interests, were ranged against me.

[5]Rajinder Puri, *India: The Wasted Years*, Chetana, New Delhi, 1975.

On 12 November Nijalingappa expelled her from the Congress, and the break was complete when two parallel AICC sessions were held in Delhi on 22 November. In December rival Congress sessions were held at Ahmedabad (Nijalingappa) and Bombay (Mrs Gandhi). The *Hindustan Times* noted that "there was little specific to differentiate them." K. Rangachari, economic analyst, writing in the *Statesman* on 5 January 1970, agreed that "the economic manifestoes of the two Congress factions have much in common as they both take the 10-point programme of the undivided Party as their starting point. In the context of the controversy raised over the sincerity of their pursuit of socialism, neither wished to yield to the other in its desire to appear more radical. . . ."

Rangachari detailed the economic steps the undivided Congress had taken toward socialism, comparing them with the measures taken or proposed by Mrs Gandhi's Congress at Bombay. The first social measure taken in independent India had been the nationalization of the Imperial Bank of India, which gave the state

a commanding height in the banking system, which along with the Reserve Bank's control of monetary policy, gave all the power it required to make the banking system subserve the needs of planning and industrial development. The takeover of fourteen more banks last year has merely extended the public sector's share in banking from one-third to four-fifths . . . achieved at the cost of creating misgivings in many quarters about future policy, and jettisoning the principles of the mixed economy . . . the nationalisation of life insurance in 1956 . . . transferred large public funds to Government; the proposed nationalisation of general insurance [by Mrs Gandhi's Congress] is unlikely to provide anything equally substantial either in terms of resources or of opportunities of improving public welfare, since general insurance does not touch the life of the ordinary citizen in the way life insurance did.

The right of property had earlier been modified:

The exemption of 64 State laws on land reform from the scope of the fundamental rights, the exclusion of the courts' jurisdiction on questions of adequacy of compensation, sanction for interference with the rights of joint stock companies, and for modification of mining leases, and the wide definition given to the term "estate", together constituted a major assault on property rights. It is significant that on the present occasion the radicals could only think of abolishing the fundamental right to property altogether.

He listed the tax measures already taken towards the socialist orientation of economic policy: estate duty (1953), capital gains (1956), taxes on wealth, expenditure, gifts, company dividends, and bonus shares. In 1960 Morarji Desai had introduced the corporation tax as a separate entity and the super profits tax. Desai was responsible, too, for the Gold Control Order, initiated when he was Finance Minister in Nehru's cabinet, "as a measure of social reform to discourage the craze for gold ornaments."

And the outstanding contribution to the socialist ideology was, of course, the massive investments in the public sector under three Five Year Plans which gave the State a dominant position. . . . State undertakings in industry alone have claimed more than Rs. 3,000 crores; to this has to be added large outlays on irrigation, power, shipping, air and railway transport. The commanding heights are now all in the public sector. The State Trading Corporation occupies an important position, in both the import and export trade. . . . Her [Mrs Gandhi's] theory of obstruction cannot therefore stand scrutiny.

The Congress split, and the way it was brought about, transformed the political atmosphere. Nehru and Shastri, inheriting the Gandhian approach to politics, with its marriage of ends and means, had peasonally practised and upheld a meticulous standard of political behaviour. Mrs Gandhi's role in the presidential election had been one of manipulation and intrigue, and her strategy to gain control of her party had displayed a militancy foreign to Congress tradition. She represented something ruthless and new. She had astonished people with her flair for cold assessment, shrewd timing, and the telling theatrical gesture; above all, with her capacity for a fight to the finish, even to bringing the 84-year-old party of liberation to rupture. She had made use of realpolitik, suiting the action to the moment's need, undeterred by any backlog of sentiment or ethics. Her own emergence from an image of extreme withdrawal and reserve was now complete.

The effect on her party was immediate. A swing to the winning side began, with the majority deserting the sinking ship of the Old Congress. Morality was not, in any case, the order of the day, Jagjivan Ram, one of Mrs Gandhi's crucial supporters during the split, had not, it now appeared, filed tax returns for ten years. Questioned about this at a meeting of the Press Club in New Delhi, Mrs Gandhi remarked that he was a busy man and had probably forgotten. Jagjivan Ram, who controlled the Untouchable vote, was an important ally. He was obliged in the glare of publicity to pay his taxes, but at a time when stringent laws for default existed, not penalized for the delay. His forgetfulness provided excellent material for the cartoonists and more acid comment on the political scene.

The shine had rubbed off most politicians for a country that was tired of their calls for sacrifice from their own safe and comfortable berths. Mrs Gandhi evoked considerable public admiration for having outmanoeuvred them all, the exponent of a tough new breed. She later described herself in much the same terms: "My father was a saint who strayed into politics. I am a tough politician." The public hoped that her toughness, along with fresh blood in the organization, might provide the momentum the country needed. She had sympathy in abundance for her fight against bossism and the enthusiasm of many who hoped for the "new dawn" she had spoken of at the Red Fort. As a child she had imagined herself a Joan of Arc, leading her people into battle. To this her public relations office now added the more relevant Indian image of Rani Lakshmibai of Jhansi who had so valiantly led her army against the British during the Revolt of 1857. She was no longer the mere leader of a party but projected as the agent of a historic process, woman of destiny, champion of the poor, in touch with the people's urges and aspirations, and uniquely qualified to lead them. She was now in command over a thoroughly roused public to whom she had promised a new era in socialism in the language of incitement and emotion. The outward resemblance to her father was over, and this showed most clearly on the public platform. Nehru's speeches had had a quality of intimacy with the crowd. A huge assembly became for him a person and a "speech" a conversation. He was given to displaying his doubts, to self-searching, to taking the people he addressed into his confidence. It is likely that the unsophisticated, who formed the bulk of his audiences, came to listen to a chat, albeit about grave and solemn affairs of state. The political air one breathes affects the talk in streets, market places, and drawing rooms. The talk had flowed over a scene extraordinarily lacking in political tension. Mrs Gandhi's pent-up intensity, finding release on the public platform, charged the atmosphere with peculiar tension.

Her successful disregard of the proprieties had paved the way for her to begin to exercise a degree of open authoritarianism. On 13 December 1969 the Union government issued a directive to state government at their annual conference in Delhi, telling them they had "unfettered freedom" to use their ultimate weapon: President's rule. The dictatorial use of powers by governors became the subject of Opposition protest in the Lok Sabha. The directive contrasted with Nehru's to governors in 1949 and 1952, reminding them they were constitutional heads and that a governor "should not and cannot override or interfere with the decisions of his cabinet who are responsible to the State legislature."

A month earlier, Mrs Gandhi's younger son, Sanjay, had applied along with seventeen other applicants for a licence to manufacture an indigenous small car. The following November he became the sole recipient of a licence and undertook to produce 50,000 cars a year, equivalent to the whole annual production of cars in India in a good year. His principal backer was K.K. Birla. The Birla family's best political investment had been Mahatma Gandhi, and it had continued close to the Congress leadership after independence.

CHAPTER FIVE

THE NEW CONGRESS REVEALS
ITS STYLE—1970

When Parliament opened on 17 November 1969 the government, represented by Mrs Gandhi's New Congress, found itself in a minority, with sixty MPs of the undivided Congress now sitting in the Opposition. But it had a working 'majority with the support of regional parties and some Independents. Its vital support came from the CPI, whose style and slant began to be felt in some of the ministries. In spite of her reduced numbers Mrs Gandhi was in a buoyant mood. The Congress split had secured for her an independent identity, status, and following. She told the Indian Science Congress on 4 January 1970: "The last few months have been exciting ones. Swift and dramatic events have taken place. As a result, you will find everywhere a sense of quivering urgency, an atmosphere of heightened expectations and a demand for quick results." She delivered a uniform message at mass meetings through the year: the need for reducing disparities, and for ceilings on property and land. The country faced danger, she said, from those who wanted to block socialist policies. She would implement these undaunted by the canards spread against her.

She did not specify the "canards" except on one occasion after the emergency of 1975, when she told a delegation from Nehru Youth Centres of "baseless canards" spread by the Opposition that she smoked and drank. Her opponents, referred to in her Letter to Congressmen on 8 November 1969 as "the forces of the status quo, with close links with powerful economic interests," could not by definition include the Socialist Party and the CPI-M, committed since their inception to radical change. It did not apply to the Old Congress, till yesterday her own party, dominated till the end of his life by her father, and responsible for the vistas of change since independence. With all its scope for elasticity and interpretation, it was avowedly a socialist party and would not have sur-

vived as a credible entity but for this. The terminology she employed did not apply even to the Jan Sangh, whose interest in the
status quo was based on religion and culture rather than economics, and whose "links with powerful economic interests" were
negligible, nearly non-existent, compared with those of the undivided Congress, and later so publicly identified with Mrs Gandhi's
party. Her forceful, insistent, and repetitious language, when ana-
lyzed, seemed puzzlingly remote from actual data. What did Mrs
Gandhi mean? What she meant was further complicated by the
pervasive personal element in her statements. Her Letter to Congressmen said there was an opposition to her personally, bent on
keeping her out of power. Earlier she had construed the vote of
the Congress Parliamentary Board for Reddy (rather than Jagjivan
Ram) as an insult and a "plot" against her, not the prosaic procedural exercise it was, of outvoting the leader as leaders are regularly outvoted and replaced by their parties. The dislike and distrust her former colleagues had of her—dull, inadequate material
for drama—was converted by her intensely imaginative faculty into the grander stuff of hate and fear of a more-than-leader, a
national symbol. Her own utterances invented the beleaguered
heroine, fighting the shadowy forces of evil, one whose victory or
defeat would be the victory or defeat of socialism in India.

Did Mrs Gandhi's colleagues mean the same thing she meant?
The confusion arising at times out of official statements blurred
issues and debates. A haze descended on argument and was, it
seemed, deliberately held there. The New Congress had broken
with the old so that it would be free to move decisively Leftward,
but Left was most of the modern Indian horizon from the Mahatma's
socialism to that inspired by Marx. Where in the spectrum did the
New Congress lie and what did it want? What was needed, at this
time of absolute break with the old party, was clear explanation,
and this was lacking. Cries against the "rich," the "big," and the
"monopolists" rose with a great stir and beating of wings like
flocks of birds into the air and vanished. No one quietly nailed
problems to the ground. "Commitment" was demanded of the
civil service, the judiciary, and the press. Yet it meant not an
educated sensitivity to what was best for the common welfare,
but government control, an idea so repugnant to free India that
it had stormy repercussions. On 9 February Mrs Gandhi was obliged to say: "Recently my remarks that we needed government

servants with commitment have been, perhaps deliberately, mis-interpreted to mean that I want civil servants to support me and my political ideology. On the contrary, I do not want politically convenient or servile civil servants." Yet Mohan Kumaramanga-lam, distinguished CPI theoretician now in Mrs Gandhi's Cong-ress, and credited with having an increasing influence on her poli-cies, said plainly that the government needed "civil servants who thought like us."[1] Kumaramangalam, who entered the cabinet as Minister for Steel and Mines in April 1971, and was probably its chief spokesman after Mrs Gandhi, gave "commitment" its final seal of authority on 2 May 1973 in the Lok Sabha, when he defend-ed the supersession of three judges of the Supreme Court—Jus-tices Shelat, Hegde and Grover—and the appointment of a junior judge, A.N. Ray, as Chief Justice. In naming a Chief Justice, he said, "the government is entitled to look into his philosophy and outlook and decide that we must have a forward-looking and not a backward-looking man." It was clear what a communist meant when he said this, and in government pronouncements only its CPI spokesmen spoke in understandable language and with recogniz-able intent. This particular step, designed to bring the Supreme Court in line with the government, proved crucial in later events for Mrs Gandhi's political survival. A.N. Ray, chosen for his ac-ceptability to the CPI coterie in Mrs Gandhi's camp, was a good example of the "commitment" required of the judiciary. Had the principle of selection of a Chief Justice, on the basis of quality rather than seniority, been explained and suitably canvassed, it is probable that it would have won many adherents and been hailed as a reform in the judicial system. Ray's appointment had no such high purpose to recommend it.

In 1970, at the beginning of the controversy, events had not yet forced definition, and confusion reigned supreme. Mrs Gandhi told the Rajya Sabha in early March 1970 that she believed in democracy and an independent judiciary. What she meant was again in question when the Governor of West Bengal, S.S. Dhavan, speaking to the Bar Association and Bar Library Club of the Calcutta High Court, held up the Soviet legal and political system as an example to his audience. Mrs Gandhi's own actions clouded her meaning in what was becoming a simmering confrontation

[1]Kuldip Nayar, *India After Nehru*, Vikas, New Delhi, 1975.

with the Supreme Court. On 10 February 1970 the Court had struck down as invalid the Act of 1969 nationalizing fourteen banks. Mrs Gandhi overcame this by a Presidential Ordinance on 14 February renationalizing the banks with retrospective effect from 19 July 1969. This was the first of several Presidential Ordinances used to enact business outside the parliamentary process, with Parliament in due course endorsing the measure taken. Government by ordinance, used at first to push through measures she could not get accepted by Parliament for want of a majority, and her otherwise free use of presidential powers, became a marked feature of her style, and demonstrated how valuable a cooperative President was to her concept of government. In September 1970 a Presidential Order was used to derecognize the princes when the Government Bill to abolish privy purses and privileges failed by one vote to get a two-thirds majority in the Rajya Sabha, though the Lok Sabha adopted it. On 1 October President's rule was imposed with undue haste on Uttar Pradesh and the proclamation suspending the state legislature signed on Russian soil, the President being on a visit to the Soviet Union at the time. An obvious and unseemly political manoeuvre, it had to be revoked after sixteen days of controversy when Charan Singh, BKD (Bharatiya Kranti Dal) leader whose coalition had fallen apart with the sudden desertion of its New Congress members, formed a majority government without them.

The privy purse issue and the vote concerning it in the Lok Sabha provided a contrast with the receding values of the Nehru era. The abolition of privy purses had been raised at the AICC in 1963. Nehru had opposed abolition on the ground that the figure of Rs 50 million was automatically going down, each successor inheriting a reduced purse. Another more fundamental consideration ruled his approach: the Government of India had a convenant with the princes, and a government must keep its word. Writing to his sister, India's High Commissioner in London, on 3 April 1955 on the subject of foreign investment and the Government of India's attitude to it, he had expressed much the same sentiment:

It never pays to destroy one's credit in the foreign market, and we have no intention of doing anything which might have that effect. Also, all major investments by foreigners are usually by contract with the Government of India. For the Government to break its own contract would be bad. Governments do not do this kind of thing. Therefore there is really no question of apprehension on the part of foreign investors in India. I have made this clear already in Parliament and elsewhere. This evening I spoke at length at a huge public meeting in Delhi and again made this clear. I shall refer to it when the Bill comes up before Parliament again.

The Bill to abolish privy purses got the required two-thirds majority in the Lok Sabha by a narrow margin of eight votes. Opposition members discovered six were invalid, as five voters had recorded their vote twice "by mistake," and one vote had been recorded for a member not present in the House. The Speaker agreed to hold an enquiry but declared himself satisfied that the majority had not been affected. An episode which for its impropriety would have had repercussions of shock under Nehru and Shastri, and would have been cleared to the satisfaction of the Opposition in order to restore faith in parliamentary procedure, was glossed over. The Speaker's reputation for impartiality suffered as did the standards expected till now of Parliament.

In March 1970 Mrs Gandhi told the Rajya Sabha: "At any moment if any privately owned industry is operating against the national interest or is impeding social progress, we should not hesitate to take it over." But since "national interest" and "social progress" had not been reduced to directives, it was not predictable what direction government's economic policy might at any moment take, and in what context industry should plan to operate.

In contrast with this (perhaps deliberate) lack of philosophy, a specific direction was taken by the government during the year in matters concerning information and culture. On 20 February 1970 diplomatic missions were required to close culture centres other than those located at their headquarters. This followed the discovery of an unauthorized Russian building under construction in Trivandrum, but the effect of the order was to shut down five USIS and two French centres. The Soviet embassy gave the running of its Trivandrum centre to the Indian government on whom it could rely for patronage to its programmes. By the end of 1970, although foreign culture centres had been closed, there were 115 embassy journals in circulation. The government's Publications

Division annual *India 1971-72* listed 47, the highest number, produced by the USSR, and 17, the second highest, by the USA.

On 23 August the BBC was ordered to close its office in India for showing Louis Malle's film on India, with its reported concentration on the grimmer sights of Calcutta. Later the import of American movies was stopped on the ground that there was no reciprocity in the film trade between the two countries. Film selection and imports were to be channelled through the State Trading Corporation. Later (1973) the STC was authorized to take over the import of textbooks and it was suggested the control might be extended to general books to prevent "pornographic" and "politically offensive" books from entering the country.

The free circulation of information and ideas had been a cardinal principle of India's leadership. Mrs Gandhi's incursions, actual and projected, into the fields of knowledge, information, and culture were evidence of another value system altogether. She was heavily dependent at this time on communist support, and had former CPI members as ministers and advisers. This may have accounted for the categorical line she took, and her monotonous espousal of the obstructionist theory, calculated by sheer repetition to gain credence, especially among the uneducated population. There was a communist stamp also to her violent aversion to the "uncommitted" intellectual, the Opposition and the press. Yet she had herself earlier advocated greater government control of the media. Radio and television had during the presidential election effectively projected V.V. Giri as the candidate with her blessing, and herself as the symbol of a mass upsurge against vested interests. It is reasonable to assume that her mind and its direction were her own. She displayed an awareness of the vital levers of power once again when on 26 June 1970 in a major cabinet reshuffle she took the Home portfolio herself (giving Finance to Chavan), with its supervision of the intelligence network, the police and the Election Commission. The Research and Analysis Wing (RAW), as the intelligence network was named, operated, in part, under Mrs Gandhi's direct command though in name it was made accountable to the Cabinet Secretariat. RAW did not remain an anonymous, behind-the-scenes agency, but became an actor on the political stage, with the press commenting on its activities, including the bugging of telephones of government's political opponents, censorship of their mail and impressive growth within a few years of its five-crore rupee budget to 100 crores. RAW was also reported to provide Mrs Gandhi with dossiers on Union and state ministers and officers of the rank equivalent to brigadier and above of the armed forces. Commenting on its methods, Jyotirmoy Basu (CPI-M) told a meeting of the Home Ministry's Consultative Committee in Parliament:

> On April 20, 1972 while speaking during the demands for grants for the Ministry of Home Affairs, I said 'that the Research and Analysis Wing formulates, operates and executes through fascist methods; with it came subsidiary bureaus and other sister organisations. The function is to keep Left forces out of power, destroy democratic methods and oppose by all possible means the persons and political parties which are against the ruling coterie headed by Mrs Gandhi. . . . My information is that seven unprinted, unmarked crates arrived in Bombay dockyard a few months ago which weren ot even touched by the customs or port authorities under instructions from the top. The same day these boxes disappeared for Delhi. The Research and Analysis Wing is being organised purely on the lines of the Hitlerite forces and its sole job is to destroy democracy in the country, and a White Paper on this organisation is absolutely essential.

Jyotirmoy Basu's warning against a sinister and unaccounted growth of extra-constitutional power in Mrs Gandhi's hands was soon backed by other parties. Mrs Gandhi's personal interest in surveillance extended to finance. Intelligence relating to revenue, though formally under the Finance Ministry, took its orders from the Prime Minister's Secretariat operating both from South Block, New Delhi, and her house at 1 Safdarjang Road.

The aura of personal fealty to Mrs Gandhi surrounding RAW came from its head, R.N. Kao, one of the Kashmiri Brahmins[2] in her confidence. Here, as elsewhere, she provided a marked con-

---

[2]Other Kashmiri Brahmins in the administration were: P.N. Haksar, Principal Private Secretary to the Prime Minister; T.N. Kaul, Foreign Secretary, later Indian Ambassador to the United States; P.N. Dhar, Economic Adviser to the Prime Minister's Secretariat, later her Principal Private Secretary; D.P. Dhar, Indian Ambasador to the USSR, later chief of the Planning Commission.

trast with her father's relaxed tread and his approach to the tasks of governing. The Kashmiri Brahmin clique implied a strong, almost tribal suspicion of the "outsider," a prejudice that found its ultimate expression in her later unabashed promotion of her son, Sanjay.

In July 1970 the Opposition brought a no-confidence motion in Parliament, charging Mrs Gandhi with rigging the state election in Kerala. She replied: "It is obvious that the entire motion is designed as a personal attack on me, on the supposed concentration of power in my hands. . . . I have been compared, not for the first time, to Hitler, Stalin and Mussolini. I think the people will laugh at the preposterousness of these comparisons." Her persistent reduction of all criticism to "a personal attack on me" had the effect of slamming a door, much as tears or an emotional outburst put an end to argument. Mrs Gandhi's public speeches through the year had a strong defensive flavour, the lonely furrow ploughed against mighty and dangerous forces.

The forces visibly at work in the country were not, however, vested interests obstructing socialism so much as those demanding speedier and more radical change (as with the Naxalite movement) by violence, though communal violence had also taken its toll at Bhiwandi, Jalgaon, and other parts of Maharashtra. It was to the theme of obstruction by reactionary and communal forces that Mrs Gandhi returned in her broadcast of 27 December, announcing a mid-term election. She was insecure in Parliament with her reduced majority and her dependence on other parties, besides being up against a far from docile Opposition. Her reliance on extra-Parliamentary devices showed her path had not proceeded smoothly. In February the Supreme Court had struck down bank nationalization. In April the Government Bill to end the special privileges of the Indian Civil Service (ICS) had not secured a two-thirds majority in Parliament. And on 15 December a Special Bench of the Supreme Court had ruled the Presidential Order on the princes as ultra vires of the Constitution. Mrs Gandhi had also had occasion to complain on 26 September at a Chief Ministers' conference in New Delhi that all chief ministers were not cooperating on the subject of land reform. She would go to the polls to get a fresh mandate for her policies. For their implementation some amendments to the Constitution would be necessary: ". . . I want to be clear. . .we are not in favour of removing all the fundamental rights nor are we even against the right to property, but we do believe in having a certain ceiling on property, whether urban or rural."[3]

At her news conference on 29 December a journalist asked: "Your broadcast speech on television and radio [on the 27th] the Opposition claimed was a political speech and wanted equal time. Do you forsee in this election campaign that All India Radio will be open to the Opposition to make political speeches?" The Prime Minister replied: "Well mine was not a political speech at all. I was exceedingly careful not to say anything that could be counted as Party propaganda. As far as the other question is concerned, it has been debated and we just could not get agreement on the subject."

The proposal of the Chanda Committee to make All India Radio (AIR) an autonomous corporation on the lines of the BBC had been rejected by the government on 21 October 1970. The Opposition was to complain of government's unfair and unprincipled use of the media at its disposal. After the election Mrs Gandhi brushed this aside in the Lok Sabha (2 April 1971): "The complaint of some Members about the functioning of All India Radio and TV, that they were used by the Government for Party ends, need not be taken seriously." Two years later, the Minister for Information and Broadcasting, I.K. Gujral, announced the Prime Minister's "firm and irrevocable" rejection of the Chanda Committee recommendations and said AIR would be run "in the manner that served the country best."

At her news conference the Prime Minister was questioned about the contradiction of her party's electoral pact with a communal party, the Muslim League, in Kerala. She agreed the Muslim League was a communal organization, but said the way to meet it was to try and solve some of the genuine grievances of the minorities. She closed her conference by wishing the correspondents a happy New Year, "and, I hope, a less jaundiced view of the Indian situation."

This period marked the end of a convention that a caretaker government functioned once an election was announced. Patronage was freely distributed by Mrs Gandhi's government and licences "worth millions of rupees" were issued to industry. Kuldip Nayar

[3]News conference, 29 December 1970.

adds in *India After Nehru* (1975): "One conscientious objector in the Prime Minister's Secretariat was Haksar, who at least stopped the distribution of brochures containing Mrs Gandhi's speech which she broadcast on the day of the Lok Sabha dissolution."

CHAPTER SIX

THE MID-TERM ELECTION

India prepared for its first mid-term general election in a tense and fevered atmosphere dominated by Mrs Gandhi rather than issues. Her party fielded a large number of unknown candidates, "lamp posts" to the press, with the appeal that a vote for the candidate was a vote for Mrs Gandhi. The Prime Minister's picture and personal message accompanied their posters. A loose alliance formed to oppose her, the "grand alliance" to the press, was not able to unite under a common programme. The men in it were uncomfortable in each other's political company, and agreed only in their shared alarm at Mrs Gandhi's style and their determination to remove her. Their slogan *Indira Hatao* (Remove Indira) contrasted miserably with hers, *Garibi Hatao* (Remove Poverty).

Most voters wanted a stable government and felt the New Congress with enough majority would not be at the mercy of extremists, even those in its own party. The constitutional amendments Mrs Gandhi had said would be necessary caused no concern. She had repeatedly said she was a democrat. Her statements had always carried the assurance of a democratic framework and civic freedoms, whatever constitutional changes were made. The legacy of Nehru, of the democratic norms and conventions he had established and scrupulously served, was such that few anticipated any threat to democracy as India had till now understood the word and system, least of all from Nehru's daughter. It was felt there had been pressures on her during her quarrel with her own party and her year of reliance on other parties. Once free of these she would show good judgement and balance. The Gandhi-Nehru-Shastri era, for all its mass participation, had also been an age of the educated in politics. Gandhi had welded the educated with the mass, convinced that progress to freedom required a true identity o interests between the different sections of society, a tradition carried on after independence. Gandhi's war had been against India's most ancient injustice—caste. Philosophically this was the reverse of class war. The challenge was projected not as rich against poor, but as civilized men against the injustices of their society. The Indian intelligentsia had, by and large, played a responsible role in independent India, in its contribution to the wide-ranging development Nehru had termed "adventure." The welding had survived principally because Indian leadership had nurtured it. It was not yet obvious that it was being taken systematically apart.

The question arises: Was Mrs Gandhi trying, within the framework of existing democratic institutions, to blaze a new trail toward an egalitarian society against the combined weight of an outdated bureaucracy and legal system inherited from colonial times? Or were her intentions of a different kind? Was she using the credentials of her father and Mahatma Gandhi to play on the feelings and understanding of the masses, and to take in the process a calculated turn toward an authoritarian order? A singleminded woman, with a categorical sense of good and bad, for and against, not given to self-examination, forgiveness or compromise, if she saw any contradiction in her role, she may have believed herself capable of resolving it. For above all, she believed she knew without the shadow of a doubt what needed to be done. Mission and opportunity met in her in a blaze of purpose. She had once listed the four most important influences on her character and thinking as Motilal and Jawaharlal Nehru, Mahatma Gandhi, and Rabindranath Tagore. Her genuine yearning towards the vision, humanity and universality of these men may have found fulfilment in another career. The road to power distorted and finally destroyed it.

The election raises some points worth considering, inextricably connected with Mrs Gandhi's highly personal style in politics. In 1969, before the Congress split, donations to political parties had been banned. The ban had worked since, without much secrecy, to the advantage of the ruling party. Industry knew it must invest in a winner. This alone seemed to assure permission to carry on business in a system of complex controls and lengthy delays, now surmounted by threat of takeover, and the credo that to oppose government was to be a reactionary and an enemy of the people. Ajit Bhattacharjea wrote in the *Illustrated Weekly of India* on 15 July 1973:

Money had been collected for election and other party purposes before, but never on the scale and in the manner it was for Lok Sabha elections in 1971 and the State assembly elections a year later. Crores are known to have been extracted from the business community, but there is no account of these transactions. The entire sum was paid in black money; no legal accounts were kept. . . . So a premium was placed on massive dishonesty and corruption and the parallel black money economy—with all its degrading social and economic effects—was legitimised.

There was a procedural change in the conduct of this election. Up to now each ballot box had been separately counted at the end of polling. This time ballot boxes from several polling stations were mixed, resulting in a lapse of time, sometimes of days, before counting could begin. The reason given was that no one should know how a particular area had voted. This innovation had been considered and rejected by the Election Commission in its report on the fourth general election. The change in procedure, which involved a change in rules, should have been placed before Parliament for scrutiny. It was, however, introduced after Parliament had been dissolved and the notification for the election had been made.

The change applied to parliamentary constituencies, not State Assembly constituencies. It did not affect the three states, West Bengal, Orissa, and Tamil Nadu, where Assembly elections were held simultaneously with the general election, a fact of some significance later.

Mrs Gandhi's victory had been expected, though no one, including her own party's best forecasts, had predicted a two-thirds majority. The Opposition parties had been expected to win in areas where they existed in strength, and enjoyed a good reputation on the basis of their past performance. Their almost total rout, an abnormally clean sweep, even in these areas, had an unreality, particularly when they were defeated by unknown New Congress candidates who themselves had expected to make a scant or mediocre showing. The Opposition held that deviation from established election procedure gave scope for mischief on a vast scale, particularly as this deviation, unobtrusively introduced, coincided with an election where a leader's political reputation and future were linked to an unusual degree with the outcome.

The Prime Minister, who as Home Minister had Intelligence, Police, and the Election Commission under her supervision, told the Lok Sabha after the election on 2 April 1971: "The complaints against the Election Commission have already been dealt with by my colleague, the Minister of Law and Justice." The Jan Sangh leader, A.B. Vajpayee, retorted: "Not satisfactorily." But in the aftermath of Mrs Gandhi's victory, and the awe created by the pendulum swing of power, criticism died away and questions remained unanswered.

The only nationally known Opposition leader to take rigging charges to court was Balraj Madhok of the Jan Sangh, defeated in his South Delhi constituency, who claimed evidence of a plan to ensure a New Congress coup. The following extracts from his book _Murder of Democracy_ (1973) have some significance in view of the dictatorship Mrs Gandhi launched with ease in 1975:

The first information about the projected fraud on the Indian electorate accidentally reached a Delhi school teacher when he was going around for enrolling new voters in the Karol Bagh area of Delhi. When he approached an officer of the Government of India who lived in that area but whose name did not appear on the electoral rolls . . . [the officer] casually remarked, "You may enrol me and I will vote for your party but you are not going to win. This time chemicals will be employed and all your candidates will be defeated ." . . . Nobody, including the officers of Delhi State Jan Sangh, took serious note of the information. . . . A few days before the polling a letter reached the Jan Sangh office at Lucknow. It said that the writer of the letter was staying in a dak bungalow in the Rae Bareilly constituency from where Mrs. Gandhi was contesting. He overheard some Congress high-ups staying in the adjacent room talking about the certainty of Mrs. Gandhi's victory because of the use of a certain percentage of chemicalized ballot papers which would be pre-stamped in her favour. He thought it his duty to convey the information to the major opposition party in the State and so he wrote that letter. . . .

On March 2, three days before the polling was to begin in New Delhi, a chit came on the stage of a public meeting organised by the Jan Sangh in Karol Bagh which was to be addressed by A.B. Vajpayee. The chit said: "I am a senior officer of the Election Commission. I want to warn you that some serious mischief is being done in regard to ballot papers. Be on guard." . . . On March 3, a young man met Vidyarthi Jan Sangh candidate from Karol Bagh] in his office and gave him detailed information about the modus operandi of the contemplated fraud on the electorate. He told Vidyarthi that a certain percentage of ballot papers will be chemically treated and an invisible stamp will be affixed on the cow-and-calf symbol of the Indira Congress. Stamps put by the voters in polling booths on such ballots will disappear because of that chemical, and the invisible stamp on the cow-and-calf symbol will become visible after some days. . . .

It is difficult to believe how responsible people who got this information dismissed it as fantastic and took no step either to inform the public about it or even to tell their senior colleagues, some of whom also happened to be candidates in the election, about it. . . .

The first concrete evidence of rigging . . . came to light at the time of counting. A number of opposition candidates and their counting agents in Delhi, Bombay and elsewhere noted that stamp marks on the cow-and-calf symbol on a large number of ballot papers appeared to be uniform, fresher and brighter than the stamps on other symbols. It was also noted that the colour of such ballot papers was somewhat different from other ballots. The matter brought to the notice of returning officers by a number of people including Madhu Mehta, General Secretary of the Swatantra Party, who was present at the counting of votes in one of the Lok Sabha constituencies of Bombay. But the returning officers expressed their inablility to take legal cognizance of these observations. . . .

The first definite information about the fraud . . . came on the night of March 11, when a senior officer of an important department of Government burst into tears before two other officials and told them the whole story to unburden the load on his conscience.

This was followed by a spate of unsigned letters giving details of the fraud to important leaders of the Opposition, including Nijalingappa . . . Charan Singh and the writer. The details given in some of these letters coming from authoritative sources were startling.

As the information started pouring in, the first thing the writer thought of was to apprise the President of India of all the facts, with the request to act in the interest of the Constitution which he was under oath to uphold . . . urging him to order a judicial probe into the conduct of the elections and appoint a commission of scientists to make chemical examination of ballot papers. . . .

Madhok received an acknowledgement of his letter to the President, but no reply. He sought the Chief Election Commissioner's permission on 30 March 1971 to inspect the ballot papers of his own South Delhi constituency. Permission was refused. On 24 April Madhok filed an election petition in the Delhi High Court, setting forth his case for an inspection of ballot papers in his constituency. The trial judge, Justice Andley, ordered an inspection. The New Congress candidate appealed against inspection to the Supreme Court. Madhok notes that Supreme Court judge, Daftary, who categorically opposed any kind of inspection, and particularly a chemical inspection of ballot papers, was not long afterward nominated to the Rajya Sabha. Two Supreme Court judges, Hegde and Khanna, however, ordered a sample inspection of a few hundred ballot papers before any general inspection was ordered. In the course of their judgement they observed:

The march of science has shown in recent years that what was thought to be impossible just a few years back has become an easy possibility now. What we would have thought as wild imagination some years back is now proved to be reality. Hence we are unable to reject the allegations of the election petitioner without scrutiny. We shall accept nothing and reject nothing except on satisfactory proof.

In compliance with the Supreme Court judgement, Justice Andley of the Delhi High Court made a sample inspection of 800 ballot papers cast in favour of the New Congress candidate and 550 cast in favour of the Jan Sangh candidate (Madhok), taken at random out of bags containing them. Madhok writes:

At the very first sight of the two sets of ballot papers, they revealed some difference in colour. While all but five ballot papers cast in the writer's favour were found to be white, almost all the ballot papers cast in favour of the ruling Congress were found to be "off white" in the language of the court. . . [The trial judge] also asked the writer to keep his scientist and formula ready for chemical examination and reserved his order for November 12. . . . But the judgement could not be delivered on November 12 as the court was closed that day because of the sudden death of a judge of the Supreme Court. Prime Minister Indira Gandhi who had been abroad also returned to New Delhi on the same date.

Madhok records his astonishment that the judgement when it came was a complete reversal of the trial judge's stated position. He rejected the request for chemical inspection of ballot papers. He also struck the issue off the election petition.

Unwilling to let the matter rest, Madhok took his case to the Supreme Court with the plea that the suspect ballots be chemically examined. He argued the case himself on 9 August 1972, saying the ballots were the only evidence of a calculated coup, which if the evidence were borne out, would reveal the extent the ruling clique had gone to ensure a sizable victory. If tests could be undertaken in cases of forged documents or currency notes, the ballots, on which a country's fate depended, should be tested. The Supreme Court now refused the plea.

The voting pattern did indeed reveal that in the states where Assembly elections had been held at the same time and where, in accordance with past election procedure, there was no time lag between polling and counting, the Opposition had done well. In Tamil Nadu where the Congress did not contest, the DMK swept the Assembly poll. In West Bengal the CPI-M did better than the Congress,[1] and in Orissa the Swatantra Party made a good showing. Losing candidates lost with fairly narrow margins in these states. As against this, in other states Congress candidates won by uniformly high margins of about one lakh votes.

Madhok did not get his party's support in his charges and was expelled from it on differences of ideology after the election. He

[1]In the West Bengal State Assembly election in 1971 the New Congress won 105 seats (29.8 per cent votes) and the CPI-M won 111 seats (33.8 per cent votes).

was considered a die-hard and the Jan Sangh was anxious to relax
its conservative image to combat the "Indira wave." A fierce critic
of Nehru, whose policies the Jan Sangh had adamantly opposed,
the observations Madhok makes in his book about Nehru and
Mrs Gandhi are interesting for their contrast:

> Pandit Nehru's greatest contribution for which his memory will
> be cherished by every democrat was that he gave respect to
> democratic institutions and kept the structure of democracy alive
> when he was in a position to destroy them if he so wanted . . . .
> by showing due respect to fundamental rights, particularly to
> freedom of thought and expression, and by preserving the inde-
> pendence of the judiciary and sanctity and fairness of elec-
> tions. . . .

Of the mid-term election and Mrs Gandhi he concludes:

> The allegation was not about any electoral malpractice but
> about rigging of the election on a large scale. . . . The plan to
> rig the elections must have been a closely guarded secret, and
> no non-Communist colleague of Mrs. Gandhi, including her
> Party president and Defence Minister, Jagjivan Ram, was privy
> to it.

Madhok's account is painstaking and pedestrian, and carries no
breath of the sensational. Born in the Ladakh division of Kashmir
State, he became a history professor in a Delhi college in 1950,
and Secretary of the Jan Sangh after its founding in May 1951. He
first entered the Lok Sabha through a New Delhi by-election in
1961. The handling of his charge makes strange reading, with its
inexplicable reversal of the stand taken both by the High Court
and the Supreme Court after a sample inspection of ballots had
been ordered and carried out, the results found revealing enough
to merit a chemical examination, and that examination ordered. If
the whole issue was a crank's fixation, thorough scrutiny would
have shown it up for what it was. Instead, the legal process was
suddenly halted and reversed. A tradition of investigative reporting might have served India well at this time, but if any newspaper thought it worthwhile to pursue this line of enquiry, it did
not do so in the glitter of Mrs Gandhi's victory and her well-

known intolerance of opposing opinion. Madhok's charge, moreover, had the ring of fantasy about it. Though two Supreme Court judges were on record as saying that not even the most fanciful possibility could be lightly dismissed in this age of sophisticated technology, most people did so dismiss it. Four general elections had taken place since 1952, and the public believed in the fairness of elections. Even those politicians who, according to Madhok's account, received information about a "conspiracy" beforehand, did not imagine so brazen a scheme could be perpetrated, though they were opponents of the regime. It is perhaps a strain on the imagination to suggest that a familiar process is going to be subverted under one's gaze while the sun shines. The average person, who has come and gone in freedom, spoken, written, and voted as he pleased, does not recognize the alien chord struck on just such an ordinary day.

If one were to give credence to the possibility of a coup through a certain number of spurious ballots, the election of 1971 could become a link in the chain starting with Mrs Gandhi's charge of the Home Ministry, and the unorthodox manner of change in election procedure. One question would still remain: Why was a "coup" necessary, if indeed it took place? The New Congress was, in the general assessment, more than likely to win. The element of chance hung only on its majority. Yet Mrs Gandhi needed a two-thirds majority to control Parliament and to carry through her amendments to the Constitution. Anything less would have put a continued brake on her functioning. She had gambled for high stakes when she broke with her party on the question of unfettered command, a meaningless gamble if lack of majority at the polls were to render her ineffective once again. That the stakes in the power game became higher, until in June 1975 she wiped all element of chance off the scene, imprisoning her opponents within and outside her party, seems to suggest that the 1971 election might have been a stage in a process.

The character of this election may also explain the subservience of Parliament in accepting and consolidating the dictatorship after June 1975. If many MPs—"lamp posts"—were her creatures rather than known and accepted personalities in their constituencies, they would have a vital interest in prolonging their tenure and displaying the perfect obedience that would keep them in the leader's favour.

CHAPTER SEVEN

"THE NEW DAWN"

The *National Herald* commented on the election on 12 March 1971 result: "It is a mandate for carrying on the socialist processes to the climax of a social revolution with vigour and speed. . . . It is not a mere mandate, it is a strong wind of change that has swept the country. . . ." The *Patriot* called it "a forceful assertion of popular opinion in favour of radical change that . . . will provide equality of opportunity for all and enable equitable sharing of the fruit of economic development."

These comments represented the general enthusiasm that marks the beginning of a political era promising great new momentum. If the methods by which Mrs Gandhi had routed the Old Guard of the Congress had created a thrill of apprehension in neutral observers, if the controversy over "commitment" and the rousing vocabulary of class war during the past eighteen months had raised a wild wind of speculation about the government's intentions and direction, there was now an expectation of concrete programmes and efficient administration. Mrs Gandhi's landslide victory gave her an un-cluttered opportunity with virtually no Opposition in Parliament to hinder it. The New Congress had won 350 out of 518 seats in the Lok Sabha. What remained of the opposition consisted chiefly of the CPI-M, followed closely by the CPI, and in Tamil Nadu, the DMK. Such pressure as could now be exerted on the govern-ment in Parliament would come from the Left. A Leftward trend began to be noticeable in the Right wing parties, too, in whom the "Indira wave" had produced some rethinking. The Jan Sangh had since its founding in 1952 been linked in sympathy with the Hindu Mahasabha which it had substantially replaced, but it had moved steadily away from orthodoxy after 1957 in wooing a wider electo-rate. The mid-term election accelerated this trend toward a mode-rate, liberal approach. The Swatantra Party, later further reduced by a split, debated at its 1973 convention the need to shed some of its antipathy toward socialism and not condemn it outright. Region-based parties of varying hue had to take note of the "wind of change." A clamour for "socio-economic" innovation and drive filled the air.

Not all was enthusiasm for Mrs Gandhi's victory. The *Statesman* treated it with frank foreboding:

What distinguished the present poll from any other is the degree in which it has been dominated, as a matter of deliberate calculation, by a cult which subordinates all considerations of principle, party programmes and manifestos to the image of a single leader. That it has yielded dividends is not too surprising. The simplistic message of Mrs. Gandhi as the guardian of the underprivileged and as the only genuine advocate of socialism was an incomparably more efficient gatherer of votes than anything the Opposition was able to produce. The latter suffered from the initial disadvantage of being burdened by a heavily intellectualized and argumentative thesis, unsupported by the charisma of an all-India personality. Whether such charisma exploited with ruthless determination is in the long run compatible with a healthy democratic system is something on which some thought is clearly overdue . . . Congress-R candidates from whom little was expected have blossomed into successful competitors under the general benediction of a leader with a masterly grip on the techniques of the emotional appeal . . . the line between an election and a referendum can no longer be seen. . . .

From this point of view the nature of the election, and events preceding it, boded ill for the future. Moral example, expected of those who lead, had been deserted by Mrs Gandhi flamboyantly during the Congress crisis. The performance had been exciting and inflaming, creating a leader-image bound by no rules or restraints. The election was proof that the performance had succeeded. A roused and restless student population, trade unions, taxi and transport operators—these and other elements, potential fuel for the fires of a growing lawlessness—had now to be persuaded into channels of work. Yet the election triumph had released a fresh militancy in the ruling party. In New Delhi a crowd led by its office-bearers marched on the disputed Congress headquarters

at Jantar Mantar Road and took forcible possession while the
police remained spectators on the scene. The Supreme Court had
earlier decreed that ownership was for the courts to decide and
until such time, it remained by law with the Old Congress. A
Congress election majority was no novelty. There had been no
effective challenge to the government in Nehru's time. But the
framework for challenge had been strong. In the present political environment its main pillars had been under attack. The fundamental rights, an independent judiciary, the freedom of the press,
clearly did not carry the same meaning for Mrs Gandhi they had
had for her father.

The government began its fulfilment of election pledges by a
Presidential Ordinance nationalizing general insurance on 13 May
1971. Its programme in Parliament centred on amendments to
the Constitution. These went through during the year amid cheers
and applause in both Houses. The 24th Amendment (August 1971)
gave Parliament the sovereign right to alter the Constitution, including the fundamental rights. The 25th Amendment (December
1971) provided that compensation for nationalized properties would
no longer be based on market value. The word "compensation"
was replaced by "amount," to be fixed by Parliament, and not
challengeable in a court of law. The Articles of the Constitution,
giving the citizen the right to acquire, hold, and dispose of property,
and to protect it against arbitrary seizure, were no longer valid.
The 26th Amendment (December 1971) ended the privy purse,
and extinguished all rights, liabilities, and obligations in respect of
the princes.

In the pursuit of social justice, the Government of India had
earlier set limits on the right to property with the first Constitutional amendment in 1951. The right to property could not be
invoked at all against specified Acts passed by state governments
relating to land reform, while the government could interfere in a
specified area of property rights, where these conflicted with the
general public interest. Compensation for nationalized property,
based on market value, could not be challenged in a court of law.
The 1971 amendment avoided a definition of government's powers
altogether, making government subject to no principle and no responsibility regarding its incursions into property rights and the
compensation payable in cases of takeover. A meticulously defined procedure was thus abrogated. The word "amount" in place

of "compensation" made compensation a matter of government's whim. Nationalization, in these circumstances, amounted to confiscation and expropriation, as the takeover of general insurance companies and coal companies soon afterward demonstrated:

> Some companies found that the amounts they received were less than the value of their government securities and the amounts of their currency notes and bank balances after providing for all liabilities. . . . One insurance company was paid Rs. 10,000 for acquisition of its *net* assets worth more than Rs. 2,300,000. . . . All assets of nationalised coal companies are taken over by government but none of their liabilities. . . .[1]

It was this lack of definition and responsibility, with no limits placed on government's powers, that sent a spasm of doubt and fear through the thinking public. The Amendments, including government's power to axe the fundamental rights—free speech, press, occupation, worship, and assembly—reflected a wide-ranging unaccountability, that was the chief feature of the new era. Instead of concrete proposals for change, even considered changes within the political system, it was the checks and balances within the system that were being demolished, leaving it unprotected against the dictatorial designs of this or any future government. Mrs Gandhi's grandfather, Motilal Nehru, had, during the struggle for freedom, defended the inviolability of fundamental rights. Thirteen out of nineteen fundamental rights listed in the (Motilal) Nehru Report had been included in the Indian Constitution in 1950. With reference to the future Constitution of free India, Motilal Nehru had said in the Central Assembly in 1928: "It is obvious that our first care should be to have our fundamental rights guaranteed in a manner which will not permit their withdrawal under any circumstances." The statement, quoted by an Opposition MP during the Lok Sabha debate on the 24th Amendment, represented a philosophy closer to the moderate opposition than to New Congress thinking. The government spoke another language. Mohan Kumaramangalam, piloting the Bill along with the Law Minister, H.R. Gokhale, said it would "clear the road blocks" to progress "erected

[1]N.A. Palkhivala, *Our Constitution Defaced and Defiled*, Macmillan, New Delhi, 1974.

by the Supreme Court" (by an earlier judgement). Supreme Court judges, he said, had "an inbuilt conservatism born out of the class from which they come. . . . Judges in our country come from the class of men with property." K.D. Malaviya, New Congress MP, defined democratic socialism as state control of all sources of production and distribution. The Prime Minister presented no argument. She merely condemned the scare created about the Bill as another of the unending attempts by vested interests to divide the people and mislead the minorities.

The notable fact about the Amendments and the debate accompanying them was their communist inspiration. The effect was of an unexpected transplant, set up on the body-politic without the groundwork, and certainly without the political system, to ensure its acceptance and success. The transplant had, as it were, sprung up noiselessly overnight, and now ruled the political daylight, yet Mrs Gandhi firmly denied communist influence or direction. With no clarification available from her, only guesses could try to explain this anomaly. With her election majority she no longer needed CPI support. The CPI's presence at the power feast indicated a larger political bargain, a friendly price paid in return for hemispheric considerations, a pointer to the assiduously cultivated and steadily growing Soviet alliance. There was, too, Mrs Gandhi's own Leftist posture, which had been her reason for the Congress split, but this appeared, as time went on, vague, romantic and adolescent, without the hard supporting structure of thought or programme.

While thought was not her strength or style, Mrs Gandhi's thorough grasp of the nuts and bolts of politics was. Philosophy, i.e., a clear statement of what she stood for, drifted cloudlike, irridescent and insubstantial above her hard-headed businesslike strategy in the control room. In his admiring *Profile of Courage*, Trevor Drieberg says of the post-election period: "[Mrs Gandhi is] on a political pinnacle, holds absolute power. . . . She speaks direct to the people today, over the heads of her own partymen, who need her much more than she needs them." The "pinnacle" was ensured by the control she established over the bowels of the Congress machine, indispensable to effective, centralized power. The apparatus for choosing candidates for the State Assembly elections due in early 1972 was replaced by groups appointed by the Working Committee. The Prime Minister herself decided which of the state ministers would get party tickets. Four veteran chief ministers, Mohanlal Sukhadia of Rajasthan, Brahmananda Reddy of Andhra Pradesh, M.M. Chaudhury of Assam, and S.C. Shukla of Madhya Pradesh, each powerfully backed in his state, were replaced by her nominees, respectively Barkatullah, P.V. Narsimha Rao, S.C. Sinha, and P.C. Sethi. Political lightweights in their states, and dependent on her favour, their chief qualification was their allegiance to her. Drieberg writes:

> This set the stage of things to come. When Congress candidates were chosen for seats in the State legislatures, the heads of six more Chief Ministers rolled. In drawing up lists of candidates, only three Congress Chief Ministers, in addition to the four whom Mrs. Gandhi had chosen in the months preceding the [Assembly] elections survived. . . .

Posts for the party's state units (Pradesh Congress Committees) were similarly operated by Mrs Gandhi. The Congress constitution empowered state units to name and elect their own office bearers. Nominations and election had been the responsibility of a Returning Officer chosen by the State Congress. Returning Officers were now selected or approved by Mrs Gandhi and lists decided by her. Elections were a foregone conclusion. Office bearers thus "elected" could be as easily unseated without reference to the state units they represented. Pradesh Congress Committees, District Congress Committees, and lower down party units upon which rested the party's local base and strength were shorn of their rights under its constitution, and could be appointed or superceded at Mrs Gandhi's pleasure.

An atmosphere of fealty, feudal in texture, descended on the Congress. Her colleagues and associates, with few exceptions, had no political bases of their own and were dependent on her for their positions. Nehru had been surrounded by an aura of deference, even reverence, but his ministers had been personalities in their own right, some of them powerful and impressive men. The contrast extended to the Secretariat. Nehru, often impatient and short-tempered, tended, all the same, to support his civil servants, and they were sure of the ground beneath their feet. The government's intentions and objectives were known. Mrs Gandhi's lack of a defined philosophy left those working with her in uncertainty.

There was no clear-cut framework within whose rhythm and logic they could take decisions without getting clearance from her, no orchestration of men and ideas to produce teamwork. There was an ad hocism, a compartmentalization of subjects, and long delays in making senior appointments that often lay vacant for months. And with Mrs Gandhi's instinctive antagonism to criticism, known or suspected, only a show of loyalty guaranteed a career.

Lining the outer atmosphere of radical rhetoric, the tightening of the nuts and bolts of power continued. During the summer of 1971 the government made its first move toward control of the press when Mrs Gandhi's own Ministry of Information and Broadcasting prepared a draft scheme to "diffuse" ownership of newspapers with a circulation of more than 15,000. This climaxed Mrs Gandhi's bias, faithfully reflected in her Minister of State's (Nandini Sathpathy) pronouncements about the "monopoly" press. The draft scheme proposed that 95 per cent of a newspaper's shares would be offered to journalists and other employees, and 5 per cent to existing shareholders. But each shareholder would exercise only half a vote per share, their combined voting rights amounting to 50 per cent. The remaining 50 per cent of voting rights on the management would go to a government appointee. The management would thus bear the final imprint of government authority and decisions.

The most anguished cry against the scheme appeared in a three-column editorial in the *Hindustan Times* headed "Freedom is in Peril, Defend it with all your Might." B.G. Verghese, calling it "a monstrous perversion that will destroy the freedom of the press," wrote:

It amounts to a scheme of backdoor nationalisation and projects an extraordinary concept of workers' management that entails a unique separation of responsibility from control. It is astonishing that such an unworkable and destructive piece of legislation should be contemplated by a democratic government. ... The whole exercise is a frightening warning that wild men enjoy wide rein within the administration ... the Bill proposed by the government would ... strike a deadly blow against the most vital aspect of the freedom of the Press, namely the right of dissent and the duty to defy uninformed opinion brought out on the streets as a demonstration of "the will of the people...."

The highest duty of a free Press is not to follow the mob but to lead it and educate it. . . . We would appeal to the Government, and to the Prime Minister in particular, to repudiate the vicious and undemocratic principles underlying this unworkable and incomplete draft scheme . . . which constitutes a diabolic attack not merely on the Press but on the citizen by seeking virtually to extinguish . . . the fundamental right to "freedom of speech and expression."

Verghese's appeal "to the Prime Minister in particular" was part of a genuine public belief that Mrs Gandhi herself was not directly associated with, or responsible for, authoritarian proposals or measures. The newspaper "diffusion" scheme was drafted by the Secretary to the Information and Broadcasting Ministry, R.C. Dutt, and the stinging backlash of criticism against it was absorbed by him and by the Minister of State. Nandini Sathpathy, whose opinions on newspaper control had been forthright, had also been made responsible for answers about the control of film imports. Mrs Gandhi herself preserved a democratic image, remaining untouched at the centre of controversy, and could be appealed to whenever democracy appeared to be in danger—an oasis of moderation in the extreme views and proposals around her. During the mid-term election she had portrayed the fighting radical, yet along with this she coveyed the image of a leader, centrist by instinct, and driven only by necessity to compromise with extremists. She maintained both images, which seemed to obscure the fact that each actual step she took embodied the extremist view. The "diffusion" scheme struck at a 100-year-old tradition of intellectual vitality and individualism in Indian journalism. It had given the community respected and influential citizens. Its spirit of independence had flowered in opposition to British rule. Men like Verghese found themselves up against something new—a threat to freedom of expression from the Indian rulers of India. The reaction to it was strong. The scheme was adversely compared with Nehru's attitude toward the press. D.R. Mankekar, former editor of the *Times of India*, wrote:

Nehru's distrust of the so-called capitalist press, if anything, was even stronger than that of his daughter. But so deep and unshakeable were his democratic convictions that he would not dream of taking any step that directly or indirectly encroached upon the freedom of the press. A Government flushed with a spectacular electoral victory and believing that it had the mandate to turn everything upside down in the country, has embarked on an assault upon the press. . . .

Nehru's own words were quoted: "I have no doubt that even if the Government dislikes the liberties taken by the press and considers them dangerous, it is wrong to interfere with the freedom of the press."

Nehru, inaugurating *Shankar's Weekly* (of political satire and cartoons), had told Shankar, "Don't spare me." Durga Das, head of India News Feature and Alliance, a leading syndicate, remarked: "Mrs Gandhi does not accept the basic philosophy of a newspaper, that it has to convey the people's problems, not the Government view, that a columnist must carry the voice of dissent to the corridors of power. It is the best safety valve a Government has. Her father understood that." A letter from Nehru to his sister, Mrs Pandit, in London, dated 7 November 1959, vividly conveys his response to press criticism during a time of tension between India and China:

We are having a curious time here in India. People are worked up to a high pitch of excitement over the Chinese border issue. The principal newspapers here, which are opposed to our internal policies, have taken advantage of this to attack all our policies, internal and external, and to make me a target of attack. They dislike me for our internal policies and for trying to go too fast toward what they call socialism. . . . So you will observe that I am having a fairly interesting time!

Commentators pointed out the total circulation of 755 dailies, variously owned, did not exceed 7 million, and government already exercised control through newsprint allocation and the supply and import of printing machinery. Mrs Gandhi was, therefore, perhaps disproportionately sensitive to the power of the press and the damage the "big" newspapers could do if they disagreed with her.

The measure was shelved as opinion against it rose to a crescendo, and government's understanding of fundamental rights remained unexplained. A religious trust in the south took the issue, relating to its property, to the Supreme Court. In October 1972 the fundamental rights became the subject of a debate before a 13-member Bench of the Supreme Court.

Mrs Gandhi's hold on party members including senior ministers, and her ability to ease them out of long-occupied berths, came from her use of the Intelligence apparatus at her command. The deeper currents she manipulated in men and money came to light by accident through the Nagarwala affair.[2]

On 24 May 1971 Ved Prakash Malhotra, chief cashier of the State Bank of India, received a phone call instructing him to deliver Rs 6 million in cash to a man who would identify himself as "Bangladesh ka Babu" on a road in New Delhi. The call, Malhotra later told the police, came from the Prime Minister. Taking a taxi he delivered the money as instructed and hurried to the Prime Minister's house to report the completion of his mission. The Prime Minister's Principal Secretary, P.N. Haksar, who met him, denied absolutely that Mrs Gandhi had made the call and advised the astonished Malhotra to go to the police immediately. The money was recovered on the same day. Captain Nagarwala, the man who had taken delivery of it from Malhotra, seemed to have left an open, easy trail for the police to find and arrest him. He confessed he had wanted the money for support to Bangladesh and had impersonated the Prime Minister's voice to obtain it.

Nagarwala's case was conducted in a highly unorthodox manner and with record speed. In three days three different magistrates dealt with it. On the third day, 27 May, he was sentenced to four years' imprisonment and a fine of Rs 4,000. The police did not produce as evidence in court the tape they said they had taken of Nagarwala's impersonation, and Nagarwala's account of it was very different from Malhotra's earlier account. Malhotra was not examined in court.

On the day of Nagarwala's arrest, Opposition MPs demanded, an answer in Parliament to the question: Had the Prime Minister spoken to Malhotra on the telephone? A member, drawing attention to her sudden exit from the House, was sternly reprimanded by the Speaker and told to "desist from making any allegations."

[2]For a full account of the Nagarwala case, see Rajinder Puri, *India: The Wasted Years*, Chetana, New Delhi, 1975.

The uproar raised by New Congress benches prevented a discussion.

Malhotra, arrested after Nagarwala had been convicted, clung to his story. He wept, insisting he had only obeyed the Prime Minister's instructions. Nagarwala, docile and cooperative enough until his conviction, seemed to have second thoughts in jail, showing signs of disillusion and despair. He appealed for re-trial, saying his trial had been rushed through contrary to all principles of justice, and asked that Malhotra's story be fully investigated first. This request was refused, though a re-trial was ordered. In November Nagarwala tried to get an interview with D.F. Karaka, editor of the Bombay weekly, *Current*, and a fellow-Parsi. Karaka, too ill to travel to Delhi, sent a representative, but Nagarwala would speak to no one else. In February he was removed to hospital, reportedly complaining of a pain in the chest. He died on 2 March 1972. In the army before independence, Rustam Sohrab Nagarwala is believed to have been employed as an intelligence officer in RAW at this time.

The case was closed. The money was returned to the bank. Malhotra was dismissed. He later appeared on the Delhi scene as owner of a transport operation and fully supported the official version of the story. The Prime Minister's role in the affair remained a mystery. Had she spoken to Malhotra on the telephone? Could Malhotra carry Rs 6 million out of the bank on receipt of a phone call unless there were some precedent for it?

The public had other questions: Was Nagarwala made a scapegoat when Haksar inadvertently (unaware of the arrangement) exposed it by sending Malhotra to the police? What use was made of funds such as these, so casually removable from the vaults of a bank? Had Nagarwala died a natural death? Had D.K. Kashyap's death been accidental? Kashyap, Assistant Superintendent of Police, the officer most closely connected with the investigation, had died in a car collision on the Grand Trunk Road near Mathura on 20 November 1971.

The code phrase in the Nagarwala affair had been "Bangladesh ka Babu" and events across the East Bengal border were, along with her consolidation of control over the Congress Party machine, Mrs Gandhi's chief preoccupation in 1971. The Opposition closed its ranks solidly behind her when on 31 March she moved a resolution in both Houses of Parliament expressing "... deep anguish and grave concern at the recent developments in East Bengal." Sympathy for the stream of refugees becoming a flood of millions was mixed with alarm at the severe strain they were imposing on India's resources, and the danger to stability in West Bengal, always a vulnerable region. If for a time Mrs Gandhi seemed robbed of initiative, her announcement of the Indo-Soviet Treaty of Friendship and Co-operation, signed in New Delhi on 9 August, put a stop to all such conjecture. In keeping with her government's style, which did not include open discussion or parliamentary debate about issues affecting the country, the Treaty was presented as an accomplished fact. Consummate showmanship marked its announcement at a rally at India Gate, New Delhi's most spectacular vantage point and scene of Republic Day parades. At another time its full implications would have provoked more thought. In essence a security-based alliance, it represented a complete reversal in foreign policy, while its other clauses would intimately and diversely affect internal affairs. But in the tension and anxiety caused by events in East Bengal, it spelled relief for India, for the first time since independence provided with a powerful ally in case of war. Coming upon the official indifference of most governments to the tragedy of genocide across the border (there were notable exceptions whose support, however, did not count in the international power game), the partisan pro-Pakistan policy of America, and the grave danger to which India felt exposed, the Treaty came at the psychological moment when it would find an enthusiastic welcome. Very few were concerned in this context with analyzing the extent to which it brought India's defence, economy, and culture under Soviet influence and pressure for the next fifteen years. Those who attempted analysis were denounced as unpatriotic.

Mrs Gandhi was able to go abroad at the end of September, cushioned by the Treaty, to try to rouse heads of governments to the calamity on the subcontinent. The Prime Minister abroad exhibited a normality and balance she lacked at home, though she carried her annoyance at Indian critics with her and displayed it on occasion. Speaking to the Society for Foreign Policy and International Relations in Austria she said: In our fifth general election last March, 152 million people went to cast their votes, in spite of the fact that . . . there was great deal of mischievous and false propaganda about our policies and programmes." In the Soviet Union she said, "There are some, in India and abroad, who

are trying to misinterpret its [the Treaty's] meaning and purpose."
At President Nixon's banquet for her she spoke of "the people" as
distinct, by implication, from those who opposed her: "So the
campaign became not a campaign of a political party, but a
campaign of the people . . . people came to the fore and said. 'If this
is a candidate belonging to Mrs Gandhi's party, we will make him
win'."

The efficient conduct of the Indo-Pakistan war of 1971 was both
balm and stimulant to a nation humiliated by the Chinese in 1962
and, in the hope of peace, persuaded into an indeterminate conclusion
with Pakistan in the war of 1965. Mrs Gandhi's handling of this period
of crisis and danger, during the tense months preceding the war,
and the war itself, illustrated that when reality had to be faced,
when it could not be obscured by rhetoric, or enveloped by the
slide and slither of innuendo, she could come to grips with it. In
the process, and through war, Mrs Gandhi attained the recogniz-
able leadership that continued to elude her in her inability to
come to grips with daily realities on the home front. The unilate-
ral ceasefire she declared immediately on Pakistan's collapse in
East Bengal was an act of statesmanship. Her broadcast announcing the war's end was quiet and calm, and had the added grace
of restraint in victory: a restraint she had not been able to exercise
after her election victory at home. The two fronts, external and
internal, continued divided. Precise, if ruthless and insensitive
action, marked Mrs Gandhi's style in her incorporation of Sikkim
into the Indian Union. A pattern of cordial relations began to be
efficiently established with neighbours. Wounds with Pakistan
began to be healed and ties resumed. China and India reopened
full diplomatic relations. Yet at home a state of "war," narrow,
unyielding, and locked in inconsistencies, went on. Neither conces-
sion nor discussion had any part in Mrs Gandhi's politics at home.

A news conference on 31 December 1971 warmly congratulated
Mrs Gandhi on her leadership through the Bangladesh crisis and
directed its questions at the war's aftermath, the future with Pakistan, and the safety of Mujibur Rahman. The dazzle of a victory,
this time a military one, once again left its deeper implications
unexplored. India's role in bringing it about had meant an involvement far beyond any yet undertaken in foreign affairs. The Indian
army, along with Bangladesh, had taken the Pakistani surrender.
The massive Soviet support that had made this possible meant the

end of non-alignment and brought India into the politics of compe-
titive power. The long-term effects on Bangladesh did not take
long to appear.

The direction now taken by foreign policy was partly the result
of America's policies in Asia, and more recently its stand on
Bangladesh. But it coincided, too, with Mrs Gandhi's leap to individual recognition in 1969, and her consolidation of her position
thereafter.

The CPI, until it became Mrs Gandhi's ally in 1969, had enjoyed
little credit or credibility in Indian politics. Founded in 1925, in 1933
it had 100 members. Banned by the British Government, it struggled
for survival during the Stalin years when revolution outside the
Soviet Union found little besides moral support. Between it and the
peasant-worker masses stood the figure of Mahatma Gandhi, a one
hundred per cent Indian obstruction, clasping India to him through
religion, tradition, and continuity, recognizing no class distinctions,
and piloting a movement for freedom that did not tolerate violence. The CPI lost further ground with World War II, when an
"imperialist" war became, with the Soviet entry into it, a "people's"
war, and enlisted the CPI's full cooperation. The mood and tide
in India were fiercely nationalist, and Congress leaders in jail for
refusing to participate in the Allied war effort unless India's freedom
was granted. After independence Nehru's position in the ruling
party and the country could not be upset by conspiracy or manipulation. He invited the cooperation of all "socialists" but he did
not need political allies. Mrs Gandhi did. The Soviet Union's
interest in the CPI New Congress alliance was not one of ideology.
Mrs Gandhi's struggle for power in her party was backed by the
Soviet Union for more important considerations. There were giant
global considerations in the balance. With the birth of a new country, Bangladesh, blessed by India and the Soviet Union, and the
enfeebling of Pakistan, a bloc encompassing the land mass from
the Soviet Union to the Indian Ocean could become a reality. In
Mrs Gandhi there was an Indian leader of the style and temperament required, herself unburdened by ideology or conscience, to
play with great flair the game of power.

At Mrs Gandhi's news conference no reference was made to
the new law, Maintenance of Internal Security Act (MISA), passed
in June 1971 giving the government "deterrent powers against anti-
social elements" and providing for arbitrary arrest and imprison-

ment without trial for six months. The emergency (against external danger), declared when the war broke out in December, remained in force, although by mid-1972 the Simla agreement had been signed, and relations between India and Pakistan had never been more cordial or promising.

The CPI leadership in government showed its customary energy when it invited "intellectuals"—actors, writers, singers, dancers, painters, and academics—to a meeting arranged by the Education Ministry in the capital to discuss ways and means of strengthening "national solidarity." Mohan Kumaramangalam, and not the Education Minister, was in the chair. The procedure and terms employed differentiated it from similar gatherings in the past when plenty of time was allowed for a ventilation of opinion. Kumaramangalam called upon the assembled company to elect a "presidium" of five, and these were named and elected with obviously rehearsed speed. The head of the presidium, the distinguished communist writer, Sajjad Zaheer, took the chair. Selected members of the audience were called upon to speak, leaving no time for discussion. The "manifesto," to be drafted by the presidium during the coffee break and discussed after coffee, had, the invitees discovered, already been drafted. Copies of it lay in front of Kumaramangalam. A few writers heatedly objected to being hustled, but the manifesto was duly adopted.

In January 1972 Mrs Gandhi used the opportunity provided by Mujibur Rahman's halt in Delhi (from London en route to Dacca) to address a mass rally jointly with him. In her Letter to the Voter, appearing as an advertisement in national newspapers on 10 March 1972, she reminded people of the Bangladesh victory and the return of the refugees to their own country, and urged voters to return her party to the State Assemblies in overwhelming strength in the coming elections. The Congress, backed by a mood of national excitement and euphoria, had an impressive success. The Congress-CPI electoral pact in Bihar, West Bengal, and Punjab had its most spectacular result in Bengal,[3] where the CPI-M was reduced from 111 to 14 seats. The Congress-CPI landslide was preceded by an eventful history.

President's rule, imposed on Bengal on 19 March 1970, had

[3]Bengal is used from now on, rather than West Bengal, as with the end of the 1971 war with Pakistan, East Bengal became Bangladesh.

ended a year later, with the 1971 election giving the CPI-M 111 seats in a House of 280, and the position of single largest party in the Assembly. The Governor, S.S. Dhavan, however, was directed to favour the formation of a "Democratic Front" 6-party coalition, supported by the New Congress. During the next two months the Democratic Front was reduced by defections, while the CPI-M improved its position by two more seats in constituencies that had held late polls. The coalition announced its inability to continue without a fresh mandate, and President's rule was imposed on the state once again.

An organized police terror subjected the CPI-M rank and file to arrests and killings. The revival of the Preventive Detention Act by ordinance in May 1971, and the enactment of MISA in June, facilitated this campaign, described by a Bengali film director as the Second Great Calcutta Killing—the first having been the country's most ferocious communal orgy in 1946. In the course of it the CPI-M was lamed and the Naxalite movement broken, its members hunted and jailed, or killed. A bloodied CPI-M contested the Assembly election in 1972. In July 1973 the death of the activist Charu Mazumdar in a "police encounter" completed its rout and crippled its impact. According to an Amnesty International report[4] published in 1974, the Bengal government held 20-30,000 political prisoners, apart from 17,800 "under-trial detainees." Among the methods of torture it listed were: (*i*) severe beating, sometimes resulting in fractured limbs, (*ii*) hanging prisoners upside down with pins inserted into their nails and other sensitive organs of the body, including genitals, (*iii*) electric shock, (*iv*) burning with cigarettes, (*v*) denial of medical aid to tortured prisoners. Justice Sarma Sankar, heading a commission to investigate the deaths of five Naxalites in Howrah Jail, concluded that "firing inside Howrah Jail in 1975 violated the jail code, the penal code and the human code."

There was irony in this formidable blood-letting to end the established hold of the CPI-M in Bengal and make way for a Congress[5] victory at the polls. Its chief beneficiary was the CPI, Mrs Gandhi's ally, whose avowed goal was a political system identical

---

[4]Amnesty International Report published in the *Economic and Political Weekly*, Vol. IX, No. 38, 21 September 1974.

[5]Congress is used from now on rather than the New Congress.

to that desired by the CPI-M. It bolstered an alliance based on a degree of opportunism that was beginning to repel sensitive sections of both the CPI and the Congress. Communist critics would have preferred the dignity of an ideologically reliable partnership with the CPI-M, or a neutral role between it and the Congress. Congress critics found communist philosophy and methods altogether alien and unpalatable. Mrs Gandhi's indifference to political principle, so graphically illustrated by her partnership with the CPI, had already been seen in her electoral pact with the Muslim League in Kerala and later in Congress collaboration with the Shiv Sena, a militant mafia-type organization in Maharashtra. In her pursuit of immediate political advantage the Congress was smearing its respected stand on basic issues, and through the widespread use of police terror forfeiting its claim to just and decent political functioning. Scrupulous sentiment within her own party surveyed this debris of a high moral and political stand with apprehension and dismay.

The campaign against the CPI-M represented Mrs Gandhi's violent answer to political violence. It also effectively crippled the legitimate functioning of this particular adversary. In 1974 a campaign as thorough was mounted against a non-violent movement in defence of parliamentary democracy that threatened Congress rule in Bihar, and ultimately in India.

CHAPTER EIGHT

REAPING THE WHIRLWIND—I

Victory in Bangladesh and the return of the refugees gave the country a psychological lift unequalled since independence. Mrs Gandhi's prestige and popularity were at their height. To the mandate she had received in the 1971 election was now added the resounding success of the Congress in the 1972 State Assembly elections, reflecting the country's hope that stable majorities in the states would provide the base for economic improvement. With an immense fund of goodwill and no political challenge to impede her, Mrs Gandhi could begin her programme for the removal of poverty. Urban unrest, the growing militancy of organized labour, the general impatience of the electorate all demanded it. Yet this proved to be a period of total political involvement for Mrs Gandhi, to the neglect of economic affairs, though her party kept up a high temperature of vocal demand for "radical" change, along with a denigration of those said to be obstructing it. This may have been useful strategy where, in the nature of things, lightning changes cannot take place, while it also furnished a smoke-screen for measures that had profoundly altered the body-politic under the guise of "constitutional" change.

India's political system, a marriage between the British liberal constitutional tradition and Mahatma Gandhi's humanitarian ideals, was also a deliberate choice at independence. It rested on the belief that a country so large and diverse could most humanely preserve its unity, as well as its legitimate diversity, within a parliamentry and federal system. While Mrs Gandhi functioned within the system she had inherited, an obsessive concern with her own importance led her progressively to tamper with the brakes and balances it provided, and to block the vents that might in time and in the natural course of events give the system a chance to replace her. She did not openly challenge it. She simply maintained the continuous contradiction of publicly professing concern for parliamentary institutions, while undoing their inner scaffolding: a style that had significantly altered the Indian landscape.

She had used Parliament to endorse ordinances promulgated when she encountered resistance to a measure. An assembly in which Nehru's meticulous regard for democratic principle and procedure had produced a high level of debate had descended to the bulk and intimidation of sheer numbers, blunted to, or contemptuous of an opposing opinion. Nehru had run government on big majorities, but much of the modification or acceptance of policy had come from an exchange of views within the party as well as criticism outside it. Mrs Gandhi treated the Opposition as illegitimate and this inevitably affected fresh air and freedom within her own party. The strict conformity demanded as patriotic paralyzed expression and ideas. The civil service was similarly affected. Administrative reform, accented by her as a vital need, had in actual working become an arbitrary exercise, with administrators dependent on government favour, instead of an overhaul of administrative procedures themselves.

The atmosphere for magnanimity and cooperation, now that her own political strength was secure, was vitiated by a cultivated arrogance. Congress MPs were told not to foregather with Opposition MPs in the central lobby of Parliament, traditionally a meeting place for politicians and journalists, where political cross-currents met in a relaxed exchange of views and humour. The directive was condemned as absurd by A.B. Vajpayee (Jan Sangh), Hiren Mukerji (CPI), and Madhu Limaye (Socialist Party) but the absurdity had a sombre touch. The ruling party behaved not only as dominant but permanent and the Prime Minister seemed temperamentally unable to adjust to the very concept of Parliament. In an article published in August 1973, Hiren Mukerji wrote:

Unlike her father, who rejoiced in Parliament, Mrs. Indira Gandhi, though Leader of the Lok Sabha, apart from being Prime Minister, has an allergy to it. One may understand a certain personal reticence, for Parliament today is a peculiar and sometimes repellant kettle of fish, very different from what it was till ten years ago; but it is representative of our people's soured mood and the Prime Minister must come to terms and make friends with it. She prefers, however, to let hordes of people interview her, and listen rather than talk, keeping away even when most needed in Parliament sessions. One wonders if she prefers the Presidential form of government, but meanwhile the business of the country suffers. Her massive majority and the fact of the Opposition being miscellaneous and very differently motivated, has enabled a gloss to be placed even over what can be called a political enormity, namely, the phenomenon of unprecedentedly heartless treatment of political prisoners, large numbers of whom have been beaten up and killed, inside and outside of jails, without anything like a judicial process, without conformity with routine regulations regarding post mortem and other investigations.

Her style had affected the balance between the states and the central government. With many, and eventually all Congress chief ministers her nominees—not the choice of the party's state units—the Centre's detailed interference became the norm in state affairs. While this enormously strengthened Mrs Gandhi's own grip on her party's state units, and made reward and punishment in the form of loans and assistance from the Centre to state governments, or their witholding, her own prerogative, the damage to the federal structure soon showed. State politics released an instability resembling the period of unsteady coalitions after the 1967 election, with bargaining and defections confined now to factions of the Congress. A jungle of intrigue and intra-party feuding sprounted, unlike the factional differences of the Nehru era when state leadership and considerations had resolved crises. The rungs of the ladder of command now dispensed with, all decision issued from the top. The results were detrimental to both party and country. In her grasp of the nuts and bolts of the machinery of power, so essential to control, Mrs Gandhi exhibited a curious lack of overall vision, if power is to be vested in a community and not in the person of a single leader. She installed a strategy of command that depended entirely on personal loyalty. It did not train a leadership for the future, taking care to remove or subdue any sign of emerging leadership. Her vision stopped at the machine, and her unrelenting hold on it produced near-chaotic conditions in the states. Faction quarrels in Orissa forced Nandini Sathpathy (sent there by Mrs Gandhi as Chief Minister in 1972) to quit. Kedar Pandey in Bihar and

Ghanshyam Oza in Gujarat followed suit. In Madhya Pradesh P.C. Sethi fought the rebel faction in order to retain control as Chief Minister. In Andhra Pradesh where a separatist agitation started, Mrs Gandhi's nominee faced rough weather. By 1973 faction fighting in many states was endemic, with state units in disarray and their leaders abandoning deteriorating conditions of law and order and economic decline while they sought the Prime Minister's intervention to keep their seats from rivals in their own party. Shaky on their own ground, each problem sent them hurrying to Delhi for orders, a recurring event not without its comic aspects. R.K. Laxman's cartoon, in his *Times of India* series "You Said It," showed two plane wrecks with a chief minister peering out bewilderedly from each. One had been heading for Delhi, the other back to his state when their planes collided. On 23 May 1973 the *Times of India*, in an item referring to questions in the Madhya Pradesh Assembly, revealed that P.C. Sethi, Chief Minister, had flown to Delhi twice a week during his first year in office, his trips costing the state exchequer 1.3 lakhs.

The props and conventions of political behaviour had been set aside by Mrs Gandhi during 1969, and her own party felt the recoil. She was acknowledged leader over its mushrooming indiscipline, but did not seem able to prevent it. There was disgrace in the spectacle of the ruling party in its exalted, unrivalled position, fallen into a snarl of schemes and intrigues. The *Patriot* lamented editorially in July 1973:

While the Congress factions were busy cutting each other's throats, Ahmedabad witnessed a shameless outbreak of communal violence, a gruesome reminder to the ruling party that communal gangsters, if not the more unscrupulous elements in its own ranks, are ever on the prowl to exploit every unstable situation for their own ends.

In another July editiorial the *Patriot* described the condition of the ruling party as an

. . . . epidemic of petty factionalism that is spreading in the Congress from State to State, paralysing its organisational structure, benumbing whatever mind it had and threatening to create a mortal political crisis when the country is reeling without any sense of direction in a chaotic economic morass. . . .

These indictments by a CPI-owned newspaper and supporter of
the Congress were almost indistinguishable from the Right wing
Jan Sangh organ, *Motherland*'s comment on Madhya Pradesh affairs:

> Mr. Sethi's personal fate or the outcome of the Congress fac-
> tion fights, however, is of little concern to the people. What is
> really tragic is that the destiny of the nation should be in the
> hands of these morally sick leaders of a sick political party.

There was an increasing awareness of corruption at high levels.
The public was convinced of authority's lucrative alliance with
corrupt elements in the country, important smugglers among them,
and with the "black money" that flowed from sections of industry.

It was finally the state of Bihar that showed the dire effects of
federal corrosion when, in 1974, the state government gave up all
pretence at decision-making during a period requiring the most
careful judgement and action.

Tension mounted within the Congress over its alliance with the
CPI. The Nehru Study Forum considered it unnecessary and harm-
ful to the party's image in the country. The Young Turk, Chandrasekhar, spoke scathingly of communist "management" of the
Congress, violently objecting to this new political elite, the control
it exercised, and the communist stamp that flourished under Mrs
Gandhi's umbrella. It was feared the extent of Indian commitment to the Soviet Union was cutting out other options when
India needed wheat and skills. Yet the alliance with the CPI was
officially and publicly affirmed in March 1973 when CPI and Congress took part in a New Delhi seminar organized by the Congress Form for Socialist Action, presided over by Congress President
Shankar Dayal Sharma, to alert the people against "the Rightist
counter-revolutionary challenge." Mrs Gandhi ordered both forums
to wind up when they clashed in open recrimination. But the
tension continued.

As the bloom faded from the ruling party's image, disillusionment focused on two of its prominent figures: Lalit Narayan
Mishra, Union Minister for Railways, and Bansi Lal, Chief Minister of Haryana. The 53rd Report of the Estimates Committee of

the Bihar Assembly had recorded that L.N. Mishra and his famiiy had made substantial fortunes out of contracts connected with Bihar's Kosi project. Specific charges of corruption and misuse of authority had been brought against Bansi Lal by Opposition leaders. These, addressed to President V.V. Giri, were contained in three documented memoradums, calling for an enquiry. As the demand for an enquiry gathered force during the 1972 monsoon session of Parliament, Mrs Gandhi gave the charge-sheet against him to a subcommittee of the cabinet, of which D.P. Dhar, Kashmiri head of the Planning Commission, was an important member. It exonerated Bansi Lal and dismissed the charges. If Mrs Gandhi was disturbed by the reputations of these colleagues she gave no indication of it. Her public references to them were warm and appreciative. The expectation that she would replace or reprimand them did not materialize. The impression grew that these were key figures in her confidence whose services could not be easily replaced. Her patronage of them made them flashpoints of a rising resentment. While L.N. Mishra, associated with fund raising for the party, remained in the background, Bansi Lal, a cruder and more colourful political figure, was involved in open controversy, and known to have the Prime Minister's special protection in return for his staunch support and some 300 acres of requisitioned land provided for her son's car factory in his state.

In her capacity as leader, Mrs Gandhi apparently did not feel accountable to her party. She cultivated a monarchical remoteness, above and beyond the growing uproar of factionalism and criticism, untouched by and oblivious to it. Indeed she denied any interest in leadership. She had told the Congress Parliamentary Party on 13 March 1972: "I am not one of those who believe in leadership. My whole attempt is to create a society in which people do not need leaders." The society she was creating showed all the grotesquerie of the opposite trend. For those who had long known it there was a peculiar pathos in watching the Congress, once a national movement inspired by high ideals, in its best days devoted to hard work and a constructive purpose, thus succumb. The idea of a leader as the focus of admiration and adulation was not new to Indians, a people more willing than most to follow a leader. But modern India's leadership had been built and based on professional excellence or on great example, not on the emblems or actuality of power. Mrs Gandhi's citadel attracted an older similie, a reigning medieval monarch surrounded by the panoply of a court, its flattery, its intrigue, and the swift retribution that visits offendors. Backed by the modern machinery of state power, in a country where the majority were uneducated and could be easily manipulated, her scope for the exercise of arbitrary leadership was almost unlimited. The pedestal she occupied, high above the party, served her well. Indicative of her lack of the common touch, her inability to tolerate equals, her trust of no one—failings of tragic proportion in ordinary life—it created the necessary regal distance between her and the party, her and the crowd, so that though the muddy tide of corruption and confusion lapped at her, it could not overwhelm her. She could remain unsullied by it.

This became harder to do as questions rose and a storm broke in Parliament over the non-appearance of Maruti, her son Sanjay's car project, his failure to account for the delay and his personal financial gains from government contracts. There was critical comment in the press and talk in marketplaces and coffee houses, where most controversial issues and political scandal ended for dissection. Industry was called to account and penalized for failing to produce under a licence. No strictures had been served on the Maruti factory, built in record time at a period when building was handicapped by shortages of cement and other materials.

One newspaper, the *Hindustan Times*, was expected to withold both unfavourable comment and neutral assessment. K.K. Birla, its proprietor, and financial backer of Sanjay Gandhi, conveyed Sanjay's annoyance to the editor. B.G. Verghese replied on 19 September 1973 with his customary clarity and composure:

Dear Mr. Birla,
Following your telephone call yesterday I checked through our file of items published on Maruti. According to our library clippings there is only one item recently published and this is an interview with Mr. Sanjay Gandhi published in the *Evening News* of September 5. This interview gave Mr. Gandhi an opportunity to project his project in the best manner possible.

Earlier in July we had published a news item about the automobile industry in which the opening reference was to Maruti. Wing Commander Chaudhry of Maruti Ltd. sent us a letter discussing some of the points contained in our news report.

This was published extensively. The clippings are enclosed. Some time later Wing Commander Chaudhry sent us a second letter apropos of nothing, which very largely repeated the points contained in his earlier letter. This we did not publish as it made no new point and came within a few weeks of the publication of the earlier letter.

I am, therefore, surprised that Mr.'Sanjay Gandhi should feel that we have been unfair to him or his project. On the contrary we showed great forbearance in accepting the letters send by Wing Commander Chaudhry although these were sent to us personally through a senior information official of the Prime Minister's Secretariat. This was very improper and is the kind of thing that arouses a great deal of suspicion, and lends credibility to the various public charges being made about official favours being bestowed on Maruti Ltd. . . .

> With kind regards,
> Yours sincerely,
> (Sd.) B.G. Verghese

Verghese's dismissal (officially on 22 September 1975) had to await the Delhi High Court's stay order. It became a cause celebre with a macabre twist. The issue it raised against proprietal interference gave a handle to the government's "diffusion of ownership" scheme, and later its steps to "restructure" the press, while in fact Verghese had been dismissed on Sanjay's order and with Mrs Gandhi's knowledge and tacit consent. The proprietor, K.K. Birla, was to emerge in 1976 with hold over a larger newspaper "monopoly" than before, when in recognition of his services he was made Chairman of the Board of Directors of the *Indian Express* group of newspapers.

The failure in 1972 of the monsoon was the beginning of a severe economic crisis laying bare the government's lack of programme. Prices rose by 14 per cent, essential supplies fell short, drought and famine gripped large areas. Constant and crippling power crises affected vital areas of public and private industry. The anxiety over food and unemployment set off agitations, often violent, at nine universities. These had to close for a time, including Delhi University and the prestigious Indian Institute of Technology in the capital. Government's announcements that disparities must end, "crash" programmes would be launched for employment and agriculture, "big" business would be drastically limited in its scope of manufacture and would have to abandon the profit motive, got no further than cutting off existing initiative and performance. The excitement of bank nationalization had died away, and with no clear credit policy had become a non-event. The optimism following the Bangladesh victory was turning into shock and anger. Remedy, or even an attempt at it, seemed blocked by an atmosphere of moral decay surrounding and supporting political functioning at the highest level. No one expected purity of politicians, but the conviction that things had gone too far was not confined to critics of Mrs Gandhi's party. Addressing a convocation of Jawaharlal Nehru University in Delhi, of which Mrs Gandhi herself was Chancellor, film actor Balraj Sahni, a star in the Left firmament, created a stir when he named Union and state ministers as corrupt. The sins of the undivided Congress looked pale and sedate compared with the lawlessness of Mrs Gandhi and her lieutenants and their assumption of non-accountability at the bar of any opinion.

In October 1972 a debate on fundamental rights began before a 13-member Bench of the Supreme Court. Counsel for the petitioners who challenged the validity of the recent Amendents was N.A. Palkhivala, eminent constitutional lawyer and authority on tax law. The government was defended by a galaxy of State Advocates General in addition to the Attorney-General. The judgement, a mixed one, was delivered on 23 April 1973. The main issues before the judges were: (1) Can Parliament amend fundamental rights under its normal amending power consisting of a two-thirds majority in both Houses of Parliament? (2) Assuming it can, are there any areas affecting the use of these rights which the amending power cannot override? The majority of judges decided that fundamental rights can be amended by the normal amending power, but that essential features of the Constitution cannot be so changed. These, however, were not demarcated, leaving the fundamental rights in a grey legal area to be variously interpreted. A bulwark against possible dictatorship was heavily eroded and the government's use of its mandate became a palpable anxiety.

The annual Congress session at Bidhan Nagar near Calcutta, held in December 1972 amid flourish and display during India's worst economic crisis, aroused comment, both desparing and caustic, from leading newspapers. Some of its severest critics were

Congressmen themselves, the ebullient younger element, unawed and unsilenced, whose crusading fire had helped to raise Mrs Gandhi to her powerful pedestal, and on whom they had pinned great hopes for the fashioning of a clean cohesive instrument to bring about change. They led the attack against malpractices during organization elections. Krishna Kant's accusation that 50 lakhs had been spent on party elections in one state alone was not taken up for discussion. Shashi Bhushan resigned from his State Congress Committee in disgust against its undesirable election practices. Mrs Gandhi's own ministers were believed to be involved in manufacturing votes to win elections.

Key speeches at Bidhan Nagar took no searching look at the party's ills or the economic crisis. The Congress President, Shankar Dayal Sharma, spoke instead of "the forces of reaction eager to take advantage." Defence Minister Chavan called the violent agitations in Andhra Pradesh and Assam the efforts of Right and Left extremists to obstruct socialism: "We have to do everything possible to frustrate their machinations. They are not yet reconciled to the massive victory of the Congress in the last two elections." Mrs Gandhi predictably declared: "We are with the people. Neither the capitalists nor the press can detract us from our path." This monotonous chant added thin comfort to what the *Tribune* editorially called:

> . . . a year of less hope and more despair, of rich rhetoric and poor performance, of more bogeys and less realism in India. For Mrs. Gandhi personally and the Congress generally, it was in some ways the worst year since the historic split in 1969. Both were at the crossroads again, totally uncertain of the future.

CHAPTER NINE

REAPING THE WHIRLWIND—II

The ruling party had framed a national policy on argicultural land ceilings, with urban ceilings to follow, and had announced it would "extend the public sector" in areas where "state ownership is vital." These included coal, sections of foreign trade, and food-grains. The Bidhan Nagar Congress session decided to eliminate the wholesale trade in foodgrains, making government the sole buyer of the wheat crop of April 1973 and the rice crop in October, through a government agency. Some chief ministers advised delay for a massive operation that would need careful preparation, not only for procurement from the farmer, but for distribution over a vast population. These misgivings were hesitantly put forward and not freely aired in party councils for fear that doubts about policy would mean a reactionary label and a black mark. An incomplete plan, conceived in haste, driven by the need to maintain a radical posture, resulted in long queues for bread in cities, the disappearance of grain altogether at intervals, and conditions bordering on anarchy in some areas. Discussing its failure, E.N. Mangat Rai[1] describes it as twofold: (1) Government made exceptions to its own monopoly, allowing retailers, and then consumers to buy privately, thus drilling leaks into the system; (2) an effective distribution system to ensure grain to the public was not created. The resulting panic put a strain on monopoly procurement that broke it:

> ... if government as the sole controller of grain creates a monopoly ... it must create a distribution agency for all persons to be fed. .... The responsibility to supply and the obliga-

[1]E. N. Mangat Rai, *Patterns of Administrative Development in Independent India*, University of London, The Athlone Press, 1976.

tion by the consumer to accept no other supply were both lacking. In the absence of rationing, which provides precisely these twin points of security to system and consumer, there was a vacuum. The government met the situation by allowing retailers to purchase limited amounts from the market to feed their customers, and by allowing customers to buy direct from the farmer for personal consumption. The farmer was convinced that he had not one buyer . . . for his wheat, but several. In places the consumer, when he could not lay hands on supplies, panicked. . . . As the season advanced there were food riots, first in Nagpur, then in Bombay, later in Mysore. In Kerala education was shut down after students attacked grain trucks. Supplies were rushed to distress areas; the movement of "special trainloads" was publicized in the press and over the government-operated radio. There was drama about the movement of food. The wheat "monopoly" had become a shambles within weeks of its start. On 31 August Fakhruddin Ali Ahmed, the Food Minister, reporting to the party said that the government had purchased to that date 600-700,000 tonnes less than it did in a free market in the previous year. The buffer stock (of 9 million tonnes on July 1, 1972) had been reduced, after accounting for new purchases, to 4 million tonnes.

Some of the chaos could have been avoided if the experienced wholesale trade had been retained as government's agent and paid at a fixed price, as had been done in a streamlined operation following the Bengal famine of 1943, and continued for some years after independence. But policy-makers had now labelled the wholesale trade a "vested interest" and earmarked it for destruction.

As the government lost control of the food situation, a mixture of incentives and threat were belatedly held over the farmer, further confusing the takeover operation, and the country driven to import more than 6 million tonnes of grain at a high international price in the very year that self-sufficiency was to have been proclaimed. The rice crop takeover by the government, scheduled for October, was "postponed." The intention to take over the wheat crop of April 1974 was abandoned. Mrs Gandhi's statement that the people would have starved but for government action did not explain why the action had been abruptly discontinued. She laid the blame for its failure on the bureaucracy's ineptitude. On 29 July 1975, when dictatorship had silenced dissent, efficiency was the government's proclaimed watchword, and blame could no longer be passed on. Food Minister C. Subramaniam said in the Rajya Sabha, quietly disowning a past disaster: "The idea looks all right on paper. But taking over the entire surplus grains would burden the system, leading to its collapse. Instead efforts should be made to build up a public distribution system for specific areas."

This manifest economic failure was accompanied by a rude shock to stability in Uttar Pradesh, the country's most populous state, with the largest number of seats in Parliament, and Mrs Gandhi's constituency. Chief Minister Kamalapati Tripathi was clearly not in control as a lightning revolt of the Provincial Armed Constabulary (the state's special police force) succeeded to the extent of capturing arsenals and refusing to surrender. President's rule was imposed on Uttar Pradesh. The Governor, Akbar Ali Khan's letter on 12 June 1973 to the President, reporting economic crisis and police revolt halted only by the army's intervention, spoke glowingly of the Chief Minister:

You and your Government have been in touch with the recent happenings in the State. The power shortage and scarcity of essential commodities had already created considerable difficulties for the general public and the State government was trying to grapple with these problems, as well as with the growing student unrest, when it had to face quite a serious situation caused by some sections of the civil police and the PAC. The incidents of grave indiscipline on the part of the subordinate ranks in some companies of the PAC had to be dealt with firmly, and assistance of the armed forces of the Union Government had to be requisitioned to meet an unprecedented situation. . . . The voluntary resignation of the Ministry headed by Shri Kamalapati Tripathi has come in spite of his unchallenged leadership of the Congress Legislature Party. . . . I would like to place on record my deep appreciation of Shri Tripathi's record as Chief Minister, the crowning glory of which consists in what he has rightly described as his act of self-abnegation in the larger interests of the State and the nation.

This letter is perhaps unsurpassed as an example of the mythical air state governments breathed, bland and benevolent towards such stark realities as "the power shortage and scarcity of essential commodities," "growing student unrest," and even the "unprecedented situation" of actual police revolt. A state seething with political and economic discontent headed by a chief minister known to tolerate corruption—twin evils creating a volcanic resentment against Congress power in many parts of India—appear to have left the Governor blissfully undisturbed. It is possible Akbar Ali Khan was aware a more factual report would have angered New Delhi, placing him in a position of critic towards Tripathi, a favourite. With President's rule the legislature was not, according to normal practice, dissolved. No risk could be taken with the Congress majority, which showed signs of being heavily eroded if another election were held, and MLAs continued to enjoy their perquisites. Despite the Governor's assertion of Tripathi's "unchallenged leadership of the Congress Legislature Party," the Uttar Pradesh Congress presented a classic picture of political talent and vigour kept in check by an ineffective leadership obedient to the Centre.

This travesty of a governor's responsibility for assessment and report reached its climax with the dismissal of Kamalapati Tripathi's successor in 1975.

H.N. Bahuguna, one of the state's younger politicians, was appointed Chief Minister in Tripathi's place on 8 November 1973. In active politics since his student days at Allahabad University, Bahuguna set about with energy, ambition, and drive to restore efficiency. His solid political base in Uttar Pradesh and his confident stride attracted unfavourable notice. He was reported as having less than the requisite ardour for Mrs Gandhi, and dismissed without cause in November 1975. No effort was made to cloak this executive order in constitutional guise. It had been preceded by the appointment of a new Governor, Chenna Reddy, whose brief included a close watch on Bahuguna's "loyalty" to Mrs Gandhi, a mission he took no trouble to hide, taking over executive functions in the process that were not within a governor's province. S.C. Kala reported in the *Times of India* on 13 March 1975:

He [the new Governor] has called officials of the intelligence

departments of the State and Centre to report to him and also
issued orders directly to State government officials. . . . The
Governor, who is hardly discreet in his utterances, has often
made remarks which betray his hostility to Mr. H. N. Bahuguna.
. . . There is no doubt his behaviour has not been constitution-
ally correct.

On 29 November 1975 Chenna Reddy reported to the President
simply that Bahuguna who enjoyed an "absolute majority in the
State Assembly, has tendered the resignation of his Ministry to me
this morning. . . ." By this time the imposition of President's rule
on a state bore no relation to the reasons stated for it in the Constitution: the actual or imminent failure of constitutional government. In fact, the frequency and transparent unconstitutionally of
its exercise had deprived it of its meaning. In an article "Misuse
of President's Rule" in the *Times of India* (16 July 1973), Ajit
Bhattacharjea had commented:" Since Mrs. Gandhi became Prime
Minister 7½ years ago, the Centre has invoked President's Rule 22
times to take over the administration of States. In the previous
16 years, after the Constitution took effect, these emergency powers
were used 10 times."

Among the rising stars Mrs Gandhi was to cut down from their
heights before long were two Young Turks about whom a special
splendour shone as they took up fighting positions to demand a
clean and dedicated Congress. Mohan Dharia and Chandrasekhar
(born in 1925 and 1927 respectively) had both come to the Congress via the Socialist Party, home of some of the most original
intellects in the country. Like many of their generation now cele-
brities in politics, they had been student activists. Dharia, a graduate of the Law College, Poona, had organized a youth march
during the Quit India movement of 1942 to capture Mahad Tehsil,
and had been associated with the liberation struggle in Janjira
State of the Konkan region. Chandrasekhar, educated at Allahabad University, had been President of the District Students' Congress in Ballia (UP) in 1947, and Secretary of the Samajvadi Yuvak
Sabha (Socialist Youth Organization) in Allahabad in 1950. During
1959-62 he had been on the national executive of the Praja Socialist Party. Both were of the calibre a political party normally regar-
ds as leadership material. Dharia had charge of the party's election campaign in Maharashtra in 1962 and 1967. He had been

elected to the Rajya Sabha in 1964 and 1970, and to the Lok Sabha from Poona city in 1971. Mrs Gandhi had appointed him Minister of State for Planning in that year. Chandrasekhar had been a member of the Congress Working Committee since 1967. He was elected to the Central Election Committee in 1971, to the Rajya Sabha in 1972, and re-elected to it in 1974. His immense popularity and political flair had won him elected party posts against determined attempts to defeat him.

A third rebel who incurred his leader's displeasure was Krishna Kant, born in 1927, and educated at DAV College, Lahore, and Banaras University. He had been Secretary of the Students' Federation, Jhelum, in 1940-42, and had been imprisoned for two years during the Quit India agitation. He was elected to the Rajya Sabha in 1966 and re-elected in 1972. During 1971-72 he was Secretary to the Congress Parliamentary Party.

All three shared an independence of speech and outlook and a dogged disregard of whom these might offend. In the sea of conformity, even servility, around Mrs Gandhi, they were irrepressible, identifiable, attractive individuals, each with a capacity to go far in the party. A child of privilege herself, with special courtesy and consideration shown to her as Nehru's daughter by the party and the country, Mrs Gandhi had entered politics at the top and not through the rugged school of competition. Her insistence on her unique position revealed her insecurity on her pinnacle and her distance from the true metier and experience of the natural politician, which her inbred disposition did nothing to overcome. She felt safe with the mediocre, uncomfortable in the presence of outstanding political talent or personality, and threatened by aspiration that sprang from the ground and did not need her permission to succeed. It was simpler for her to deal with the elders in her party, no longer willing or able to do open battle. Any show of political virility alerted her to danger. To disagree with her was unpatriotic. In her own party it was to become *lèse majesté*.

In a country so diverse culturally, where the problems of poverty and integration demand solution, a charismatic leader may well be an insurance of political stability and the will to get things done. Nehru had been one in his time. Mrs Gandhi, however, introduced authoritarian trends and ideas into the Indian polity very different from the values of her two predecessors. It is possible that in her hunger for leadership, and without the solid apprenticeship this required, she became involved in more than she bargained for: a complex human situation, not merely a political one, and that a turn away from freedom became the inexorable course in reducing the human to malleable material. By the end of 1973 India's political and constitutional future were uncertain, without any balancing assurance of economic gain. And this was the consequence not of a "people's" urge but of a particular character driven by its own urges, in search of fulfilment. Power has been sought for a variety of reasons. Mrs Gandhi was not unusual in thus using "the people." The people serve, especially in a society such as India, patiently and often passively as the raw material of power. It is the leader who invents, or authentically articulates, their demands. How he conceives and articulates them is a matter of his own belief and temperament. What he draws from them reflects in part what he himself is. Thus Mahatma Gandhi could get mass participation through an appeal to suffering and make it a platform for dynamic political action. Jawaharlal Nehru could sustain democracy partly by sheer faith, upholding a vision of the future beyond present difficulties, so crucial for the courage all voluntary effort needs. Indira Gandhi understood the leadership of India as a relation between the ruler and the ruled, a rigid formula that left out the noblest and richest possibilities in human development.

CHAPTER TEN

JAYAPRAKASH NARAYAN

In March 1974 a student movement in Bihar, originating as a demand for educational reform, created, under the leadership of Jayaprakash Narayan, the conditions for a powerful political challenge to Mrs Gandhi. Jayaprakash, the most unusual figure in Indian politics, and for twenty-four years, 1930-54, the most important in the age-group under Nehru, had a career more fully representative of India's three-cornered political tradition than any other Indian. Three streams—British liberalism, Marxism, and Gandhism—met in it to evolve a personal philosophy. If Jayaprakash arrived finally at Gandhian interpretation and action, it was because Gandhism alone involved the whole human being and all aspects of his striving.

The challenge to Mrs Gandhi was led by a man as different in background, experience, and temperament from her as can be imagined. Jayaprakash was born, the fourth of six children, on 11 October 1902 into a lower middle class family in Sitabdiara village on the UP-Bihar border, where his father was a revenue official in Bihar's canal department. There were few comforts at home but the Kayastha caste prizes learning, and there was plenty to read. He saw a city for the first time when, aged twelve, wearing the villager's dhoti, shirt, and flat cap on his head, he arrived in Patna to join school. He lived with his sister and brother-in-law and had an allowance of three annas a day, one anna for lunch and two for transport. Matriculating with high marks in 1919 he got a government scholarship of Rs 15 a month to Patna College. At about this time, he was married by arrangement to 14-year-old Prabhavati whose father, Brij Kishore, had helped Mahatma Gandhi to collect data on indigo plantation workers in Champaran and had supported his Champaran satyagraha campaign.

Jayaprakash left college two years later when Maulana Azad and Jawaharlal Nehru made a stirring appeal to students at a public meeting in Patna to work for freedom. JP wrote later:

I ... was one of the thousands of young men of those days who, like leaves in a storm, were swept away and momentarily lifted up to the skies. That brief experience of soaring up with the winds of a great idea left imprints on the inner being that time and much familiarity with the ugliness of reality have not removed.[1]

His family persuaded him to take his examination, due in a month, from the Bihar Vidyapeeth, a college just established for students who had walked out of institutions aided by the British Government, and later to continue his studies outside India. In 1922 he sailed for the United States with $ 600 which he would have to supplement with what he could earn. He told a public meeting in Patna on 5 June 1974:

I worked in mines, in factories, in slaughter houses. I worked as a shoeshine boy and even cleaned commodes [toilets] in hotels. During vacations . . . three or more boys lived in a single room and we cooked our own food. After graduation I got a scholarship and three months later an assistantship in my department which made it possible for me to live in some comfort.

He spent seven years in America, his studies interrupted by a long illness and a variety of jobs, and attended three universities, leaving California (Berkeley) where he could not afford the fees, for Iowa, and later Wisconsin. Saul D. Ozer, a classmate at Wisconsin, told Nageshwar Prasad of the Institute of Gandhian Studies, Varanasi, in March 1968:

I had never met a person who was more awake and intellectually alive to the implications of what ever anybody in that class said. He was always like an architect, developing his case and argument to its logical conclusion. And as a logician he was

[1]Ajit Bhattacharjea, *Jayaprakash Narayan: A Political Biograhy*, Vikas, New Delhi, 1975.

superb. . . . We all felt there was greatness in Narayan.

Ozer remembers JP as tall and strikingly handsome. When they entered the library, "it wasn't more than five minutes before every seat was filled with girls looking at Narayan." His habits were monastic. He did not smoke, drink or date. He did, in his own words, try "to learn to dance at the Recreation Room. I didn't have enough time, and never became any good." At a farewell party given by his Indian friends in New York before he left for home, they insisted that he "at least smoke a cigarette before leaving the shores of the United States."

The certificates his professors gave him when he applied for a fellowship in New York reveal the wholeness of his impact on them, and a sustained academic brilliance that seemed as much a trait of character as a quality of mind. Ajit Bhattacharjea lists three in his biography:

Intellectually, it seems to me, Mr. Narayan ranks as high or higher than any student I have ever had. He is a careful and critical thinker, and a searcher after truth; of course he is a wide reader. He is, in every sense, a scholar in the making. (Professor F.E. Dumley, Sociology Department.)

In his class work on theoretical psychology I think he is one of the brightest students I have ever had. My impression at this time is that he has in him qualifications which under favourable conditions will lead to an outstanding position as a social theorist. (Professor Albert Weiss, Psychology Department.)

Perhaps Mr. J. P. Narayan's most remarkable trait . . . is his idealism. It infuses his daily life as well as his world outlook. It has been my experience in living with him to be surprised again and again by little unexpected acts of unselfishness. (Professor Richard Steinmetz.)

JP's Hindi biographer, Lakshmi Narain Lal,[2] lists three others:

He shows distinctly an enquiring turn of mind and a critical capacity rare even in the better class of graduate students. He is a fine-appearing man, a thorough gentleman, and in my opi-

[2]Lakshmi Narain Lal, *Jayaprakash: Rebel Extraordinary*, Indian Book Company, New Delhi, 1975. (Translation of Hindi biography.)

nion, a thorough student. I have noted that he always has an interest in the larger and deeper problems of economics, rather than in matters of technical detail. . . . (Professor A.B. Wolfe, Economics Department, May 1, 1929.)

His work with me is consistently A grade. He is openminded, eager to make intellectual contacts and has plenty of originality. In short, Mr. Narayan belongs to the highest class of graduate ability. . . . (Professor Charles A. Dice, May 2, 1929.)

Mr. J. P. Narayan is a fine candidate for a Moral Leadership fellowship. He is one of the ablest students I have ever had, both keen and deep. His whole outlook is based on a desire to know how to do something to help society. . . . (Professor Millar, May 7, 1929.)

JP's American experience was both varied and profound. At Wisconsin, Polish-born American communist, Abram Landy, introduced him to the communist creed and classics. Convinced. Marxism was the solution for change in India, JP found its paradoxes hard to digest. Ozer called him: ". . . a strange mixture of Marxism and Gandhism. . . . He told me that the major thing that bothered him was the morality, character, integrity of the Communist. . . ."

At home he joined the Congress, not the Communist Party. The Salt March in early 1930 impressed him deeply with the discovery that while the ideologues propounded ideology, Gandhi, with neither ideology nor manifesto, took the people with him. The Mahatma's mission, freedom without violence, transcended political programmes, yet concerned itself minutely with the human springs of social and economic change. Stalin's excesses disillusioned and repelled JP as they did his contemporaries, Ignacio Silone and Arthur Koestler. Yet his belief in Marxism and his admiration for many aspects of the Soviet experiment remained integral to his thinking, even after a brief abrasive collaboration between his Congress Socialist Party and the Communist Party decided him against any further link with the communists. Differences between the two became bitter in 1939 when the CPI justified the Soviet invasion of Finland. The partnership broke when the CPI joined the British Government's war effort, ignoring the nationalist mood in India and the Congress demand for an assurance of independence before it could actively support the Allies.

Prabhavati had spent the years of her husband's absence at Mahatma Gandhi's ashram in Wardha. JP's Hindi biographer records:

> Seven years later, when JP returned, they began to live together; but Prabha's vow of *brahmacharya* and her involvement with Gandhi's programme caused its stresses. . . . [JP's] intellectual bias was Western; rationalism was an unfailing yardstick, dialectical materialism a tenet. . . . On the public platform, Jayaprakash would tirade against Gandhi, subjecting his arguments to a searching scrutiny. Behind him on the same platform, Prabhavati quietly spun raw cotton on a charkha. . . . Yet there was a strong emotional bond that held them together.

JP's association with the Congress Party began in 1930. His intellectual calibre, integrity, and ardent commitment to feedom endeared him to Nehru, thirteen years his senior, while Kamala Nehru and Prabhavati were drawn to each other. When Gandhi launched civil disobedience in 1932 and the government arrested Congress leaders, JP took charge of organizational work until his own arrest in September. He had made enough impact on the party and the public by then to merit Bombay's *Free Press Journal* headline: "Congress Brain Arrested."

His fellow prisoners in Nasik Jail were, like himself, impatient young men afire with ideas, eager to give the Congress a Leftward direction and a firm economic programme. They inaugurated the Congress Socialist Party, a radical group within the Congress, in Bombay in October 1934. The CSP sought the involvement of the intelligentsia as well as the peasants and working classes. JP toured the country to promote its programmes and explain its ideas. His first tract, *Why Socialism*, was published and widely read in 1936, while his four imprisonments during British rule added drama to his celebrity. His second arrest, in March 1940, for making a "seditious" speech at a strike meeting of steel workers at Jamshedpur, Bihar, provoked Mahatma Gandhi to comment in his paper *Harijan*: "The arrest of Shri Jayaprakash Narayan is unfortunate. He is no ordinary worker. . . . He has forsaken all for the sake of the deliverance of his country. His industry is tireless. His capacity for suffering is not to be excelled . . . ."

His nine-month sentence ended at the close of the year, but he

was arrested again soon afterwards. As organizer of strikes, particularly in the steel industry, aimed at impeding Britain's war effort,
he was a special target for the police and a growing legend for the
public. Detained this time in a prisoner-of-war camp near Ajmer,
he and thirty fellow prisoners went on a month's hunger strike in
protest against camp conditions. A roused public opinion succeeded
in getting the camp closed and its inmates transferred to jails in
their own states. JP was sent to Hazaribagh Jail in Bihar. On 9
November 1942 he and five colleagues scaled the prison's seven-
teen-foot wall and escaped. The Quit India agitation begun three
months earlier, sparked by the arrests of Gandhi, Nehru, and other
leaders, had led to violent uprisings in parts of the country and
caused major dislocations in transport and communications. The
sensational escape from Hazaribagh thrilled patriotic sentiment, as
did JP's underground activities. In hiding he and Ram Manohar
Lohia, who had escaped with him, raised a small guerilla band
near the Bihar-Nepal border, printed militant pamphlets against
British rule, and travelled in disguise to organize resistance all over
India. With a 10,000-rupee reward for information leading to their
capture, JP was arrested in September 1943 (and Lohia soon afterwards) and held until April 1946, a year longer than senior Congress leaders.

Crowds gave him a tumultuous welcome on the train journey
home to Patna. In the popular imagination he was a hero, covered
with a charisma and glory second only to Nehru's, and looked upon
as his successor, though now their paths diverged. The socialists
formed a separate party when the Congress took power at independence, though Mahatma Gandhi remained a link between the
two. In February 1947, on the eve of separation, Lohia, CSP president, said at Kanpur: "The Congress is our home. Even when
one leaves a home, it is not easy to deal badly with it. . . . It is
our hope that as long as Gandhi lives, he will not allow the Congress to abandon its revolutionary goals."

Gandhi was killed in January 1948. His agrarian emphasis, belief in decentralization, and in revolution as applicable to caste,
not class struggle, achievable through peaceful, not violent means,
remained a rallying programme for the socialists. The dead Mahatma
continued to light the way with a fundamentally Indian Leftism and
rationale, as against the Moscow-dominated CPI, and a Nehru

government which the socialists believed was overly influenced by Western economic concepts.

The Praja Socialist Party (PSP), as a merger of socialist parties was called after 1952, was invited by Nehru in 1953 to cooperate with his government. The move was dropped when JP wrote to Nehru saying it would have no meaning if it meant strengthening his hands "in carrying out your present policies." The party's impact was weakened and scattered when Lohia broke away with his own splinter group in 1955, and later when JP withdrew to seek solutions to India's problems outside party politics. It was yet perhaps the most intelligent and idealistic development in Indian politics. Part and parcel of the national movement and the Congress inheritance, it did not fall under the Congress spell. It rejected charisma in favour of argument, criticism, and thought. Contemptuous of the doctrinaire, it kept the pot of ideas boiling.

On a visit to Gandhi's ashram at Wardha in 1952, JP found the institutions around it were "in far greater touch with the people and their problems than any other group in the country." The following year he went on a three-week purification fast in his evolving search for answers, coming to the conclusion that: "The problem of human goodness is of supreme moment today . . . it has become patent to me that materialism of any sort robs man of the means to become truly human. . . ."[3] On 29 April 1954 he announced his intention to work for Bhoodan, Vinobha Bhave's land gift movement, a section of the Sarvodaya movement begun by Gandhi's followers after his death. In 1957 he gave up his membership of the PSP in order to give all his time to Sarvodaya: "To create and develop forms of socialist living through the voluntary endeavour of the people rather than seek to establish socialism by the use of the power of the state."

Though ostensibly this was a withdrawal from politics, it provided a broader canvas for creating awareness in the countryside, a labour intended eventually to raise political consciousness and teach people the meaning of their democracy. His basic involvement with politics remained, and his speech to the 13th Sarvodaya Sammelan in 1961 had a prophetic ring:

---

[3]Article by Jayaprakash Narayan in *Freedom First*, its ideas amplified in a speech to the First Asian Socialist Conference in Rangoon, Burma, January 1953.

It means, of course, that we do not belong to any political party, that we do not and shall not take part, directly or indirectly, in any political contest for position or power. But does it also mean that we are not concerned with what is happening in the political field; with the working of our democracy and its various institutions? If democracy were to be in peril, if there was danger of political chaos, of dictatorship, shall we sit back smugly and twiddle our thumbs on the ground that we have nothing to do with politics? Perhaps it is not understood clearly that our policy not to be involved in party and power politics is meant precisely to enable us to play a more effective and constructive part in moulding the politics of the country.

It was during his years of "retirement" from politics that at his urging Panchayat Raj[4] was set up by the Union government in the states to give a village base to the political process. During this period JP led a conciliation mission to Pakistan and worked to end rebellion in Nagaland. In 1966 he wrote to Mrs Gandhi urging Sheikh Abdullah's release and a lasting settlement in Kashmir. Of the Naxalites, active in areas of Bihar, he wrote:

. . . their attempt to precipitate a revolution here and now has rendered at least one service, in that it has aroused the social consciousness of the people in general and prodded the powers that be, in particular, to hasten the implementation of land and other socio-economic reforms.

A development in Madhya Pradesh strikingly illustrated his reputation as a leader whose human qualities and moral stature were held in high regard. At the request of the dacoit leader, Madho Singh, he negotiated with the government for humane treatment for the dacoits in return for their voluntary surrender. On condition that they would not face the death penalty, four hundred dacoits laid down their guns and ammunition in a moving ceremony before JP and his wife.

The early 1970s had seen dramatic changes in prime ministerial style and behaviour. Mrs Gandhi's drive towards centralization,

---

[4]A programme started by state governments, beginning with Rajasthan, in 1959, to create local participation at village level in planned programmes.

her concentration of powers in her own hands, and her frequent use of the new arbitrary arrest law (MISA, June 1971) gave notice of a growing authoritarianism. In 1973 JP wrote to Members of Parliament outlining ways to protect citizens' right and democratic institutions. An organization, Citizens for Democracy, was set up by him for this purpose. In an open letter to youth, dated 9 December 1973, he urged a Youth for Democracy movement: "What form their action should take is for the youth themselves to decide. My only recommendation would be that in keeping with the spirit and substance of democracy, it must be scrupulously peaceful and non-partisan."

In January 1974 a student revolt against food prices in engineering college hostels in Ahmedabad and Morvi, in Gujarat, erupted into a citizens' movement against scarcity and Congress misrule in the state. A wave of anti-government demonstrations, comparable in size to pre-independence civil disobedience, was brought under control by the Central Reserve Police and Border Security Force rather than the state's own police. An unknown member of demonstrators had been arrested and between 85 and 100 killed by mid-March when Mrs Gandhi was compelled to concede the outraged demand for the state government's resignation. The Gujarat mood stayed anti-Congress. A year and a half later an election in the state ended in the Congress Party's defeat.

The agitation in Gujarat had taken Mrs Gandhi's government by surprise. The first sign of organized protest in Bihar found it prepared, equipped, and armoured.

CHAPTER ELEVEN

THE BIHAR MOVEMENT—1974

The year 1974 saw an outbreak of smallpox in Bihar, so neglected by an administration caught in the coils of political manoeuvre that it spread to epidemic proportions. And in that year Bihar demonstrated the damage an unconfident chief minister, dependent on Mrs Gandhi, with no political strength of his own in the state, could do in crippling a state government's initiative and, in a crisis, rendering it irrelevant altogether. Matters came to a head on 18 March 1974, precipitated by two events.

The Students' Action Committee, representing several Patna colleges and youth groups, held a demonstration that day at the State Assembly, demanding a reply to a memorandum on educational reform presented to the State Education Minister at the end of February. The police took brisk action. Students who crossed the barricades set up by the police were removed and thrashed. They retaliated by throwing stones and the demonstration was dispersed by lathis and tear gas.

On the same day a mob carrying kerosene and rags set the building housing two newspapers, *Searchlight* (English) and *Pradeep* (Hindi), on fire, destroying machines, files, records, newsprint, reels and rotary. The police arrived two and a half hours after the fire started, too late to prevent damage. The editor of *Searchlight*, S.K. Rau, believed the fire was the CPI's revenge against his editorial policy, which was critical of the Congress-CPI alliance, and that the delayed arrival of the police was deliberate.

Three days of loot and arson followed, with the police firing indiscriminately on terrified running crowds. The Bihar government, under a chief minister and cabinet sworn in eight months earlier, seemed unable to bring the situation under control. Jayaprakash Narayan issued a statement from his home in Patna:

In any democratic country after such a monumental failure of administration as Patna witnessed on Monday last, the government would have resigned. . . . Everyone talks vaguely of hooligans and goondas. Hooligans, of course, were abroad in large numbers. It also seems reasonably sure that those responsible for the major incidents of arson were outsiders, probably hailing from Bhagalpur, and had a certain measure of expertise. For one thing, some of the drivers of the hijacked buses seemed to be well-trained; for another, the incendiary used appeared to be more powerful than ordinary fire and spread very quickly. . . among those arrested are members of the Tarun Shanti Sena,[1] the Secretary of the local centre of the Gandhi Peace Foundation, and the editor of *Ayeena*. Those who believe in and work for peace are being punished for the violence of others.

On 8 April, at the students' request, JP led a silent procession in protest against indiscriminate arrests and police excesses. It was greeted with flowers from silent spectators. He was 71, in indifferent health and bereaved by Prabhavati's death the previous year. He explained his decision to enter the fray after twenty years devoted to Sarvodaya, as the only possible one, in the context of recent developments. Two days earlier he had said:

Speaking for myself, I cannot remain a silent spectator to misgovernment, corruption and the rest, whether in Patna, Delhi or elsewhere. It is not for this that I at least had fought for freedom. . . .I am not interested in this or that Ministry being replaced or the [Bihar] Assembly being dissolved. These are partisan aims and their achievement will make no difference. It will be like replacing Tweedledum with Tweedledee. But I have decided to fight corruption and misgovernment and black marketing, profiteering and hoarding, to fight for the overhaul of the educational system, and for a real people's democracy.

The students had twelve demands, eight for minor reforms at the university, and four relating to corruption, unemployment, scarcity of essential supplies, and the need for fundamental chang-

---

[1]A youth brigade recruited by Vinoba Bhave to work for the Bhoodan Movement.

es in the educational system. After 18 March these were headed by
the demand for the Bihar government's resignation. JP explained
this unorthodox demand: "The argument that people have a constitutional remedy in that they can change the government at the next
election has no validity now in view of the distortions and abuses
of our democratic institutions and processes."

The students' movement expanded to include the community.
Jan Sangharsh and Chhatra Sangharsh Samitis (People's and Student's Struggle Committees) were formed to organize processions,
meetings, and *bundhs* to demonstrate the strength of the popular
demand for the state government's resignation. Non-violence was
the condition for JP's leadership. Violence, which could in any
case be crushed, would, he said, give the Union government an
excuse to launch a dictatorship.

> Everyone participating in and sympathetic with the movement
> must eschew violence in word and deed, whatever the provoca-
> tion. It is a matter of gratification that by and large the move-
> ment has remained peaceful. That has been its strength. God
> knows there has been no little provocation and it is natural that
> young men should become excited and angry. . . .

Non-violence gave the movement one of its slogans: "*Police hamare bhai hain: unse nahi.1 ladai hai.*" (The police are our brothers;
we have no quarrel with them.) The state police responded with
enough sympathy for the Bihar government to summon armed aid
from Delhi, as the Gujarat government had done. In shaky charge
of a faction-ridden party that had no confidence in his leadership
and wished him replaced, Chief Minister Abdul Ghafoor had, in
any event, to rely on orders from Delhi in handling the crisis that
now threatened to unseat him and overwhelm the state.

On 5 June, shots fired on a procession led by JP wounded 21
participants. He referred to this, as well as to an earlier incident,
at a public meeting that evening:

> The government of Bihar distrusts its own police force. We have
> a fine army which has raised the country's prestige and respect.
> Can there be a matter of greater shame than that these brave
> soldiers should be used to fire upon their own people? Is
> there no way to understand and deal with a people's move-

ment except bullets and lathis and jail? Are not the demands of the movement should be readily acceptable?

There was an incident a few days back. A bomb exploded in a room of a dak bungalow. For two days news of the incident appeared ... after that it was hushed up. It is said that the men in the building were members of the Indira Brigade. Now, today, shots were fired on the procession from the flat of an [Congress] MLA, Shri Phulena Rai. The flat also houses the office of the Indira Brigade. The police raided the place after the shooting and some men were caught redhanded, while some others managed to escape. You have learned about all the arms that were recovered from that place. Our friends in the Congress want to give us lessons in democracy, lessons in peace. I ask the officers, who should be given lessons?

His reference to the "army" was to troops of the Border Security Force, created for the country's defence, now brought into Bihar and supplemented as in Gujarat by the Union government's Central Reserve Police (CRP). The arms found with the "Indira Brigade" in "the flat of an [Congress] MLA," indicated the currents at work in Bihar at this time.

The Union government's attitude towards the Bihar Movement, starting with its tough initial handling of a student demonstration, followed by a wave of arrests under the government's arbitrary powers, showed a surprisingly weak link in Mrs Gandhi's political and psychological armour. Her view of dissidence as unnecessary here became a refusal, or incapacity, to understand and deal in rational terms with rational demands. The movement became for her a personal insult and disproportionate anger was visited on it when it became apparent that this was not a phenomenon that could be controlled by police action.

JP's speech on 5 June saw the Bihar stir as the inevitable outcome of conditions in the country, and an opportunity to channel the enthusiasm of its young supporters into constructive work:

Friends, this is revolution, a total revolution. This is not a movement merely for the dissolution of the Assembly. We have to go far, very far. In the words of Jawaharlal Nehru, the people still have to travel many long miles to achieve that freedom for which thousands of the country's youth made sacrifices. ...

Hunger, soaring prices and corruption stalk everywhere. . . . Unemploment goes on increasing. . . . Land ceiling laws are passed but the number of landless people is increasing. Small farmers have lost their lands. . . . The government has taken the path of falsehood and violence. It has only one power, that of repression. Use the police. Use arms."[2]

JP understood "total revolution" as fundamental change affecting social attitudes and economic priorities. It included decentralization, with maximum power to village communities and in towns the strengthening of institutions of local self-government. The former development began soon after independence and was followed in 1959 by Panchayat Raj for "democratic decentralization." Welcoming Panchayat Raj, Nehru had said: ". . . authority and power must be given to the people in the villages. . . . Let them function and let them make a million mistakes. Do not be afraid about it. We are restricted in our thinking and in our movement because of our way of thinking. Let us give power to the Panchayats." Institutions of local government, chiefly municipalities, were already in existence at independence with a long tradition and experience. Both developments had been neglected or eroded during the past decade. Panchayat Raj had gradually lost its independence and identity under pressure from state politicians. Municipalities had suffered from continual interference, the pattern of governmental erosion at state level being repeated at municipal and local levels.

West Bengal exemplified the trend. Sivadas Banerjee writing in the *Times of India* on 14 February 1975 noted there had been no panchayat elections in Bengal for more than a decade, and in as many as 72 out of 90 municipalities a poll had been due for four to twelve years. An example of direct intereference by the Union government itself was its takeover in March 1975 of the Delhi Municipal Corporation when it became clear that the ruling Congress would be defeated in the mayoral election due on 24 March. The Delhi Municipal Corporation became the 25th (of 32) corporation functioning without elected representatives.

---

[2]JP's statement reproduced from *JP on Bihar: A Citizen Action Pamphlet*, published by Govindrao Deshpande, 299 Shantashram, Nana Chowk, Bombay.

JP's effort to reverse this trend in Bihar began with the setting up of "janta sarkars," informal "people's governments." These were to work in cooperation with government agencies where possible, and without their help, if necessary, in dealing with local problems and prejudices ranging over caste, custom, the fair distribution of commodities, and the settlement of disputes outside the local court or police station. "Janta sarkars" would also form committees at village, block, and district level to make people aware of their importance in the voting process, set up candidates for final selection from each polling booth area, and act as watchdogs over booths at election time. Any future government would have to reckon with these "permanent organs of people's power." Bihar, JP hoped, would become the laboratory of an experiment for which the mood of the people now seemed ripe. "Total revolution" countenanced no violent change. The negative consequence of a violent revolution, he believed, was that

power comes invariably to be usurped by a handful of the most ruthless among the erstwhile revolutionaries [inevitable] when power comes out of the barrel of a gun and the gun is not in the hands of the common people. . . . That is why a violent revolution has always brought forth a dictatorship of some kind or the other. And that is also why after a revolution a new privileged class of rulers and exploiters grows up in the course of time to which the people at large is once again subject.[3]

He explained the need for "janta sarkars" to the All India Youth Conference at Allahabad (UP) on 29 June:

In countries where democracy has developed an infrastructure there are many checks on those in power: the press, the academic institutions, the intellectuals. There is strong public opinion. We have no such structure and it will take time to develop. I wish to give the people's movement a revolutionary direction so that the people develop their own power to become guardians of democracy. My interest is not in the capture of power, but in the control of power by the people.

[3]Ajit Bhattacharjea, *Jayaprakash Narayan: A Political Biography*, Vikas, New Delhi, 1975.

A conference to report on the progress of "janta sarkar" was held in April 1975 at Khadigram (near Monghyr, Bihar), a flourishing Sarvodaya settlement. Khadigram ran schools for girls and boys where they also cultivated the fields and learned crafts. The curriculum included stocking and providing seed and fertilizers for neighbouring areas. I recorded some impressions of the conference where 90 delegates representing 21 blocks in the state described their experience:

Many delegates were young men, some clear and forceful, others later scolded by JP for not marshalling their facts better. There was some dolefulness, some enthusiasm, but mainly unvarnished reporting. It ranged over issues involving village justice, land, sugar, caste and custom. Considerable success was reported in setting up courts for the settlement of local disputes, and in persuading people to give up *chotis* and *jenaoos*. A delegate from Bhagalpur said that a temple that raised funds through gambling sessions and shared the proceeds with the police had been stopped from doing so. In areas where it had become customary to marry several wives, abandoning the previous one when a new alliance was contracted, the "janta sarkar" opposed this practice but got no cooperation. It then decided to put an immediate stop to it. Its members lay in wait for the drums of the marriage party. As soon as the culprit bridegroom arrived, his attendants were ordered to scatter, he was seized, put on a donkey and sent home. This, said the speaker with satisfaction, soon put an end to 75% of these "double and treble marriages."

There were complaints that city youths considered themselves special, and few would devote time to active work. Political parties tended to be disruptive influences, diverting attention to their own camps and activities and electioneering. Talk of elections was generally condemned as an obstacle to the steady groundwork of janta sarkar. Aware that decent representatives must serve on their committes, one delegate disconsolately remarked that there were no decent fellows in the village so they had chosen "fairly decent" ones.

All of this had proceeded without confrontation with authority. But confrontation is planned by Jagannathan, veteran Sarvodaya woker, under whom the "janta sarkar" in the Bodhgaya region will launch a campaign for land backed by 5,000 women led by his wife. According to the books, a Hindu *math* there owns 7,000 acres. The largest permitted family holding is 40 acres, and the *math* can only own twice as much. It has formed 18 trusts to get around the law and has been notified by the District Magistrate that he will recognize only one of these. The matter is now in government's hands for a decision. It is further complicated by the fact that some lands donated by the *math* earlier, as Bhoodan, have since been sold and are now tied up in litigation—an example of the untidy snarl of land problems in Bihar, where the law remains on the statute books and is not put into effect. Jagannathan made a vigorous appeal for a united land programme for all "janta sarkars." Outlining his own strategy, he said mass fasts would be held on the 18th, 19th and 20th, and a petition presented to the *math* requesting the distribution of its lands, except for its legal entitlement. After this "janta sarkars" in village, panchayat and block would pass a resolution and send it to the *math*. If they had no response, they would occupy these lands when the rains came and start cultivating them.[4]

This was, by itself, no revolutionary breakthrough, nor any portend of dangerous uprising as understood by governments. But "janta sarkar" in the hands of experienced Sarvodaya workers who knew their territory and its problems might make more than a dent in specific areas, and might even become a challenge to long-established local institutions or government agencies. Its danger to the status quo was its dedication to its aims, and a determination backed, in many instances, by a thorough knowledge of the problem it was attacking. Beyond this, it possessed neither the arms nor the belief in violence to make it dangerous. The worst a hot-headed encounter with opponents could come to might be a fist fight or the use of crude weapons, no great matter for local authority to control. Yet "janta sarkar" produced a shiver down the official spine. A government claiming an exclusive relationship with the masses, and a record of service and sacrifice, with both these under fire could not but be put out by the growth of "people's" agencies outside it, at times in confrontation with it.

[4]*Everyman's* (Jayaprakash Narayan's weekly), New Delhi, April 1975.

The arguments, used to discredit the development, called it "foreign-financed" and subversive. It was stamped out with a singular ferocity under the emergency after June 1975.

In early November 1974 Mrs Gandhi told the Congress Parliamentry Party the Bihar Movement was aimed at her personally to drive her out of office. She labelled it reactionary and accused it of support by the Anand Marg, an occult religious group with political overtones. JP answered these charges a week later, after a procession led by him on 4 November was severely mauled by the police and he himself was thrown to the ground under a volley of lathi blows:

> Whether the blows . . . were meant for me or not, is best known to the Prime Minister herself, for it was the Central Reserve Police which was wielding the lathis. . . . What is of great concern to all democrats is that if this is repeated, then the people will have no chance to give expression to anything that goes against government policies and actions, however bad or evil such policies might be. . . . I am not surprised that while the common people are the target in action, truth is the first casualty in their [government's] campaign to defame the movement. . . . The Prime Minister also goes on repeating that the movement in Bihar is in the hands of the RSS and the Anand Margis. The RSS has, of course, been active in the Bihar Movement, not directly but through its members in the Jan Sangh and the Vidayarthi Parishad student wing of the Jan Sangh. But the Socialist Party, the SSP, and the Old Congress and their youth wings, the RSP and the Marxist Coordination Committee are all fully involved and active in the movement. The CPI-M has not joined the coordination committee of political parties, but has extended full support to the movement. So has the Forward Bloc. Non-existent groups are repeatedly mentioned, but the active involvement of all these parties, a majority of whom are radical, is ignored. . . . The Prime Minister should at least know this elementary principle of politics that it is the function of opposition parties to try and dislodge the party in power.

That the Bihar Movement, except for the Jan Sangh, was backed by parties of the Left and Centre was not, as JP then believed, "ignored" by the Prime Minister. Government's confrontation with it was shaped, in fact, by this realization, and the knowledge that its support was both progressive and broad-based. If Mrs Gandhi admitted it was a genuine symbol of the comman man's distress, she would have to concede a rising tide in the country against her. A "reactionary" movement that was "foreign-financed" justified its repression.

During 1974 the police were increasingly evident in civic affairs. In January civil disobedience in Gujarat was not met with violence. In May a 20-day railway workers' strike demanding parity with other public sector workers was efficiently crushed. Some 50,000 workers were arrested while negotiations were on between their representatives and the management. Another 100,000 lost seniority and other benefits, or their jobs. The treatment of these and others imprisoned for dissent gave awe-inspiring dimensions to Mrs Gandhi's display of power. An element of unreality was added to her fight against the Bihar Movement when in November the Congress and CPI began a "counter-offensive" against the "conspiracy to defeat democracy."

On 11 November a CPI procession was given permission to march through Patna carrying weapons. A cluster of onlookers who jeered the marchers were savagely attacked. Others hospitalized with injuries that day were workers of the Electricity Board and Fertilizer Corporation, dragged out of their buildings and beaten because they did not belong to the CPI Union and had not joined the procession. The Congress held its own procession at Patna on 16 November, led by its new President, Dev Kant Barooah, attended by an imposing contingent of Congress MPs from Delhi and supervised by the Prime Minister's aide, Yashpal Kapoor. The Railway Minister, L.N. Mishra, had requisitioned trains to bring participants from other states and was on hand to welcome them. This set the pattern for Congress processions in different parts of the country, costly affairs backed by government's resources importing trainloads of participants, using jeeps, motorcycles, and sometimes elephants. They did much to deprive the Congress President's office of dignity and serious purpose, while the Congress-CPI's newly affirmed partnership against the "conspiracy to defeat democracy" looked both frivolous and macabre against the neglect of the actual issues the Bihar Movement had raised. The reprisals against it contrasted unflatteringly with the movement's non-violence. Police muscle began to figure in political comment:

Democracy cannot last for long if its existence depends upon the continuous use of the State's coercive power. The strength of Indian police and para-military forces, which are used against the people, has reached the level of our military forces. People have been fired at once in every 4 days since 1971. In such a situation mass agitation and even counter-violence remain the only democratic instruments for the defence of people's democratic rights against the creeping fascism of the State. (J.D. Sethi, *Tribune*, 15 November 1974.)

. . . battalions of the Border Security Force, raised as a security line of national defence, have been permanently stationed in placid Bihar towns, hundreds of students and others have been arrested and put in jail without trial, and worse still, the news of the Bihar happenings is suppressed from the rest of the country. The question is, which is more dangerous, and therefore more reprehensible: the violence of an unpopular government in deploying para-military organisations against civil resisters or the acts of violence provoked by such developments. . .? (G.S. Bhargava, *Everyman's*, 1 December 1974.)

In October 1974 the Public Accounts Committee of Parliament published government's police budget figures,[5] showing allocations had doubled in five years. The increase was accounted for mainly by the steady expansion of three paramilitary services under the Union government's control: the Border Security Force, the Central Reserve Police, and the Central Industrial Security Force. The budget figures did not include those of the intelligence agencies, the Central Bureau of Investigation (CBI) and the Research and Analysis Wing (RAW).

I visited Patna in November:

I went to the Patna Medical College Hospital, part of which has been turned into a prison with barbed wire fencing and armed guards. The prisoners within needed no guard. They were in no condition to move, with such injuries as a bullet in

[5]Police budget figures of the Government of India:

1968-69	Rs 726 million
1971-72	Rs 1183 million
1974-75	Rs 1560 million

the throat, an amputated leg and an assortment of broken bones. They had been wounded in the act of doing no more than walking in a peaceful procession. . . . In the prison section of the hospital, food and blankets were in short supply. So were injections, X-ray plates and blood. These emergency cases had had the misfortune of falling between two stools, hospital and jail, and did not seem to be squarely the responsibility of either.

Bihar's jails, long overcrowded and notoriously lax in their observance of the jail code regarding food, clothing and prisoners' rights, cannot accommodate the swelling tide of MISA, DIR and other political arrests. I met Karpoori Thakur, ex-Chief Minister of Bihar, who, along with twenty others, mostly students, was waiting in a dak bungalow encircled by armed guards, to be produced before the Advisory Court. They had been shuttled back and forth between three crowded jails, with no provision for food or blankets, until Thakur furiously declared he was not a football and would not be kicked around any more. They were then brought to the dak bungalow. Brahmdeo Pradarshan, ex-MLA. . . said his hands had been wrenched roughly behind him and handcuffed, and he was lifted bodily by four policemen and dumped into the police van. With these indignities inflicted on the well-known, it is sad to imagine how the unknown are treated. And it is the "unknown", students and villagers, stall keepers and rickshaw wallahs, who form the backbone of the protests.[6]

It was plain that Bihar had become the scene of a spontaneous convulsion with repercussions far beyond its borders. Protest had been a feature of Indian politics. Strikes, processions, and demonstrations had been staged by interest groups and by every political party since independence, including the ruling Congress itself in states where Opposition governments were in power. Political protest was an accepted part of the system. Its origins in the national movement had given it an honourable stamp. It had been institutionalized by Mahatma Gandhi's highly organized nationwide satyagraha campaigns. Individual protest had acquired dignity and distinction with his own fasts. Agitation had vast numbers to draw on, and perhaps nowhere in the world had it drawn on so many for a variety of causes, from freedom itself to wage rises,

[6] *Indian Express*, New Delhi, November 1974.

state boundaries, and a ban on cow slaughter. Even against this background the Bihar meetings were extraordinary for their size and discipline, the more impressive because official policy was directed at obstructing them and preventing the surrounding population from arriving in Patna to take part in them, apart from the force used against them. Three-quarters of their participants were young, which may explain the ardent commitment, the quality of youthful outrage, and the special delight taken in defying authority that had forfeited public respect. From the Bihari villager, more comfortable speaking his own dialect than Hindi, to the city student, the Bihar movement had wide-ranging young support, and it seemed to find JP's credentials particularly apt and attractive. A brilliant modern mind that had consciously rejected power in favour of the "Gandhian alternative" of service, he was a combination of the ascetic and practical, intellect and action, passion and poise. His quiet rational tone at public meetings was more philosophical than political. He seemed a counter-leader, a prevailing moral influence rather than a personality, at a time when many believed the leadership cult at Delhi had been carried too far. The idealistic and unequal nature of the confrontation now begun appealed to the best in youth. It harnessed an energy growing restless and combative in a deteriorating economic situation and a political atmosphere of moral decline. And it gave an outlet to students who had till now seen no way but violence to change the scheme of things.

Apart from Bihar, active participation in it was limited to neighbouring Uttar Pradesh. Ballia, in eastern UP, was JP's home district, while Varanasi had long been a base for Sarvodaya workers, an overwhelming majority of whom were now involved with the Bihar Movement, particularly its rural programme. It was also the centre for student adherents of the Jan Sangh and the Socialist Party, both constituents of the movement and well supplied with trained workers. Its success can be judged by the UP government's investigation into nine eastern districts of Varanasi and Gorakhpur for signs of its influence and a report on anti-Congress sentiment or activity in the area. Its influence extended further afield, to universities in Orissa, Delhi, and Haryana. In November, in anticipation of JP's visit, Kurukshetra University in Haryana was closed by the state government, a number of students arrested, and the President and Secretary of the Students' Union expelled for taking part earlier in a rally in Ludhiana, Punjab, in support of the Bihar Movement. Gujarat, though its own agitation had died down with the dissolution of the State Assembly, gave the movement its sympathy and support.

Why did this extent and activity of an avowedly peaceful development panic the government or make Mrs Gandhi feel gravely threatened on her pinnacle? The strong reaction it aroused in Delhi was never defined. Several reasons might be ascribed to it. The movement represented grievances that could not, now that they were being so remorselessly and publicly aired, be ignored. It could not be explained away as a reactionary or anti-people development. It looked, in fact, very much the opposite, the groundswell of a just indignation backed by profound public sympathy, if this was to be judged by the success of its programmes involving public cooperation. Its calls for *bundhs* effectively paralyzed life in Patna particularly, with a near-total shut-down of trading and academic establishments, and rendered the administration ineffective at district and sub-divisional levels. Many in the Congress tacitly sympathized with it. Bihar had been a storm centre of revolutionary agitation during British rule, and the heart of violent protest during the Quit India upheaval. That this movement was non-violent increased rather than lessened its impact. The use of force against it discredited the user, while it conferred a badge of courage on its victims. Yet a leadership caught in its own insecurity continued to use arrest, intimidation, and violence to suppress it, and to be confounded by its failure to do so. For Mrs Gandhi the movement presented major irritants. It was a rival claimant to the people's voice. The reputation it had brought back into focus had little to do with the politics of power, and much to do with character, virtue, and example. A personality reminiscent of Mahatma Gandhi's now occupied the centre of the stage, and it had arrived there without benefit of political paraphernalia, legend or lore. Next to it the cant and carnival lately surrounding Congress politics looked shoddy. A clear voice had broken through and people were listening to it. Mrs Gandhi was faced with the British government's dilemma in dealing with the Mahatma, who had been able to unite, inspire, and influence because of the human being he was. Unable to resolve her dilemma she took a whole country to task for her failure through action that proved to be the natural culmination of her style.

The movement required a long-term programme, apart from the "janta sarkar" experiment. It entered its second phase when non-partisan intellectuals—economists, educationists, editors, and social scientists—met at JP's invitation to pool their ideas and make suggestions for a socio-economic programme. On 28 November Opposition leaders[7] met in New Delhi to discuss joint political action. A move toward Opposition unity had been made three months earlier when seven national and regional parties had combined under the chairmanship of Charan Singh to form the Bharatiya Lok Dal (BLD).[8] That this development, affecting several states, took place under an Uttar Pradesh leader, had a significance all its own. Any appearance of a challenge to Congress or an impairment of its prestige carried more serious consequences to the ruling party in the state with the country's largest representation in Parliament. As the Prime Minister's home ground it was a sensitive power area, and a more decisive battleground for crucial controls than other parts of India. Charan Singh, with a mass following, was a seasoned politician, a personality to reckon with. His was one of four Opposition parties represented at the New Delhi conference. The conference approved the appointment of a High Court judge to hold an unofficial enquiry into allegations against L.N. Mishra and Bansi Lal, and a committee set up by Citizens for Democracy to study the electoral system and "to recommend appropriate measures of reform to secure free and fair elections. . . ." The Opposition claimed that a system of direct election had given the dominant party an overwhelming and disproportionate advantage in the number of seats it gained compared with the percentage of votes polled. The Congress Party had won its two-thirds majority in the Lok Sabha in 1971 with only 43.5 per cent of votes polled. The manufacture of votes and cheating at the polls had become public issues raised by Congressmen themselves at Bidhan Nagar in 1972, while the CPI-M claimed polls had been held even under the gun in Bengal to ensure a Congress-CPI victory. The demand for electoral reform was brought to a head when government evaded the consequences of a Supreme

[7]Five Opposition parties at New Delhi conference: Old Congress, Jan Sangh, BLD, Socialist Party, Akali Dal.

[8]Formed of seven constituent parties: BKD, SSP, Swatantra, Utkal Congress, Rashtriya Loktantrik Dal, Kisan Mazdoor Party of Haryana, and Punjab Khetibari Zamindar Union.

Court judgement, setting aside the election to Parliament of a Congress MP, on grounds of his exceeding permitted election expenses. An ordinance was promptly issued altering the People's Representation Act to exclude party expenditure from a candidate's permitted election expenses.

On 3 December the *Indian Express* reported Bihar's jails as "bursting at the seams with students and political workers" on the eve of the Assembly's winter session. Ten Opposition and Sarvodaya leaders had been externed from the state. Barricades set up by the police extended into rural areas. Forty-three Assembly seats were vacant, 37 of these due to resignations in response to the movement. A harassed Chief Minister, the polite and inoffensive Abdul Ghafoor, obediently carried out Delhi's instructions while he tried to hold his factious party together and to prevent some members from resigning their Assembly seats. Supporting the validity of the demand for the Assembly's resignation, G.S. Bhargava commented in *Everyman's* on 1 December 1974:

> Richard Nixon had received a massive mandate in 1972, with all the States of the Federation except Massachusetts voting for him. Until June last, Nixon also used to argue that demands for his resignation, like the attempts to remove him from the Presidency, were anti-democratic because his mandate lasted until 1977. . . . It is an irony that Mrs. Gandhi who owes her pre-eminence today to the successful mobilisation of the people against the former managers of the Congress Party should pit herself against political participation by the people, which is the essence of the Bihar movement.

JP expressed it similarly in a letter to the editor of *The Illustrated Weekly:*

> . . . do you also think that Mr. Nixon's removal from the U.S. Presidentship before his term expired was wrong and against democracy? And do you think that the *Washington Post* and the *New York Times* and many other American papers were wrong in launching the campaign against Nixon? Were they enemies of democracy? . . . Some of the highest constitutional authorities in the world have said that, in such cases of misrule, the people have a right—and a constitutional right, mind you—

to demand removal of the offending government or dissolution of the offending parliament. . . .

Moscow's concern at the blaze of opposition to Mrs Gandhi became apparent when Kitsenko, *Pravda* correspondent in Madras, made a stinging attack on JP, and when on 4 December, the opening day of the Bihar Assembly session, Soviet TV cameramen entered the Assembly chamber contrary to the rule forbidding cameras in the chamber. Ilyashenko, chief of Soviet radio and television in New Delhi, said he was there "with the permission of the Government of India." In the storm of objection from Opposition benches Soviet TV withdrew and the Union Minister for Information and Broadcasting, I.K. Gujral, called upon to explain the intrusion, denied having granted permission, saying only that the Soviet request had been transmitted to the Bihar Assembly secretariat. But the Soviet weight behind the Congress-CPI campaign against the Bihar Movement was now an open fact. In December the Congress Party inaugurated a series of secret conclaves. Narora, scene of the first, was an Uttar Pradesh village about 70 miles from Delhi. Barbed wire, armed guards, and a thousand tents for military and police personnel, brought it into national prominence. Mohan Dharia, Union Minister for Works and Housing, revealed on 17 March 1975 in Poona that the Narora camp had been attended by Soviet embassy officials.

The Congress Party's feverish apprehension broke through the secrecy of its conclaves in a variety of ways. Crash plans to fulfil election pledges were called for. On 18 December a group of Congress and CPI MPs tabled a privilege move in the Lok Sabha against Ram Nath Goenka, Independent. Goenka, proprietor of the *Indian Express* group of newspapers, and supporter of the Bihar Movement, replied that he had been a target of Congress attack since he had left the party in 1969. Since his support to JP "a politically motivated campaign of calumny and vilification" had been directed against him. In late December the "Bihar University Bill 1974" replaced the ordinance of 1972 bringing the universities under the state government. The new Bill provided "a code of conduct" for teachers, forbidding them to join a political party or any political activity. On 5 February, Shashi Bhushan, influential Congress MP, demanded the expulsion of Chandrasekhar, Mohan Dharia, and Krishna Kant, who were lobbying for a dialogue with JP. On 18 February, the new President, Fakhruddin Ali Ahmed, addressing the budget session of Parliament, said the government had plans to reform the educational system and to resurrect the Lokpal (Ombudsman) Bill[9] as earnest of its intention to fight corruption.

On 1 January the *Hindustan Times* commented editorially:

It was the tragedy of 1974 that development was subordinated to politics, while politics in turn has come increasingly to be influenced by black money and the economic underworld which has established an unfortunate nexus with the country's administrative and political echelons. . . . The Government has not improved its image by its reluctance to move firmly, swiftly and openly against every form of corruption. . . . It is essentially this sense of anger and anguish that epitomises the Bihar Movement. Mr. Jayaprakash Narayan has become a symbol whose true relevance extends far beyond Bihar. . . .

[9]A Bill to hear and investigate complaints by private citizens against ministers and government officers. This legislation had been pending for many years, postponed by the Prime Minister. An amendment to the draft Bill excluded the Prime Minister from its purview.

CHAPTER TWELVE

JANUARY TO JUNE 1975

The first six months of 1975 saw a crescendo of political activity, with Jayaprakash Narayan as its centre. The main Opposition parties acted in concert in Parliament and some State Assemblies, and backed common winning candidates in by-elections. A series of Congress reverses at the polls, climaxed by its defeat in the Gujarat state election in June, brought the arousal represented by the Bihar Movement into sharp focus. Yet the new climate was fundamentally different from that of 1967 when Congress had suffered its first major electoral setback. As a result of the 1969 split in the party, followed by Mrs Gandhi's victory in the 1971 election, high hopes and expectations had been roused. These had not begun to be fulfilled and the electorate was sorely disappointed. A mood of euphoria had been dashed to the ground by grave economic crisis and the government's inability to cope with it, by the scandal and strife within the Congress and its shielding of the corrupt, and by its apparent indifference to mounting despair. The prospect of an alternative was emerging in the form of a united Opposition. But the new atmosphere was also the result of a searing psychological experience. Those who voted anti-Congress in 1975 did so because its leader, member of a revered family—no stranger to the democratic faith—had revealed how far she could go in trifling with democratic institutions and crushing dissent—a performance frightening in its implications for the country. In the cold political light of 1975, public sentiment, affection, and indulgence, long a source of strength and succour to the Congress, had given way to distrust in its leader's basic credentials. A rocky road had been travelled in six years, from assured political values to political extravaganza, from ethics to the lawless techniques of expediency and ambition, from open transactions to the politics of secrecy and violence. It was, in essence, the distance between Jawaharlal Nehru and Indira Gandhi.

Events between January and June, profound in their effect on the political landscape, are best described in sequence.

On 2 January at 5.50 P.M. L.N. Mishra was injured by a bomb explosion at a railway platform ceremony in Samastipur, Bihar. He died at Danapur, Bihar, at 9.30 next morning. The surgeon, R.V.P. Sinha, who operated on him at Danapur, later pointed out the inordinate delay in getting him to a hospital. The train carrying the wounded minister did not leave Samastipur until 8.30 P.M. Instead of being rushed to Darbhanga, an hour away, he was taken to Danapur where another 45 minutes were lost while the train shunted from the wrong platform to the correct one. When he reached the operating table, six hours after the explosion, he was a case of "grave emergency," his injuries so advanced, "it was a herculean effort to start the operation."[1]

Other related information came to light: K.P. Verma, Counsel for Mishra's family, said in his evidence before the Mathew Commission appointed by the Union government, that the failure to provide security for the minister was "deliberate" in spite of the Bihar government's instructions in 1974 to all relevant departments that special security arrangements must accompany the minister's visits to the state. After the breaking of the railway workers' strike in 1974 Mishra had apparently feared assassination and had told some colleagues he suspected a political conspiracy against his life. A private detective had informed the Delhi police in writing of a specific threat, naming Samastipur and Darbhanga as probable danger spots. In these circumstances K.P. Verma claimed the arrangements at the railway ceremony had been extraordinarily lax.

Just before the assassination, leaders of the Jan Sangh, CPI-M, and BLD had called for an enquiry into a series of "mysterious [road] accident deaths" of men investigating cases with important political implications. These included D.K. Kashyap, connected with the Nagarwala case; R.D. Pandey, a deputy director of the intelligence bureau; Anil Chopra, Collector of Daman, who had broken a smuggler gang; and recently, Ramanathan, a CBI inspec-

---

[1]R.V.P. Sinha's remarks made to newspapermen after L.N. Mishra's death, reported in *Indian Express*, New Delhi, January 1975.

tor examining the improprieties of Congress MPs selling licences to well-known firms, an affair implicating L.N. Mishra, and the subject of storm and stress in the current session of Parliament. Mishra's death by violence raised a flurry of fresh speculation about his role in the "licence scandal."

On 7 January All India Radio broadcast a portion of Mrs Gandhi's speech at a condolence meeting organized by the Congress Party's Delhi unit. Her shrill accusation that Mishra's death was a "rehearsal" for which she herself was the "real target" was as shocking as her imputation of the crime to JP's movement. An edge of hysteria was conveyed to listeners more startling than the printed account of her speech. Bewildered listeners heard her strenuously disown the crime herself, and decry attempts to link her with it: "Even Congressmen have been misled by these blatant lies."

The condolence meeting was converted into one of fervent support for Mrs Gandhi. Its most vigorous speaker, H.N. Bahuguna, Chief Minister of Uttar Pradesh, said "fifty-eight crores of people" stood solidly behind the Prime Minister. Mrs Gandhi's own wrought-up accusation had the reverse of the effect desired. On 8 January the *Hindustan Times* editorial pointed out:

> . . . those who have rushed to implicate Mr. Jayaprakash Narayan by proxy with the Samastipur outrage might recall earlier bomb explosions last May at the Bankipore [Patna] dak bungalow and the subsequent firing on JP's procession in Patna on June 5th from a government flat allotted to a Congress MLA, Mr. Phulena Rai, and occupied by workers of the "Indira Brigade" . . . the use of bombs and firearms in Bihar is older than JP's movement. . . .

There was open talk that a government agency was responsible for Mishra's death. Controversy over the minister had reached a peak in the licence case before Parliament, involving government in its most embarrassing collision with the Opposition. His death had come at a convenient time. Jyotirmoy Bosu's (CPI-M) statement in Parliament that Mishra's office and home had been searched immediately after his death to remove documents connected with Sanjay Gandhi's Maruti Company was not answered by the Home Minister. The extreme slowness of the CBI investigation created further suspicion of government involvement, while the prompt dismantling of the dais at Samastipur had destroyed primary evidence. A politician who dominated and manipulated cliques, had men and money to do his bidding, and aroused disproportionate loyalties and antagonisms, Mishra had reportedly refused to resign and had a devoted following in the party to back him up.

The event served to blur Opposition differences and feed a mounting fear. The CPI-M issued a statement on 13 January from Calcutta : "The semi-fascist and gangster tactics of the ruling party have been continuing for the last three years, and free functioning of all opposition forces, especially the CPI-M and other Left and democratic opposition, has beeome an impossibility . . . ". Marxist leader, Jyoti Basu, announced the CPI-M would, as a result, invite the Old Congress and the Jan Sangh to a conference to plan a broad-based movement in Bengal for civil liberties and free and fair elections. Each party would conduct its separate campaign but the three would be synchronized. There would be no truck, he added, with the CPI.

The CPI, also an opposition party, was not recognized as such any more. Its interests were too closely identified with the Congress. In a recent article, Mohit Sen had explained his party's objective as "unity and struggle vis-a-vis the Congress." The unity was manifest, the struggle was not. If the CPI had disapproved of the breaking of the railway strike the previous year, its disapproval had been in a low key. During the Soviet President Brezhnev's visit to India in 1973 the party had been told to back Mrs Gandhi regardless of her policies. The Soviet investment in India was political and geographical, not ideological. The Indian record showed that the CPI harvest out of this alliance, abundant in its share and spoils of power, had not added favourably to its reputation. An 8 per cent bonus to workers made law in September 1974 (and applicable to 1973) was withdrawn by the government in 1975. The wheat takeover, fully backed by the CPI, had been discredited by its failure. The projected takeover of the rice crop had been abandoned. The nationalization of coal mines in 1973, authored by Mohan Kumaramangalam, became linked in the public mind with the Chasnala mine disaster in Bihar in December 1975, one of the worst in mining history. It was judged to be due to "reckless slaughter mining endangering mine safety" in order to increase production after nationalization. The party's direct influence on the Congress had dwindled after its chief spokesman in government, Kumara-mangalam, was killed in an air crash in 1973. The Congress-CPI combine had less logic to commend it than the opposition of varying political complexion now drawing closer together. Developments in Bangladesh, with Mujibur Rahman taking dictatorial powers, added anxiety and incentive to this process. That the war to release a much heralded "Sonar Bangala" from bondage—one that so exhaustively engaged India's soldiery, resources, and idealism during 1971—should have come to this, was a reminder of what might happen next in India, with the Bangladesh Government closely advised by India. The possibility of a dictatorship, with a sudden seizure of extra powers by Mrs Gandhi, was widely discussed.

On 19 January at a youth rally in Patna JP appealed to adherents of the Bihar Movement to enlighten people about the danger ahead, and mobilize them to defeat any move on Mrs Gandhi's part to thrust dictatorship on the country. Her outburst at the condolence meeting for L.N. Mishra, he said, showed, she was realizing "people were losing confidence in her." Defending the multiparty membership of the movement, he said it had no labels. Members of the Jan Sangh and Old Congress had faced lathis and bullets and were in prison for their participation in it. He would not ask any party to leave it. Six weeks later (5 March), addressing the 20th plenary session of the Jan Sangh in New Delhi, he said he wished to communicate the conclusion after a year's work with the Jan Sangh and the RSS, that he had found them neither reactionary nor fascist. Fascism was rearing its ugly head, but it came from another quarter. A similar caution was delivered by the CPI-M General Secretary, P. Sundarayya, in Hyderabad on 12 February. Denying his party had joined hands with the Jan Sangh or the BLD, he said the danger of fascism, however, was much greater from Mrs Gandhi. It would not surprise him if she, aided by the CPI, repeated the Bangladesh development and called off the 1976 election.

The Opposition, though fragmented, had been a lively and talented presence in Indian politics. The combined votes it polled, even before the 1967 elections, its high point of achievement, had been more numerous than those polled by the Congress Party. Single Opposition parties or coalitions had formed state governments, at times under outstanding and admired leaders, as Annadorai of Tamil Nadu and Namboodiripad of Kerala. Accomplished Opposition speakers had exerted pressure on the Congress majority in Parliament and contributed to the quality and maturity of Parliamentary debate. The near-impossibility of dislodging the Congress even gave the enterprise a certain gallantry. The challenge called for discipline and dedication. Thus the Jan Sangh built up a student cadre, the Vidyarthi Parishad, a successful foil to the CPI's All India Students' Federation, and prided itself on the allegiance it commanded among the young. A quarter century of democratic opportunity had left the Opposition divided. When it surfaced after Nehru's death, it did so with a distinct regional bias. It took Mrs Gandhi's autocratic tread to goad the Opposition to unity. In this it had an advantage it had not had before: the decay of the ruling party's image and its impotence on the economic front. Unwilling to give up party identities, the Opposition formed a single bloc in Parliament and some State Assemblies, and fielded common "janta" candidates for approaching by-elections. After the emergency of 1975, prison and suppression furthered the process, with the Janata Party finally challenging the Congress in the national election of 1977. This development can best be understood in terms of a scene reduced by Mrs Gandhi's style to a warlike confrontation between the Congress and other opinion, leaving no room for compromise or manoeuvre.

Yet there was more to opposition unity than this. If Mrs Gandhi's categorical style had broken with the whole texture of the Congress past, initiated alignment with the CPI at home and the Soviet Union abroad, and in the process fundamentally altered Indian politics and the working of Indian political institutions, Opposition parties had also undergone degrees of transformation. Some old stock images had changed and no longer applied.

The Old Congress, the rump left by the split, tainted at the time by accusations of conservatism and "bossism," and expected shortly to capitulate to the ruling party and disappear from the scene, had not done so. Its President, Asoka Mehta, once a leading theoretician of the Socialist Party, had always been associated with the Left. Its elder statesman, Morarji Desai, had acquired added stature as an honourable man in the hurricane of desertion and defection encouraged by the split. He stood out now as one of the last Gandhians, recalling receding values, a symbol of dignity in the muddy political landscape. The charge levelled by Congress radicals some years earlier that Desai's businessman son, Kanti, had used his father's position to promote his business, now looked meagre next to Mrs Gandhi's vigorous sponsorship of her son and the official apparatus freely used to assist him. The conservative taint had faded in view of Mrs Gandhi's lack of radical, or credible performance, while her party's extortion and use of money on a scale as yet unparalleled had given "bossism" and "black money" a new life and dimension.

The Jan Sangh had since its founding been open to all communities. On this issue it had parted with the Hindu Mahasabha, and under the leadership of Shyama Prashad Mukherjee, had avoided the word "Hindu" altogether in its official title, using "Bharatiya" instead. Its espousal of Hinduism and Hindi as the dominant culture and language of India was, it claimed, based on statistical realities, Hindi being spoken or understood by 42 per cent of the population, as against the next largest figure, 9.24 per cent speaking Telugu. Its attitude towards these two issues had, of circumstance and necessity, become more tolerant for religion ceased to be a profitable issue in politics once the fever following partition subsided, while the search for support in the south and among the Muslims produced a modified stand on Hindi. Its expanding rural base in Uttar Pradesh had resulted in a cautious economic programme after 1959, geared to woo the cultivator with such provisions as co-operative societies for credit; ownership of land by the cultivator with compensation payable to the dispossessed landlord; a common grazing area for each village; and the use of cowdung as manure rather than chemical fertilizers. With the birth of Bangladesh, and Pakistan reduced in size, Mrs Gandhi's policies at home and her dealings with the Soviet Union engaged its concern. The Jan Sangh had its extremists, but its current crop of leaders, drawn from the academic world and the professions, closely resembled the educated middle-class leadership of the early Congress with its moderate liberal approach, though unlike the early Congress it was more Indian than Western in inspiration. Lalchand Advani, its President, was a lawyer by training and a journalist by profession, measured and accurate in his pronouncements. Atal Behari Vajpayee's gift for language had early made him Parliament's star speaker. Respect for his political quality was not confined to his party. Subramaniam Swamy, Harvard-educated economist and a teacher at Delhi's Indian

Institute of Technology before he entered politics, was an example of the younger minds and talent the party now attracted. Mrs Gandhi's angry militancy towards the Jan Sangh showed its front rank leadership up in a sober balanced light by contrast. Even the RSS, noted for militant activities in the past and denounced for its anti-secularism and cultivation of the Hindu mystique, now contrasted favourably with the growing aggressiveness of the Youth Congress, protected when it transgressed the limits of law-abiding behaviour.

The Socialist Party, always anti-doctrine and experimental, felt vindicated in its demand for a redistribution of economic priorities and more decentralization. Mrs Gandhi's drive for world recognition and her definition of "achievement" as victory in war and the explosion of a nuclear device did not accord with these.

The Old Congress, the Jan Sangh, and the Socialist Party found common ground with Congressmen who opposed the alliance with the CPI and feared the consequences of Mrs Gandhi's present unyielding posture.

The CPI-M, its ideological purity intact, kept out of the Opposition bloc, but extended its cooperation where it thought fit. Battered by police action, its chief enemy was the "fascism" of the Congress-CPI combine.

Mrs Gandhi had two choices. Influential members of her party were urging a reconciliation with the Opposition, and a basic programme inviting the cooperation of all parties to meet the urgent needs of the population. She chose her second option, rejecting a conciliatory course. This meant the manufacture of a "right reaction" obstructing her, with which no talks were possible.

That the time had come for a new political combine, ignoring conventional Left-Right divisions, was apparent to the public, for the effect of jointly fielded "janta" candidates was immediate and electric. The Congress had already lost two by-elections when in the third week of January the Opposition won a spectacular victory in the important by-election to the Lok Sabha from Jabalpur (Madhya Pradesh). The seat had been a Congress bastion for fifty years, vacated by the death of Seth Govind Das, who had held it since his membership of the Central Assembly during British rule. The New Congress candidate was his grandson, Ravi Mohan, backed by the Chief Minister, P.C. Sethi, who put state transport (including helicopters) and resources to lavish use in the campaign. Mohan was defeated in all eight segments of the Lok Sabha consti-

tuency, all eight of whose Assembly seats were occupied by Congress MLAs: an anti-Congress wind the *Times of India* described as
"a veritable tornado." The "janta" candidate, a virtually unknown
gold-medal engineering student, Sharad Yadav, became Parliament's youngest member. Welcoming the victory, JP told an interviewer in Bombay on 22 January that the people's force now at
work was more powerful than the "greatest and grandest alliance":

> The "grand alliance" seems to have become for Mrs. Gandhi
> the same kind of cry as Bonaparte had become for British
> mothers in those times. . . . Mrs. Gandhi makes herself out as
> radical and suggests she stands for policies and ideals of which
> Jayaprakash Narayan and the Bihar Movement are afraid. But
> the people of Bihar, or for that matter, the people of India,
> would like to ask her what she has done in nine years of her
> reign. What radical change has she brought about?

The Opposition's "janta" candidate won next at the Govindpura
by-election (Madhya Pradesh). February brought further defeats
for the Congress in two (Meham and Rori) out of three by-elections to the Haryana Assembly. The victories of the "janta" candidates, one of them a young lawyer new to politics, were particularly galling to Chief Minister Bansi Lal who had campaigned
extensively with several cabinet colleagues. The Barpeta (Assam)
by-election to the Lok Sabha on 20 February revealed a degree
of panic in the Congress Party and the government. The seat had
been vacated when Fakhruddin Ali Ahmed was nominated to the
Presidency. Now President, he paid a visit to Assam timed to
coincide with the Congress election campaign. The "janta" candidate, B. Goswami, with a dramatic lead of 41,000 votes in a constituency of 100,000 was declared defeated by 28,000—more votes
than the constituency had—in favour of the Congress candidate. Goswami's messenger, on his way to Delhi to lodge a complaint with
the Election Commission was, detained at Gauhati (Assam) air-
port and not allowed to proceed, though the ballot papers he was
carrying as evidence bore the signature and seal of a presiding
officer.

Mrs Gandhi described the new wave as "certain outside forces"
taking a deep interest in India's internal affairs, a theme she ex-
pounded for newspaper and magazine interviews, and in open and

closed-door meetings with selected academics, businessmen, and other groups. Her remarks were repeated as part of the news bulletin, or following it, over radio and television. She did not support her statements with facts, figures or precise information. Along with secret "Narora-type" conclaves being held by the Congress Party in parts of the country, her remarks shrouded the atmosphere in insinuation and vague menace, but presented no argument.

Indira Gandhi's view of JP as a mere epiphenomenon or a shadow, or a puppet controlled by sinister forces is a typical attitude of the established reaction against the rising forces of revolution. . . . Each day a new scandal, a new Watergate that exposes the ruling party and the government confirms the absurdity of JP's caricature at the hands of our rulers. Almost all the forces of fascism, such as big business, black money, bureaucratic power, secret police etc. are all lined up against JP's movement, and on the side of the Congress-CPI alliance. Indian fascism will have a radical face, as is the case of many other countries in the Third World.[2]

The above comment, by no means isolated, represented the opinion of several distinguished non-partisan commentators that Mrs Gandhi was pursuing a neurotic line, unrelated to facts. In her view of a black-and-white, either-or world, peopled with elements "for" and "against" her, it is probable she could not see the situation objectively. The act of coming "down from the clouds" her father had seen the need of years earlier, had never been accomplished. She had continued to be "extraordinarily imaginative and self-centred or subjective," and the line between fact and fantasy was one she was unaware of. "A great actor when he is acting, never forgets that it is all a game," Ignacio Silone wrote of the distinction consummate actors and politicians make between deceiving others and themselves. Mrs Gandhi had, however, fully identified herself with the fictions she was playing. Her opening speech at the Jamaica Commonwealth Conference in May made admirable reading, showing a touching idealism divorced from her own reality: "I was brought up in an atmosphere where

[2]J.D. Sethi in *Everyman's*, 23 February 1975.

politics denoted neither power nor riches. . . . But as I look around I find that politics are taken to be the art of acquiring, holding and wielding power. International relations are said to deal with power equations among nations. . . ." It was precisely her expert use of the levers of power, her realization that its capture and continuance outside democratic channels depends on planning, conspiracy, surprise and ruthlessness, that marked her own success in the politics she herself had initiated—a far cry from the upbringing she had had when "politics denoted neither power nor riches."

The dictatorship in Bangladesh cast a shadow over India. On 15 February addressing a meeting of government employees in New Delhi at the Boat Club, JP reminded them they were permanent public servants, unlike the President, the Prime Minister, MPs and MLAs, who were temporary, and that they should not obey illegal, immoral or partisan orders: "Your loyalty is to the country, to the people, and to the Constitution, not to the Government, the Prime Minister or the Home Minister. Use your rights and do your duty without any fear." It was over half a century since Mahatma Gandhi had launched his first civil disobedience campaign in India. This appeal seemed to arise out of an even grimmer and more urgent need. In view of the adverse publicity given to this statement during the emergency, and the excuse made of it to launch the emergency, I quote my own comments on it in March 1975:

> Satyagraha is a moral principle, only employable when the cause is just. Its essence is that truth, be it represented by the individual or the mass, can shake an empire. . . . In a purely religious context the message of Christ on the cross is somewhat the same, for how could the suffering and death of one man save millions unless the truth he stood for had the power to affect and influence for beyond him?
>
>   . . . In British times we broke laws we considered unjust, made by a government to which we did not give our allegiance. Today we have a Constitution and laws of our own making and a government elected through them, but one which almost daily violates them either in fact or in spirit. We . . . do not wish to depart from either the Constitution or the laws, but to see that they are observed by those in authority. The aim of satya-

graha today is to demand their proper observance. We are in the very curious position where the government of the country needs this reminder.

. . . the politician or his mouthpiece must be disobeyed when he plays fast and loose with the laws or with decent practices and conventions. The civil servant who is told to arrest 25 people who are squatting in a peaceful demonstration knows very well that there is no ground for arresting them, that the demonstrators are breaking no law, and that the executive order is arbitrary and unjust. In such a case the civil servant is not bound to carry it out. There are too many such cases nowadays where the civil servant, particularly the young and sensitive, fresh from their training or their first experience of field work, and earnest about their responsibilities, are thrust into terrible situations of being driven to act against the law and against their own conscience. The ritual enactment of MISA must put this kind of strain on many an official conscience, as it must also on the police, who must at times be confused and bewildered at what they are asked to do. The ferocious use of force, or on the other hand the total absence of the police when they are urgently needed, are signs of confused, and at times unscrupulous executive orders.[3]

JP's appeal was bound to stir interest and controversy, especially when it was repeated on other occasions, and addressed to the army and police as well. He was interviewed[4] in Delhi in May:

Question: At Bhubaneshwer your appeal to the army and police have been described by the Home Minister as "treasonable," because it may cause disaffection in the armed forces and police. Can you explain the context in which your remarks were made? And what is the role you envisage the armed forces and police to play?

Answer: What I said at Bhubaneshwar about the army and the police, I have said earlier also at some places. Let me take up the army first. On March 3 I had said at the mass rally at the Boat Club, New Delhi, in the context of the possibility of

[3]"The Return of Satyagraha," *Indian Express*, New Delhi, 6 March 1975.
[4]Interview reproduced in *Indian Express*, New Delhi, May 1975.

some sort of authoritarianism scuttling our democracy, that the loyalty of the army was to the country, its flag and its Constitution. The Indian people have given themselves a democratic constitution of the parliamentary type. The President of India in his capacity as Supreme Commander of the armed forces is pledged to protect and uphold the Constitution of the country from authoritarian threats. If any party, government or party leader intends to use the army as a means to further their party and power interests, it is the clear duty, to my mind, of the army not to be so used. . . . If the rulers do venture to use the army to suppress a peaceful revolution, then the army should not allow itself to be so used. I have also decried sometimes the use of armed personnel to deal with civil disturbances, for which the civil armed forces, like the armed police and the para-military forces, should be enough. If all this amounts to committing treason, I shall not mind being prosecuted for this offence.

As for the police, the circumstances in which I have made references to them are these: Sometimes in the course of the [Bihar] Movement, the police commits excesses, no doubt under orders of superior officers. For instance, on November 4 last, when I, with a large number of students and citizens in Patna deliberately broke prohibitory orders, the Central Reserve Police personnel present were asked to lathi-charge. The demonstration was entirely peaceful. Not even a pebble was thrown by any demonstrator, and not a single policeman or magistrate was injured, and yet there was a lathi-charge. It would have been perfectly legal if we had all been arrested. But when there was no violence of any sort, in fact even when I was hit and fell to the ground, young men kept shouting the slogan "*Police hamare bhai hain, unse nahin ladai hai*" [The police are our brothers; we have no quarrel with them], a lathi-charge was wholly unjustified.

There have been hundreds of cases where policemen have been ordered by their superiors to commit illegal acts. Take the Calcutta incident of April 2. While thousands of hooligans milled around my car, hit it with sticks, reducing its sunshade to smithereens, and some of them got up on the hood and others on the roof, and jumped and danced on it, badly damaging the car, the police looked on disinterestedly. I saw Samar Guha MP being struck on the face with a stick just two or three yards from my car. Yet the police did nothing. Is it wrong in such cases to tell the police what their duty is? . . . I consider it my duty to explain to the police that . . . they must not obey orders that are illegal or go against their conscience.

Mrs Gandhi's refusal to draw a realistic conclusion from the "janta" poll victories and her relegating the national tide to "the forces of reaction" and "certain outside forces" amazed her younger colleagues. Leading radicals, Chandrasekhar, Mohan Dharia, and Krishna Kant, rejected this day-dream utterly with the stern reminder that the Bihar Movement was a result of Congress failure to fulfil its promises. They made repeated forceful pleas for a national reconciliation and an all-party effort to tackle the country's urgent problems. The blank they came up against in Mrs Gandhi, who adopted the simple expedient of no-response, was perhaps the first sign they had of a frozen irrationality in the leader they had so exuberantly raised to power, Finding it difficult even to meet her for discussion, they continued their efforts to defuse the situation. Their independence released a long-dormant animation in their party. The steady hum of controversy and speculation—meat and drink to Congressmen until Mrs Gandhi's rule—returned. In the new situation the Opposition could not be dismissed as unnatural, unpatriotic or outcast. Contacts were resumed. The processes of give-and-take that people and parties live by were set in motion again. The non-partisan record and integrity of JP gave these a more than political purpose. The time had come for a talk on fundamentals, an all-India debate long postponed. Mrs Gandhi's displeasure struck Mohan Dharia first.

On 1 March 1975 Dharia, speaking at the Harold Laski Institute in Ahmedabad, had renewed his plea for talks between Mrs Gandhi and Opposition leaders, and strongly condemned the brutal treatment of youth demonstrations. He had also said "the CPI design to replace the tricolour with the red flag would be frustrated." In a letter of the same date Mrs Gandhi informed him: "It is not proper for you to continue in the Council of Ministers since your views are not in conformity with the thinking of the Congress Party." Dharia replied, expressing his astonishment at this abrupt dismissal. He tendered his resignation to the President and said he would explain it in the Lok Sabha: "Had the Prime

Minister shown the courtesy of indicating to me her intention, either directly or indirectly, I would have immediately and willingly tendered my resignation." On 5 March in Parliament he denied the Prime Minister's charge of disagreement with party policies. Where his views on implementation or behaviour had differed, he had repeatedly used party forums, or conveyed them personally to the Prime Minister, to make them known:

On October 7, 1974 I personally conveyed my feeling that the continuance of persons with dubious reputations in the Ministry would erode the credibility of the government. . . . To adopt a callous attitude toward rising doubts in the public mind is easy, but to ignore them is very dangerous. . . . The period between 1969 and 1971 was one of making promises and giving assurances . . . 1971 should have been marked by the determination of the Congress and the administration to enter upon an era of performance. . . . I have been of the view that the cooperation of all such parties and people should be sought who are willing to contribute in the implementation of the policies in the interests of the common man.

Dharia said he had sent a letter and note to the Prime Minister on 19 November 1974, requesting a timebound programme of action. In a letter of 26 February 1975, he had further elaborated his views. Before writing it he had tried, from 11 February onwards, to get an appointment with the Prime Minister, and had failed to get one. He did not know what greater efforts he could have made to keep her posted with his thinking.

Dharia's statement was heard by a rapt Parliament and warmly welcomed by his constituency. Instructions to Congressmen of Poona city and district to boycott a reception and public rally arranged for him were blithely ignored. Dharia's dismissal had enormously enhanced his reputation and brought him a wider celebrity. Opponents of Mrs Gandhi within her party noted the fact.

On 6 March JP and Opposition leaders led a mammoth citizens' procession to Parliament and presented a charter of demands to the Speaker. The *Indian Express*, comparing its significance with Mahatma Gandhi's Salt March, reported that "when the head of the procession reached the Boat Club, its tail was still near [its starting point] the Red Fort," a distance of about five miles. JP addressed a public meeting at the Boat Club, announcing similar meetings at state capitals until 6 April. The 6th would be observed as "Revoke Emergency Day"—(this referred to the war emergency declared in December 1971)—as it was becoming evident that the Prime Minister would use this emergency to call off the 1976 elections and declare a Bangladesh-type dictatorship. He categorically denied inciting the people or the army to revolt, and charged Mrs Gandhi instead with wanting the movement to turn violent, so that she would have an excuse to crush it under a dictatorship. "You should not give her this opportunity." So far, he said, the Bihar government had killed 200 peaceful participants in the movement, yet they had the "temerity" to call the movement violent.

Delhi wore an armed look on 6 March. A Marxist MP described it in the Lok Sabha:

. . . the entire police force of Haryana seems to have tumbled into the capital, and blank-faced policemen wielding anything from lathis and batons to rifles stood in their hundreds at every point. Between the Boat Club and Parliament House it was a human wall of policemen and one could not move an inch without being challenged.

Police barricades had been erected outside the Prime Minister's house, far from the procession's route. That morning the state-owned Delhi Transport Corporation cut its bus services from about 1200 to 336—explaining the stoppage as being caused by the need for repairs—to prevent citizens from joining the march. Haryana Roadways suspended all its bus services to Delhi. Private buses were halted and delayed at three points along the Gurgaon-Delhi route for checks "to prevent overloading." Trucks were denied permission to carry passengers to Delhi. Along with contingents of the state's police force sent to the capital, these measures brought Bansi Lal's militant authority and loyalty to the Prime Minister into flamboyant display.

At Ahmedabad (Gujarat) on 6 March 79-year-old Morarji Desai led a procession to Raj Bhavan and handed the Governor a petition for an election to the State Assembly, due following its dissolution in March 1974. It was given a rousing ovation along the way.

2 April Congress and CPI youth organizations, led by Information Minister Subrata Mukerji, stopped JP's party on arrival at Calcutta University. Demonstrators climbed on his car and smashed the windscreen. Those who came out of the university building to receive him were surrounded, beaten, and had their clothes torn. The meeting had to be abandoned but the orgy continued as JP addressed a teachers' convention while the hall was stoned and glass panes broken. Coming out he faced a barrage of stones and missiles and was trapped with his companions for half an hour in his car before it was allowed to move. He told newsmen before leaving for Patna:

> I could have been killed. . . . I am sure this kind of thing could not have happened without the clearance of the Chief Minister and also of Mrs. Gandhi's government. . . . I don't think any single organisation is strong enough to face this menace because the Bengal government is behind this menace. . . . I appeal to all parties in the opposition, and all student and youth organisations in Bengal to bury their differences and join hands, and before anything else destroy the rising menace of fascism.

Methodical and open violence against workers of the Bihar Movement now appeared. On 27 April JP called attention to an incident in Arrah town in Bihar the previous week, when six of his student workers had had to be hospitalized and 12 others had received injuries:

> It seems that the government being unable to put down the Bihar Movement by the forces at its command, is hiring goondas and ex-criminals to do the job. . . . It should be a matter of joy for everyone in the State, whether he agrees with the Bihar Movement or not, that all through the time that the students were being beaten up they kept on raising slogans like *"Hamla chahe jaisa ho, hath hamara nahin uthega"* [whatever the violence used against us, we shall not retaliate]. I myself feel proud of these students. By their heroic and peaceful action they have set an example for others to follow.

In Delhi Morarji Desai informed the Prime Minister that unless correct constitutional procedure were adopted in Gujarat, and an election announced in the state, he would fast to death. He began his fast when Mrs Gandhi replied the election could not be held until after the monsoon. She set no date. A reader's letter in the *Indian Express* on 14 April commented on this development:

> We all know that of late Mrs. Gandhi and the Congress have been losing political ground very fast. . . . In the wake of the JP movement which is giving her sleepless nights, Mr. Desai's fast has become another nightmare for her. Thus the only alternative left for Mrs. Gandhi, if she wants to hold on to power, which she obviously does very desperately, is to go the Mujib way. . . . People feel that there are ample indications that things are gradually being manoeuvred into such an eventuality. This is what makes Mr. Desai's fast very crucial. Had there been faith in the plighted word of the ruling party's spokemen, Mr. Desai perhaps would not have staked his life for advancing the election schedule by a mere three months. But unfortunately he knows, as do others, that there is no such certainty about the promise held out by the ruling party. Hence the urgency to force the issue. (Ramadhar, New Delhi.)

Mrs Gandhi announced an election in Gujarat in early June. The death by fasting of a veteran Congressman, once her father's cabinet colleague, might have provoked shock and outrage. Her own popularity, according to opinion surveys, was low. A reader's letter in the *Indian Express* on 31 January 1975 conveys the flavour of public disenchantment:

> With the kind of massive mandate and unstinted support the Prime Minister has received from the people, which has been the lot of very few politicians in history, any shrewd and sagacious statesman could have virtually converted the country into a veritable heaven. But she has failed miserably to deliver the goods. . . . If the Prime Minister is the repository of all dynamism, radicalism and wisdom . . . why should she at all have given quarter to this corrupt clique? Secondly, having somehow done so, why should she find it difficult to extricate herself from their clutches? It is indeed odd that some six years ago she required to be protected against the so-called "syndicate"

which fettered her hands against the radical measures she wanted to take. Today she must be rescued from the inefficient clique that surrounds her and nullifies all her efforts. At this rate, some other hurdle may crop up tomorrow! (Badlu Ram Gupta, Sonepat Mandi).

Raj Narain's (Socialist MP) court case against her election to the Lok Sabha in 1971 was being reported in detail in the press and her replies in court made ambiguous, evasive reading. Her agent, Yashpal Kapoor's testimony did nothing to clear the air. His rise from average means and obscurity to sudden wealth and commanding political authority during the last few years had made him a highly controversial figure. In these circumstances Mrs Gandhi was ill-advised to campaign in Gujarat herself, accompanied by the impressive paraphernalia of her official position. Dressed in a Gujarati-style sari she called herself a "daughter-in-law of Gujarat." (Her husband, a Parsi, came from a Gujarati-speaking background though his family had settled in Uttar Pradesh.) Her speeches carried the hint that Gujarat's need of central assistance for its fertilizer and other schemes would be judged against how the state voted. The Congress was defeated by 12 seats in an Assembly of 182, a particularly humiliating blow after the loss of every critical by-election in 1974 and 1975. The Opposition Janta Front, the largest single party, formed a government with the support of the Kisan Mazdoor Lok Paksh (KMLP), a group that had earlier broken away from the Congress.

The last election result was announced on 12 June, the day of the Allahabad High Court judgement indicting Mrs Gandhi on two corruption charges in the conduct of her 1971 elections, declaring her election invalid, and debarring her from holding political office for six years. The verdict was not unexpected. Yet it made a sensation. Much of the public argument and coffee house debate had revolved around whether the judge would, if he found her guilty, be fearless enough to indict the Prime Minister. Public opinion had been less concerned with "technical infractions" of the election law than with Mrs Gandhi's scant regard for rules and proprieties in general, and the uses she had made of authority over a period of years. Could judicial freedom survive this process? Justice Jagmohan Lal Sinha had been as much on trial as Mrs Gandhi.

The news that Mrs Gandhi had been unseated by the Allahabad High Court judgement was announced on All India Radio at 10.25 A.M. The police had prepared for the possibility by erecting iron barricades around Mrs Gandhi's house and closing all roads leading to it, with heavy police patrolling of the area. This left a clear field for rallies and "upsurges" in her favour while it prevented public demonstrations against her from approaching. The *Times of India* reported: "The capital wore the look of the days of the 1969 Congress split. In the afternoon of June 12th about 2,000 Congress demonstrators assembled near the Safdarjang Road roundabout shouting Indira slogans and "*Justice Sinha murdabad*". . . . The report added that between 3 and 8 P.M. the Prime Minister came out of her house three times to address rallies at the roundabout. Each time she warned the gathering against internal and external threats to the country and said, come what may, she would stand by the people to usher in socialism.

The scene was, however, different in important respects from 1969. Some of her crucial supporters during the Congress split—the best known and most popular of the Young Turks—were now absent. By 1969 Mrs Gandhi had antagonized and alienated the Old Guard. Six years later she had dissipated her credit with key radical supporters. In 1969 there had been risk and chance in Mrs Gandhi's battle with her party. In 1975 she stood securely at the head of it through her control of its organization, while her command of the nation relied heavily on the country's intelligence and paramilitary forces.

There was one vital similarity to 1969. Realizing then that her chances of succeeding against her opponents in the party were not certain if she proceeded through accepted political channels and observed the political code, she had set conventions aside and turned to street agitation to create the drama of a leader demanded by the people. The High Court judgement debarred her from office. Correct procedure ruled that she resign her seat in Parliament and her leadership of her party with immediate effect. However the High Court had granted her a 20-day stay order— a gesture of courtesy and accommodation to the party in power— to allow the Congress to choose another leader. Mrs Gandhi turned this interval to account, once again through street agitation. The slogan "Death to Justice Sinha" and the burning of the judge's effigy gave it the drama of "the people's" judgement as against the court's. The drama continued with the stoppage of bus services for the public the next day, and Delhi's entire transport system diverted to carrying demonstrators to Mrs Gandhi's house. This major dislocation in the capital evoked very similar accounts in leading newspapers:

The public transport system here was virtually paralysed today (13th) as hundreds of buses were unauthorisedly diverted to points near the Prime Minister's house to carry demonstrators affirming support and loyalty to her. Not a single DTC bus operated till 1 P.M. Some buses made their appearance around 2 P.M. By 5 P.M. only 380 vehicles out of 1400 were operating on scheduled routes. . . . There were heated exchanges between rival DTC workers' union representatives . . . workers of the union controlled by the CPI-M protested against the sudden dislocation of the bus services. (*Times of India*, 15 June 1975.)

As DTC buses went off the roads this morning leaving lakhs of commuters stranded, Congress volunteers were pouring into the capital from Punjab, Haryana and UP in buses and trucks, hired or comandeered by State units of the Party. This followed an understanding between Chief Ministers of these States who met here yesterday, that they would flood the capital with party volunteers to march to Mrs. Gandhi's house to demonstrate that the people were with her in this "hour of travail". . . . Over 200 DTC buses were used to ferry people from Gurgaon and adjoining Haryana areas to Delhi. . . . A resident of Akhumpur village told this reporter that five DTC buses visited his village to collect people, but all of them went back without a passenger. Only a handful of people from some areas went to Delhi to join the rally. The Haryana government also allowed DTC buses to enter its territory without road permits, in direct contrast to the March event when buses carrying people to Delhi from Haryana to attend Jayaprakash Narayan's meeting were stopped from proceeding to the capital. (*Indian Express*, 14 June 1975.)

The mass upsurge, barring the DTC workers' rally, was in reality rag-tag bands of people hastily collected and carted in New Delhi Municipal Committee trucks and DTC buses that should really have been plying where they were needed most.

Squatting on the grass behind banners prominently displaying their affiliations, the demonstrators stoically suffered the scorching heat, cheering listlessly as speaker after speaker rained a considerable amount of rhetoric and made blasphemous statements against the judge and judiciary. . . . For anyone not in the party of demonstrators and without credentials to prove his ranking as a Congressman, access to the roads leading to the Prime Minister's residence was barred. The security arrangement were the tightest they have ever been. . . . (*Hindustan Times*, 14 June 1975.)

The Opposition, prevented from holding a meeting or demonstration near the Prime Minister's house, held one outside Rashtrapati Bhavan, condemning the dislocation of transport, the closure of many electricity units, and Mrs Gandhi's resort to street agitation when facts and legalities went against her. The rumble in her own party grew distinct. Shambu Nath Mishra, MP, issued a statement:

Nobody has ever been indispensable in this world and nobody can be made indispensable at the cost of morality, propriety, fair play and justice, and more so the honour of the country. If she herself wants to stick to the chair, a thousand excuses can be invented. If she is honest and sincere and has no lust for power, she must save the face of the country from the greatest ridicule of the world. . . .

Mrs Gandhi could come back with honour and dignity, the statement continued, if her appeal against the High Court judgement succeeded. It was unfortunate that rallies and propaganda had been launched to whip up public opinion and prejudice the judiciary.

The Congress Parliamentary Party was openly divided on the issue of retaining Mrs Gandhi as leader. Senior Congressmen, encouraged and emboldened by the High Court judgement, had advanced their claims. Mohan Dharia had already called for her resignation. A move to collect pledges of loyalty failed when many members refused to sign the blank sheet handed round. Some MPs vigorously objected to the burning of Justice Sinha's effigy and condemned this and other forms of rabble behaviour.

Others wanted to know for whose benefit the rallies were being staged.

On 21 June the executives of five Opposition parties met in New Delhi and passed a resolution:

> The joint meeting of the National Executives of the Akali Dal, Bharatiya Lok Dal, the Congress (O), Jan Sangh and the Socia- list Party is deeply perturbed at the stand taken and activities indulged in by Mrs. Indira Gandhi in the wake of the judgement against her by the Allahabad High Court. . . . Mrs. Gandhi is not only sticking to her position but is resorting to means and methods repugnant to democracy to maintain herself in power . . . there has been an exhibition of mounting arrogance and a cynical disregard of moral values. It is against this terrible tra- vesty and moral degeneration of the political structure that the people have to bestir themselves. The combined Executives appeal to the people to express themselves fearlessly and massi- vely through all the legitimate and peaceful democratic channels.

The national newspapers exhibited a rare unanimity, suggesting that the High Court verdict warranted Mrs Gandhi's resignation. The *Tribune* in an editorial titled "Janta on the March" had gone further: "Today the Indira Wave or the Indira Hurricane is only a distant memory, and slogans like Garibi Hatao raise only Rabel- aisian laughter. . . ." In its June 26th editorial the *Tribune* said: "A claim to rule by staking it out on the streets must, and will, invite challenge. Already there is talk of civil disobedience."

Civil disobedience did not begin. The night it was announced by Opposition leaders, India came under the emergency.

The enormity of the High Court judgement's blow to Mrs Gandhi must be understood in terms of her assessment of herself as indis- pensable to the Indian scene. She considered herself more than a politician or a party leader. She believed she had played a role of glory and sacrifice in the struggle for freedom, even been classified a "dangerous" prisoner by the British. Her background, she was convinced, had endowed her with wisdom and instincts since child- hood that no one else in the country possessed. That anyone should regard her as a politician, subject to normal political processes, was a gross impertinence and injustice. She had come to believe she was India. In 1975 "Indira is India, and India is Indira," the

Congress President's slogan, became the party's refrain. At the party's annual session in December the national anthem was followed by a new song *"Indira Hindustan Ban Gai"* (Indira has become India). By that time Mrs Gandhi had passed "through the looking glass" into the full-blown exotica of make-believe.

Yet no political leader can be a creature of fantasy alone. The shrewd politician in him sees when the tide is running against him and no make-believe attends the concrete preparations he makes to master an entirely real challenge to his power. The High Court judgement and the Guajrat election result were incontestable realities. The Opposition gave every sign of improving its strength and support as the 1976 elections drew near. Public disillusionment with Congress performance centred on Mrs Gandhi. None of this, however, is likely to have made the extreme step of declaring a second emergency necessary to Mrs Gandhi if she had been sure of her own party's loyal support. But it was becoming clear that the move to replace her, now being discussed, would allow no easy return. A party far from bankrupt of leadership, in fact restless with aspiring leadership and with leaders smarting under blows to their pride and dignity, would use this opportunity to ease her out. Its brilliant rebel corps was waiting to do so. The emergency was Mrs Gandhi's second, and this time literal coup against the Opposition in her own party. Unless this had been so, the sweep of arrests during the night of 25 June would not have taken Congressmen from their beds, including Chandrasekhar and Ram Dhan, high office bearers in the party. More revealing, these arrests did not have the sanction of the emergency provision of the Constitution. Mrs Gandhi's cabinet did not meet until the morning of 26 June to take this decision. The President signed the proclamation on Mrs Gandhi's orders during the 25th night. Clearly this sequence of events was intended to be a warning to wavering cabinet colleagues as well. By 26 June they had been provided with reinforced, heavily armed guards at their gates, and some with armed escorts, ostensibly for their own protection, when they attended official engagements. Without doubt preparations for the smooth transformation to dictatorship proceeded without the knowledge of Mrs Gandhi's cabinet. They were made in consultation with selected aides and the police and intelligence network. Her own party was as much a victim of this lightning seizure of absolute power as opposing opinion outside it.

CHAPTER THIRTEEN

THE FLOWERING OF A STYLE

Mrs Gandhi's pre-emergency measures highlights her political technique. Power failures arranged for the night of 25 June prevented most morning newspapers from appearing on the 26th. Arrests made that night gave her the advantage of surprise attack over political adversaries, both in her own party and the opposition. They also presented her cabinet with a *fait accompli* when it met on the 26th morning. The cabinet's "consideration" of a proclamation of emergency, invoking Article 352 (1) of the Constitution, came many hours after the event, when police action had been taken and an efficient network of control established.

With its official proclamation the emergency went into smooth visible operation. Presidental ordinances, later converted into law, enlarged government's powers to arrest and imprison without trial. Meetings of more than five persons without permission were forbidden, an unreal ban in over-crowded market areas where the streets teem with human beings. It was rigorously enforced where it could be. Casual groups collected on streets and outside coffee houses were roughly dispersed. Delhi's most popular meeting-and-talking place, the crowded Janta Coffee House in Connaught Place, a people's venture set up to combat the rising price of coffee a few years earlier, was demolished. On the other hand, officially backed "spontaneons" demonstrations in support of Mrs Gandhi sprouted like mushrooms, and were enacted too offen to even require permission from authority. The double standard of law already in evidence was now practised quite openly. Posters of Mrs Gandhi appeared in the streets, bazaars, and at thoroughfares proclaiming her the saviour of law and order. Shop windows were required to display her picture prominently and to post a pledge supporting the Tweny-Point Programme alongside. Delegations of teachers, writers, students, workers, lawyers, and trade union representatives were regularly summoned to her heavily guarded residence to congratulate her on the emergency and endorse her programme. Government's propaganda department claimed the police had obtained clues to secret hordes of arms and ammunition with the "discovery" of "weapons" in the offices of RSS, and skulls in the offices of the Anand Marg, an occult group not connected with any Opposition party. A connection was sought to be established in the public mind through film documentaries showing Jayaprakash Narayan and Oppsition leaders addressing gatherings, alternating with rows of skulls being "discovered" by the police, and flashbacks to Hitler rallies and goosestepping Nazis. These clumsy efforts tried to convey that something very sinister had been about to happen when the emergency saved the situation. Anthony Lukas of the *New York Times* got the following official enlightenment about published pictures of wooden swords and staves found in RSS offices:

I asked Om Mehta, Minister of State in the Home Ministry, about this and he replied vaguely, "There were some metal swords too." Even with some metal swords, I asked, how could boys with staves pose much of a threat to a superbly equipped army of about one million men, the Border Security Force of about 85,000, the Central Reserve Police of about 57,000, and some 755,000 State policemen? "Well," Mehta said, "there were undoubtedly some rifles too." "Did you seize any?" I asked. "No," he said, "But they probably kept them at home. Don't underestimate these people's capacity for mischief."[1]

In a standard speech Mrs Gandhi made, with minor variations, over the next twelve months to interviewers and different audiences, she claimed there had been a "plot" against established authority. The charge was never substantiated and no one accused of conspiracy was brought to trial.[2] The more specific charges she repeated were: the Opposition wanted to remove her and the Congress Party from office; it wanted to weaken the nation; it was insigni-

[1]Anthony Lukas, "India is as Indira Does," *New York Times Magazine*, 4 April 1976.
[2]The exception was George Fernandes, Socialist Party leader, arrested in June 1976, whom the government proposed to bring to trial.

ficant and had no following; the only following it had came from the press:

It was necessary in order to avoid any trouble because it would have been their effort to provoke violence on our part. *If* they did something, that would not have created a good situation. So it was more to keep the peace. (To a Bombay weekly, 8 July 1975.)

A large section of the press had identified itself with the Opposition. (To a group of editors, 9 July 1975.)

In the last few years a consistent attempt was being made to weaken the fabric of the nation. (To members of the Lions Club and Lions International, 10 July 1975.)

The Opposition had no support except the support of a vociferous section of the press. . . .These parties concentrated their entire energy on denigrating me and spreading the most baseless canards such as that I smoke and drink, which I do not do. (To members of the Nehru Youth Centres, 11 July 1975.)

Sections of the press had become total partners of the Opposition front . . . Censorship of Opposition newspapers had become necessary. . . . In the process other sections of the press have also had to face inconvenience. (Interview with the *Sunday Times* and the *Observer*, 12 July 1975.)

Reverting to the situation leading to the proclamation of Emergency, Mrs. Gandhi said there had been a steady effort to weaken "our system" since 1950. (To 7th biennial conference of State Anti-Corruption CBI Officers, July 1975.)

A section of the press was anti-government and it was projecting only what was anti-government. . . . Newspapers were building up the Opposition. (To correspondent of West German daily, Bild Am Sonntag, 10 August 1975.)

The press was not only a mouthpiece of the Opposition, but spearheading it too. (To Comex VII, 23 September 1975.)

The Opposition had united for the purpose of forcing me and the Congress Party out of office. (Interview with NBC, published 24 August 1975.)

The press, both Indian and foreign, were denigrating India. (At Bhubaneshwar, 27 September 1975.)

In a situation where no voice but her own could be heard, now that debate and dissent had been silenced, and there were no enemies at large, real or illusory, to react to, Mrs Gandhi's utterances laid bare a complaining naiveté. She sounded aggrieved and perplexed that the Opposition should want her and the Congress out of office, and that sections of the press should support the Opposition. Her answers to questions in an interview with NBC made her reasons for declaring an emergency sound no more rational:

Q. You yourself say the Opposition is in a small minority. Why did you really have to move in the extreme way you did? We simply cannot see that there was a national emergency.

A. Well perhaps you're just too far away. Many things could not go on because a very few people, a handful of people, were disrupting it.

Q. If you want to tell the world this, why not put the people on trial? You have a good court system. Why not let the world know what they were about to do?

A. Firstly our court cases go on for years and years. And it is very difficult to prove anything.

Q. How much real danger was there that the armed forces would mutiny?

A. I don't think that there was a real danger. But this sort of thing causes confusion in the minds of the people.

The Home Ministry's document "Why Emergency," placed before Parliament on its opening day, 21 July 1975, laboured hard. The Opposition, it said, had held a series of meetings between 21 and 25 June to work out a "grand design" to dislodge Mrs Gandhi and her government. On the 25th Jayaprakash Narayan had called on the army, police, and government employees not to obey orders they considered "wrong." He had urged the Chief Justice, A.N. Ray, not to sit on the bench to hear the Prime Minister's appeal against the Allahabad High Court judgement.

Thus these Opposition parties had irrevocably embarked upon the path of chaos and anarchy and were soon to set about executing their grand design. . . .The true justification for the present Emergency under Article 352 of the Constitution is the preservation of the social interest in peace and order and the promotion of the public good.

The document listed as "unconstitutional" methods the railway strike of 1974, and the movements in Gujarat and Bihar.

Jayaprakash Narayan, arrested before dawn on 26 June, and reduced to sudden, rapidly deteriorating illness in prison, wrote to the Prime Minister on 21 July 1975 from his solitary confinement alternating between hospital cottage and hospital ward at Chandigarh:

Dear Prime Minister,

I am appalled at press reports of your speeches and interviews. [The very fact that you have to say something every day to justify your action implies a guilty conscience.] Having muzzled the press and every kind of public dissent, you continue with your distortions and untruths without fear of criticism or contradiction. . . .

About the plan to paralyse the government. There was no such plan and you know it. Let me state the facts. Of all the States of India it was in Bihar alone where there was a people's movement . . . and you should know if your ubiquitous intelligence has served you right, that it was spreading and percolating deep down in the countryside. Until the time of my arrest "janta sarkars" were being formed from the village upwards to the block level. Later on the process was to be taken up, hopefully, to the district and State level.

If you had cared to look into the programme of the "janta sarkars", you would have found that for the most part it was constructive, such as regulating the public distribution system, checking corruption at the lower levels of administration, implementing the land reform laws, settling disputes through the age-old custom of conciliation and arbitration, assuring a fair deal to Harijans, curbing such social evils as *tilak* and *dahez* etc. There was nothing in all this that by any stretch of the imagination could be called subversive.

Only where "janta sarkars" were solidly organised such programmes as non-payment of taxes were taken up. At the peak of the movement in urban areas an attempt was made for some days through *dharna* and picketing, to stop the working of government offices. At Patna whenever the Assembly opened, attempts were made to persuade the Members to resign and to prevent them, peacefully, from going in. All these were calculated programmes of civil disobedience, and thousands of men and women were arrested all over the State.

If all this adds up to an attempt to paralyse the Bihar government, well, it was the same kind of attempt as was made during the freedom struggle through non-cooperation and satyagraha to paralyse the British government. . . . What right has anyone to ask an elected government and elected legislature to go?. . . The answer is that in a democracy the people do have the righs to ask for the resignation of an elected government if it has gone corrupt and has been misruling. . . .

. . . the students of Bihar did not start the movement. . . . After formulating their demands at a conference they had met the Chief Minister and the Education Minister. They had had several meetings. But unfortunately the inept and corrupt Bihar government did not take the students seriously. Then the latter *gheraoed* the Assembly. The sad events of that day precipitated the Bihar Movement. Even then the students did not demand the resignation of the Ministry, nor the dissolution of the Assembly. It was after several weeks during which firing, lathi charges and indiscriminate arrests took place, that the Students' Action Committee felt compelled to put up that demand. It was at that point that the Rubicon was crossed. . . . Thus the plan of which you speak . . . is a figment of your imagination, thought up to justify your totalitarian measures.

If there was a plan, it was . . . announced at the Ramlila grounds by Nanaji Deshmukh on June 25 and which was the subject matter of my speech that evening. The programme was for a selected number of persons to offer satyagraha before or near your residence in support of the demand that you should step down until the Supreme Court's judgement on your appeal. The programme was to continue for seven days in Delhi, after which it was to be taken up in the States. And. . . it was to last only until the judgement of the Supreme Court. . . . It goes without saying that the *satyagrahi* willingly invites and accepts his lawful punishment. This is the new dimension added to democracy by Gandhi. What an irony that it should be obliterated in Gandhi's own India.

It should be noted—and it is a very important point—that even this programme of satyagraha would not have occurred to the Opposition had you remained content with quietly clinging to your office. But you did not do it. Through your henchmen you had rallies and demonstrations organised in front of your residence, and posters appeared in the city suggesting some kind of link between the judge and the CIA. When such despicable happenings were taking place every day, the Opposition had no alternative but to counteract the mischief . . . by orderly satyagraha.

And why has the freedom of the press been suppressed? Not because the Indian press was irresponsible, dishonest or anti-government. In fact nowhere, under conditions of freedom, is the press more responsible, reasonable and fair than it has been in India. The truth is that your anger against it was aroused because on the question of your resignation, after the High Court's judgement, some of the papers took a line that was highly unpalatable to you. And when . . . all the metropolitan papers, including the wavering *Times of India*, came out with well-reasoned and forceful editorials advising you to quit, freedom of the press became too much for you to stomach. . . . It staggers one's imagination to think that so valuable a freedom as freedom of the press, the very life-breath of democracy, can be snuffed out because of the personal pique of a Prime Minister.

You are reported to have said that democracy is not more important than the nation. . . . It is a false choice you have formulated. There is no choice between democracy and the nation. . . . [Our] democratic constitution cannot be changed into a totalitarian one by a mere ordinance or a law of Parliament. That can be done only by the people of India themselves in their new Constituent Assembly, especially elected for that specific purpose. If justice, equality and fraternity have not been rendered to "all its citizens" even after a quarter of a century of signing that Constitution, the fault is not that of the Constitution or of democracy, but of the Congress Party that has been in power in Delhi all these years. . . .

You inherited a great tradition, noble values and a working democracy. Do not leave behind a miserable wreck of all that. It will take a long time to put all that together again. For it will be put together again, I have no doubt. A people who fought British imperialism and humbled it cannot indefinitely accept the indignity of totalitarianism. . . .

The prisoner received no reply.

The essence of the emergency was the pinnacle-power—a position above the multitude, unacountable and unchallengeable—it sought to guarantee the Prime Minister. This was accomplised by three Amendments to the Constitution and an Act of Parliament. The 38th Amendment put the declaration of emergency beyond the scrutiny of the courts. The 39th Amendment made election disputes relating to the Prime Minister, President, Vice-President, and Speaker non-justiciable. This wiped out the Allahabad High Court judgement with retrospective effect, and ensured a Supreme Court judgement in her favour. On 7 November 1975, a 5-judge bench of the Supreme Court, with no legal option but to exonerate her, upheld her 1971 election to Parliament. The proposed 40th Amendment conferred complete immunity on the Prime Minister, President, Vice-President, and Speaker, in respect of past or future criminal offences. An Act banned the publication of "objectionable matter," making criticism of the Prime Minister, President, Vice-President, Speaker, and Council of Ministers a penal offence. The inclusion of these other dignitaries resembled light musical accompaniment to the sombre theme of prime ministerial power, finally established through a drastically amended Constitution in 1976.

The emergency enabled Mrs Gandhi to move towards an institutionalized control of the press and the Opposition. "Personally I am not for censorship at all, but the Home, and Information and Broadcasting Ministries have their own difficulties," Mrs Gandhi said in an interview with a Bombay weekly. The policy she had instituted was, nevertheless, censorship, controlled by a Chief Censor at Delhi, and his counterparts at state capitals. Among the newspapers shut down by the government on 26 June were the Jan Sangh's *Motherland* and Jayaprakash Narayan's *Everyman's*, with their last issues shredded by the police. The arrest of two prominent editors, amongst others, acted as a brake on the profession generally. Official reprisal for past criticism, at first directed at large-circulation papers and journals, narrowed its attack until *Opinion*, a one-man protest paper, which had flourished since independence in criticism of Nehru's policies, was eliminated in August 1976. A series of steps including a "code of ethics" for journalists and

editors; government nominees on newspaper boards; and the "voluntary merger" of India's four news agencies, PTI, UNI, Samachar
Bharati, and Hindustan Samachar, into a single, government-
regulated agency, ensured government control of the news and
docile channels for its transmission. The Press Council, set up in
July 1966 "for the purpose of preserving freedom of the press and
maintaining and improving the standards of newspapers and news
agencies in India," was dissolved by ordinance on 8 December
1975. The Council had recently defended some celebrated cases:
the *Tribune* vs the Haryana Government, the burning of *Searchlight* in Bihar, and the dismissal of B.G. Verghese by the Birla
proprietors of the *Hindustan Times*. With the establishment of
Samachar, the government could "lift" curbs on foreign reporting
in 1976, and permit a "debate" on pending changes in the Constitution, allowing newspapers to report limited opposition opinion on
the subject. But the censorship mandate continued to operate. It
covered the writings of Mahatma Gandhi, Nehru, and Tagore
relating to freedom, and all news items and events adverse to
government, e.g., riots against sterilization measures, jailbreaks,
satyagraha campaigns, and Opposition opinion. Whether a political
opposition could survive at all became dependent on the ruling
party's favour, when the amended Constitution in 1976 gave Parliament the right to pass laws over-riding the fundamental rights,
forbidding "anti-national activity," and banning "anti-national associations." Mrs Gandhi had moved before this to bring the two
Opposition governments, in Tamil Nadu and Gujarat, under central
control, ending the last vestige of true federal functioning. Mrs
Gandhi's style and preference in this regard was aptly stated by
Congress President, D.K. Barooah, at a party symposium: "The
Central Government is the national government of India. All
other governments [i.e., in the States] are only municipal governments." Neither Tamil Nadu nor Gujarat capitulated. The
campaign mounted against each, and the resistance it met lit for
a while the last bright embers of political opposition and federal
vigour.

In Tamil Nadu the DMK was firmly established as the dominant
political force in the state. On 12 July 1975 Chief Minister Karunanidhi had addressed a mass meeting on Marina Beach in Madras,
declaring there was neither an internal nor external threat to India
and calling upon the vast concourse to take a pledge to defend

their freedoms. His public speeches caustically directed at the emergency were laced with Tamil folk humour and biting sarcasm. On 29 July the police seized all copies of *Murasoli*, the DMK's Tamil daily with a circulation of 30,000, for publishing "objectionable matter." But the party's hold on the state was confirmed in December with its conference at Coimbatore:

> The biggest crowds ever seen in this industrial city of half a million thronged the 5-mile route of a long and colourful procession taken out by DMK. (*Times of India*, 5 December 1975.)

> The Coimbatore conference clearly did not look like that of a party on its last legs. The size of the gathering assumes importance when one considers that the DMK is a party without "glamorous" leaders, that runs against popular political currents, and that it has had a string of electoral defeats in the past 3 years. (*Statesman*, 1 January 1976.)

Karunanidhi was not the only obstacle to a takeover by Mrs Gandhi in Tamil Nadu. The enormous prestige of Kamaraj, elder statesman of the Old Congress, stood in her way. Kamaraj, normally silent and phlegmatic, had expressed his horror at the declaration of emergency at a public meeting at Sholingar and in an interview with students at Tiruvellore:

> I am shocked to hear that leaders have been arrested throughout the country. This state of affairs is not good for the nation. . . . What happens in Delhi we are not able to know. The radio does not give correct news, newspapers are also not giving correct news. . . . Such an event has no parallel even under British rule. (Sholingar, 27 June 1975.)

> I feel as though I have been left in the jungle blindfolded. I cannot visualise the consequences of the Emergency. Can anyone even imagine that such an Emergency would be proclaimed. . . . During the 1971 election I had expressed my apprehension that there was danger to democracy. Mr. Karunanidhi and Mrs. Gandhi, who were then in alliance, scoffed at me. What I said in 1971 is happening in 1975. (Tiruvellore, 28 June 1975.)

Kamaraj's death on 2 October gave Mrs Gandhi the opening she needed to suck the state's Old Congress unit into her own party.

The effort had some of the ingredients of Kathakali, ancient dance drama of the south, with masks, costumes, and colour in full play, and great cymbal clashes punctuating the performance. Her spokesmen in Tamil Nadu announced that "certain outside forces, including some foreign powers, are at work in Tamil Nadu to scuttle the merger of the two Congress parties in the State." The Old Congress countered by suspending its state unit and instructing that no decision could be taken during the emergency. A committee was set up in its place, headed by Ramachandran. On 2 December 1975 D.K. Barooah told a meeting at Tiruchirapalli: "If we fail to remove [Ramachandran] we shall be treacherous to the memory of Mr. Kamaraj." The *Statesman* account of the meeting read:

> The speeches were also notable for the frequent emotional references to Mr. Kamaraj; often many were seen wiping their tears at the reference. A number of policemen stood around the meeting venue to prevent any trouble from those opposed to the merger proposal.

The mixture of tears and truncheon over Kamaraj's dead body accomplished a kind of merger with a faction of the Old Congress. On 31 January a virtual occupation army in the form of CRP contingents moved into Tamil Nadu bringing it under control. A State Assembly election was due. This could have been postponed by the Union government as the parliamentary election had been postponed, and the DMK government, with its strength of 166 in a House of 234, given an extended mandate. Both these options, and any semblance of constitutional action were discarded as the Centre's police moved in, and Tamil Nadu was brought under President's rule. On 14 February 1976 Mrs Gandhi drove in an open car under decorated arches bearing portraits of herself and Kamaraj to open the Kamaraj Memorial at Guindy in Madras. She said the merger had been his "last wish." He had sent her a message about it and she had wanted to come to Tamil Nadu to discuss it with him, but he had dissuaded her, saying this would give rise to gossip about the merger. "For me," she concluded, "it was a privilege to work with him. I sought his guidance and we discussed almost every matter of importance." Earlier, the newspapers had reported Kamaraj's gun carriage funeral attended by Mrs Gandhi, and her "great grief" at the loss of her advisor.

In an interview on 29 February with the New Delhi fortnightly *India Today*, Union Finance Minister, C. Subramanim, once Kamaraj's cabinet colleague in Tamil Nadu, said:

> My own impression was that [Kamaraj] would have taken the plunge for a merger, but he fell ill. Then this Emergency came. He again became allergic to any decision taken during the Emergency, when his colleagues were in jail.

The *Democratic World*, political and economic weekly, offered its own unmistakeable opinion:

> [Kamaraj] never concealed his contempt for the many political fortune hunters who flocked to Mrs. Gandhi's party since 1969. . . . Given his reputation for principled consistency, it is difficult to believe that during his last days he changed his stand and decided to give his colleagues short shrift.

Gujarat's Janta Front government took six weeks longer to remove. Hitendra Desai, defector from the Old Congress, took the lead in the campaign against it and secured a flow of youth support for the Congress Party from the 1974 Gujarat agitation, helping it to an impressive victory in the panchayat elections. The Union government built a "case" against Gujarat on the issue of "clandestine" literature being produced in the state, and the discovery of dynamite, allegedly being moved to Varanasi. The Janta Front died hard. In October, November, and December 1975 it won important civic elections in Rajkot, Baroda, Surat, Broach, and finally to the Ahmedabad Municipal Corporation, the largest civic body in the state. For the Ahmedabad election the bulk of Janta seats had been shared between the Old Congress (a constituent of the Front) and Majur Mahajan, the prestigious labour organization of textile workers started by Mahatma Gandhi. The Janta Front lost its majority in the State Assembly when its partner, the KMLP, was dissolved by defections on 11 February. It was defeated on a budgetary demand in the Assembly on 12 March 1976. The Congress Party secured defections of six Corporations of the Ahmedabad Municipal Corporation and gained control of this important body soon afterwards.

A third state, Jammu and Kashmir, maintained a discreet but definite distance from the emergency. Sheikh Abdullah, restored to power as Chief Minister some months earlier, refrained from joining the chorus of praise around the Prime Minister. He spoke of a national reconciliation and on 20 September 1975 told newsmen, "If I can be of any use to the Prime Minister in this regard, my services are at her disposal." Resisting Congress pressures to merge his own party with the ruling party, he said the National Conference had waged the people's struggle against Maharaja's rule. It would keep its identity, and the Congress could merge with it, if it wished. He said at a publc meeting at Lal Chowk:

Power was handed over to me when the ship of State was on the point of sinking with the loads of corruption and maladministration. We are not obliged to those who vacated office in our favour. It is they who should be obliged to us because we are being obliged to carry the mess created by them. No one voluntarily gives up power. If someone does so, it is only to save himself from the deluge. My government is determined to root out corruption. Its extent and ramifications at the moment would frighten even the devil. The image of the Congress in the State is far from healthy. But we want no confrontation with Congress.[3]

Kashmir, a sensitive border state, was paradoxically less vulnerable to "takeover" than Tamil Nadu or Gujarat. Its stability was vital to the country and Sheikh Abdullah was firmly in the saddle. At a public meeting in Udhampur on 13 March 1976, in what may have been an oblique reference to the massive security arrangements at the Prime Minister's meetings, he objected to police barricades separating him from the crowd. He said the worst that could befall him was an assassin's bullet and he would prefer that to being kept at such a distance from the people.

Mrs Gandhi had kept a group of Kashmiri Brahmins close to her. This preference for her community, and kith and kin, was climaxed by the emergence of Sanjay into the political limelight. The ease with which Sanjay was planted in the body politic was not, as it

[3]Sheikh Abdullah's speech reported by Press Trust of India (PTI) on 19 October 1975.

might have been in normal times, due to the respect Indians attach to family and tradition. Acceptance without demur by the Congress illustrated how thoroughly democratic procedures in the party had been gutted and the fear that now ruled out disagreement altogether. A party whose inner confidence had been shaken, and whose senior figures had been reduced to obedience, dully submitted.

Unlike his brother, Rajiv, a happily married airlines pilot and father of two, who stayed out of the limelight, Sanjay did not enjoy a reputation for modesty or pleasant human relations. A problem student, he had been withdrawn from boarding school and tutored at home to prepare him for the school-leaving examination, and later, had left Rolls Royce at Crewe before completing his training. Sanjay, like his brother, had never known any environment but India's select Doon School and the Prime Minister's House (first their grandfather's, at Teen Murti, and later their mother's, at Safdarjang Road), with all the privilege, prestige, and authority that went with it. Some of the most charming press pictures of the Nehru era had been of two enchanting children and three golden retrievers on the lawns of Teen Murti House. Sanjay had developed a taste for authority and a lifestyle lacking restraint. Much is forgiven a handsome young man, particularly a Prime Minister's son, and his escapades, which at one time included hijacking cars and coarse personal behaviour, were generally ignored. He came to critical public notice for the first time as the recipient of government favour with no qualifications in education or experience to justify it, "suddenly heading a huge car manufacturing industrial complex involving an investment of ten million dollars."[4] His failure to produce under license became a public issue that was, however, silenced by the emergency. The only available information on the performance of Maruti Ltd. afterward was Sanjay's answer to a question at a meeting in the south on 20 March 1976 that his factory was producing "20 cars, 15 lorries and a few road rollers each month."

---

[4]From the statement of Ram Jethamalani, Chairman of the Bar Council of India, before a House of Congress subcommittee on international relations in September 1976. Jethmalani had sought and received political asylum in the United States.

The emergency gave Sanjay wide scope for bullying command and vendetta. He already exercised authority without official position. He was now credited with ordering arrests and house and office raids. He gave direct orders to government officials and had squads of the Youth Congress to do his bidding. An aura of terror now attached to his name and it was augmented by the enforced sterilization campaign conducted by him. By the end of the year he was given the status of a leading political personality, his arrivals in state capitals accompanied by official panoply matched by his mother's. He was met by chief ministers and cabinet members, his visits elaborately arranged and attended by state politicians and officials. On a "surprise" visit paid by him to Patna on 3 December 1975 Jaggannath Mishra (brother of the late L.N. Mishra), Bihar's new Chief Minister, told newsmen "everyone was impressed by the simplicity of Mr Sanjay Gandhi and his concern for the down-trodden masses." He made his official debut as "youth leader" at the Congress Party's annual session in December at Komagata Marunagar near Chandigarh, and was projected henceforth as one who "truly understood the aspirations of the poor," gifted with brains, business acumen, vision and compassion. Not surprisingly, the halo looked incongruous and his new personality and importance had to be reinforced by a flood of rhetoric, and bestowed with a new character. The following write-up in the *Indian Express* on 12 February 1976, in anticipation of his visit to Calcutta, is one of the more sedate examples of the lavish buildup provided for Sanjay through the media:

Youth Congress leaders, Cabinet Ministers, industrialists, Rotarians and intellectuals are vying with each other to give him a big reception. Welcome arches are being erected at every turn of the ten-minute route through which he will be taken in a motorcade. At one point on the VIP road, a group of Sikhs will receive Mr. Gandhi with the bhangra dance, while at other points women will accord him a welcome in traditional Bengali style. The day-long programme is so packed with functions that Mr. Gandhi will be running from place to place to keep his engagements. The highlights of the programme are his address to a mass rally at the Shaheed Minar Maidan, the reception by the six Chambers of Commerce and two other business associations at Kala Mandir, and the luncheon meeting with the Rotarians.

Never before have the Chambers of Commerce and the Rotarians from all over the State jointly welcomed any national leader or even a Prime Minister as they would be doing to Mr. Gandhi. At the meeting with the Chambers of Commerce, Mr. Gandhi will be answering questions by the country's top industrialists—an event of unique importance.

Sanjay's undefined powers ranged over a wide area, his activities including public meetings, interviews to newspapers and magazines, and conferences with ministers. On a visit to Bombay on 11 January 1976, Sanjay, acccording to a PTI report, "spent over two hours discussing the economic and political problems of the country" with a group that included Bombay's Congress Party boss, Rajni Patel, Maharashtra Revenue Minister, Rafiq Zakaria, Union Ministers V.C. Shukla and Bansi Lal, and "leading journalists."

Asked about the powers her son was exercising, Mrs Gandhi replied in two interviews in October 1975:

> It is a big lie that the whole Emergency and so on is being run by or decisions taken by a small group including my son. (Interview with North German television, 3 October.)

> This is a systematic campaign all over Europe and America, not just in Britain. . . . My family has been very much maligned and of course my son is not in politics at all. (Interview with the *Sunday Telegraph*, 12 October.)

Private Indian comment on Sanjay's startling elevation at first favoured the view that his mother, completely isolated from her colleagues' true feelings, and beset by the actual and psychological hazards of autocratic rule, could now be sure of no one but her son. But this did not explain his natural assumption of arbitrary authority, which could more readily be understood in terms of special knowledge and information in his possession concerning his mother's political functioning. Crucially damaging to her credibility and the cult of her popularity, for example, would be any evidence of a carefully rigged poll in 1971, more believable in view of Mrs Gandhi's subsequent behaviour. His induction into the limelight served a useful purpose in projecting a new "pragmatism" while Mrs Gandhi could continue to carry the "radical" posture:

"I believe in anything that will help the poor. . . .This is a point on which there is no difference of opinion between my mother and me." (9 April 1976.) On 20 March 1976 he declared that the "ideological struggle" of Right and Left had been started by "vested interests, the very forces that had supported the British in India, only to misguide youth."

Sanjay's anti-communism was an assurance to industry and the propertied class that they had nothing to fear, that no radical economic change would take place, an assurance borne out by events. The annual budget, by convention a closely guarded secret, became the subject of Sanjay's comments and revelations at a meeting of the Calcutta Chambers of Commerce in February 1976, and provided substantial tax relief for the upper class. The *Democratic World* commented on 28 March 1976:

> If the Finance Minister's budget proposals are any indication, India has no poor at all. If anything, the people who need succour the most are the rich. Else why should the man who has wealth of Rs. 15 lakhs pay a tax only a quarter of what he was asked to pay earlier. . . .

Sanjay received Soviet recognition and blessing when he visited the Soviet Union with his mother and brother in August 1976. Soviet support for the emergency had been announced when *Pravda* lauded India's "new economic plans" in July 1975, and Brezhnev told the 25th Congress of the Soviet Communist Party in February 1976 that the Soviet Union "attaches special importance to friendship with that great country, India . . . close political and economic cooperation with the Republic of India is our constant policy."

The Congress session in December 1975, a high point of the emergency, represented Mrs Gandhi's style in full flower. Between the last session, almost unnoticed in the outcry of economic distress and the rising tide of opposition opinion, and this one, Congress had suffered visible decline in reputation and popularity. In June it would have replaced Mrs Gandhi with another leader. The declaration of emergency obviated this need. With all crucial opposition eliminated via arrest, intimidation and censorship, the one-party one-leader idea could rise unhampered out of a levelled landscape as the single political presence. The session was celebrated as a 'national" event representing "nationalism." D.K. Barooah declared the Congress a movement, not a party, and in February 1976 at a public meeting on Marina Beach in Madras, he said its doors were open to "all who believed in Indian nationalism, and were honest in personal and public conduct. . . . [Congress was] a brotherhood of patriotic Indians who fulfilled these two conditions."

"So far as I know," said Mrs Gandhi on 21 August 1975, "force has not been used at all, not even in a small way anywhere." She repeated this in an interview with a Bombay weekly later: "There is no use of force and . . . there is no show of force whatsoever anywhere in the country. The truth is that the police have had less work since the Emergency than ever before."

Political arrests had been a feature of the past five years, beginning with the powerful assault on the CPI-M, and expanding during 1974 to fill jails with multi-party dissenters belonging to the Bihar Movement. The treatment of prisoners had drawn international enquiry and reportage, and aroused shocked comment in India. Government's budget for the police had doubled in five years. Mrs Gandhi had no basis whatever for the statement she made. On 19 September 1975 it was announced that Delhi would have a sixth police district and its police force would be expanded by 900 men. Brutality figured large in suppressing protest and extorting bribes, and torture became an instrument of vengeance. The number of citizens arrested during the months following the emergency was not revealed. Estimates by some Opposition parties, based on the number of their workers arrested, along with state government figures quoted from time to time, put the arrests at 110,000. There was no way of making an exact assessment. The exception to censorship on this subject was the capture of George Fernandes, Socialist Party Chairman and trade union leader, who went underground to escape arrest. His seizure in June 1976 was headlined as a police and intelligence triumph over the underground protest he was directing.

For the majority, "preventive detention" meant punishment in primitive conditions continually strained by waves of new arrests, a policy designed to enfeeble or break opposition while the emergency lasted. The prime targets were the Jan Sangh and the CPI-M, both with a strong following and influence in the academic and professional world. But the emergency also gave Mrs Gandhi a unique opportunity to stamp out "janta sarkar" and other aspects of the Bihar Movement. Specific cases of force used against prisoners, and terror exercised by the police, were brought to her notice and that of the Home Ministry, as well as to the President of India. There is no question that she was informed about these, and it is hardly credible that she was in ignorance otherwise of the enormities and excesses of the police state she had established. I quote some cases of violence on prisoners known even during the emergency. Tihar Jail, near Delhi, was the scene of brutality on 2 October 1975 when its political prisoners chose Mahatma Gandhi's birth anniversary to protest against the conditions of their confinement. The jail authorities turned criminal convicts on them with clubs and iron rods. Two Opposition leaders in Tihar Jail, Charan Singh, Chairman of the BLD, and Prakash Singh Badal of the Akali Dal, went on a 3-day hunger fast in protest.

On 22 October, six leading Socialist Party MPs wrote to the Prime Minister: "We have already addressed a few letters to the Home Minister regarding the ill-treatment of the political detenus in various jails. We have not received any reply to these letters so far."

The letter listed, among others, the following examples:

In Muzaffarpur Central Jail in Bihar where a large number of professors and political workers are detained . . . a lathi charge was made on September 9, 1975 by the jail authorities and criminal convicts were let loose on them. A large number of them received injuries, some of them serious. The injured persons included: Professor Thakur Prasad Sinha, Head of the Department of Mathematics of SRD College, Muzaffarpur; Professor Shyam Sunder Das of LS College, Muzaffarpur; Shri Sarbadhikeshwar Mishra, Shri Ranjit Singh and Shri Satya Narain Kesari. . . . Another case of lathi charge in Begusarai Jail is reported where Shri Ram Jiwan Singh, ex-MLA, who was recently operated for hernia, received head injuries. . . . On the 15th of August police arrested Shri Anupi Raut, whose son is a jawan in the Indian army. He was brutally assaulted while being taken to prison, as a result of which he died on August 26th. . . . We are seeking your intervention not only because the Home Minister did not reply to our letters earlier, but because we feel that political detention should not amount to punishment.[5]

Letter circulated via the underground protest movement in India.

On 24 May 1976 Mrs Alice Fernandes, mother of George Fernandes, then underground, wrote to the President of India with copies to the Prime Minister and other members of the central and state (Kerala) government:

Sir:

It is with a heavy sorrow-stricken heart that I am writing this, further to my letter dated May 12, 1976 (copy enclosed for ready reference), with the hope of obtaining justice at your hands. . . .

On Saturday, May 1 at about 9 p.m., my 44-year-old second son, Lawrence Fernandes, was taken away from our residence by the police, on the pretext that they wanted to interrogate him about the Habeas Corpus petition filed in February . . . by my third son, Michael Fernandes (an officer of the Indian Telephone Industries and a trade union leader) who has been detained without trial under MISA in prison since 22 December 1975. After keeping up this pretext for about an hour, the police began questioning him about the whereabouts of my eldest son, George Fernandes, and then subjected him in a most inhuman, reckless and ruthless manner to third degree methods of physical torture, going on with this torture into the small hours of the morning until 3 a.m. Besides beating him with clubs (until five of them were broken to pieces) they used a banyan tree root to clout him with and booted him and slapped him. They also used vulgar language in abusing him and our family, and threatened him that if he did not reveal the whereabouts of George Fernandes he would be thrown on the railway tracks and killed under a moving train, leaving no evidence of their hands in his death. They were actually preparing to do so about 3 a.m. when his physical condition had deteriorated to an almost irreparable state. After thus reducing him to a condition of physical, mental and nervous wreck, he was kept in solitary confinement until May 20, during which period he was subjected to further torture and interrogation. He was kept without food for 3 days and was not given proper food on other days, nor allowed cigarettes. During all these 20 days he was allowed bath only on 3 days and made to remain in the same clothes in which he was when he was taken away on treatment. He was taken to different doctors and hospitals, each time under a different and false name, impersonating him as a police officer, for treatment to keep him alive. On one night a doctor was brought to the police station itself for treating him.

On May 9 my son was taken by police car 300 kilometres away to Davengere, and on May 10 produced before the magistrate there, as though arrested in Davangere on the previous day. He was tortured and kept in a closed lockup there until May 11, and then brought back to Bangalore.... He was refused lawyer's help and not allowed to contact home or anybody else either by letter or by phone. He was not allowed newspapers and kept in solitary confinement. He was threatened with dire consequences if he reported to the magistrate or anybody else about his torture. Finally on May 20 he was produced in the Second Metropolitan Magistrate's chambers during lunch time and then removed to the Bangalore Central Prison where he has been detained in a cell meant for condemned criminals, or for convicts who are mentally unsound, or under punishment for violation of jail rules.

In addition to oral complaints, I had lodged written complaints, sent telegrams and letters to all concerned from the highest to the lowest level of authority, but without any result and without even acknowledgement, and the whereabouts of my son, Lawrence, had not been informed to us. On May 20, upon being informed by a lawyer, I went to the prison, and although I waited along with the lawyer from 6:45 p.m. to 7:30 p.m., I was not allowed to meet my son. On the 21st after waiting for over 3 hours, from 10:45, I was taken at about 2 p.m. to the cell to see him. I found him looking dead. He was unable to move without two persons helping him about, and then too with great pain and limping. His left side is without use, as if crippled, and both his left leg and hand are still swollen. He is in a mentally and physically wrecked condition, and is unable to talk freely without faltering. He is terribly nervous and mortally afraid of the police, of anyone in khaki uniform, of the approaching sound of anyone walking with shoes on, or of any other person, all of whom he fears to be interrogators and tormentors.... As if to deal a further blow, yet another page was added to this sordid, inhuman act by serving on him in the prison in the afternoon of May 22 an order of detention dated May 21, signed by the Commissioner of Police, detaining him under MISA.

Whatever I have stated here is on the basis of what the family could gather from Lawrence during the visits to him in the cell. . . . I urge upon you in the name of all that is good in civilised conduct of human beings and their governments, and in the name of justice, to order a thorough judicial enquiry into this barbaric torture, and take suitable action against the concerned authorities. I also urge that he should be transferred to a good hospital, and specialist medical and psychiatric treatment be given to him, and daily visits to him by the family allowed so that he may regain his mental and physical health and become a human being. . . .[6]

In August 1976 an *Indian Express* editorial referred to the deaths of 22 prisoners while being interrogated in lockup. The fact was quoted from a government-instituted enquiry in Uttar Pradesh.

A victim of arbitrary arrest and indecent treatment within my personal knowledge was the social worker who tried to persuade Sanjay to delay eviction of Jama Masjid traders and shopkeepers until suitable alternative arrangements had been made for them. The emergency's eviction campaign, to clear crowded and slum areas in cities, had caused severe hardship during the monsoon. Inder Mohan was visited on the midnight of 19 September 1975 by seven policemen in plainclothes who thrashed him and said they had orders to give him the third degree if he did not go quietly with them. He was taken in his nightclothes to a police lockup in a market area, which he described as a small room with a table in the corner and a stinking lavatory "full of muck" across a low partition wall. A bucket of filthy water outside the lavatory was meant for toilet use as well as drinking. At 11 next morning he was interrogated, and alternately charged with being a Naxalite sympathizer, a backer of Muslim fanaticism, and a CIA agent. He was accused of making an inflammatory speech some days earlier and a crumpled handbill was produced as "evidence." His decision to refuse food and water worried his captors who did not want a collapsed or dead body on their hands. On

---

[6]Letter circulated via the underground protest movement in India.

the fourth day of his fast they marched him in shackles to the district court where the magistrate remanded him to judicial lock-up in Chandni Mahal at Jama Masjid. He shared the room, replete with stinking lavatory, with four petty criminals, including a bicycle thief and a pickpocket, and was grateful for their company. Well-known and respected in the area as a worker of ten years' standing, Inder Mohan had been recognized on his march to the district court. A crowd collected outside the lockup, with a change of clothes, toothpaste, and food for him. He continued to refuse food. Publicity brought the Chairman of the Delhi Metropolitan Council to the scene. In his presence Inder Mohan broke his fast with fruit juice. A lawyer friend came to his defence. He was produced in court and sent to Tihar Jail on 23 September. He watched a queue of new political prisoners slapped, boxed and kicked from behind as they entered. Placed with 58 others in a barrack meant for 20, mice and mosquitoes added to the suffocating discomfort of human crowding, heat and humidity. The barrack had three bathing places and three lavatories. The toilet was stopped up in each one. Stagnant water collected outside bred mosquitoes and an overpowering stench. This was a "better class" barrack. His lawyer obtained bail three days later, and he was released with the warning that if he wished to avoid trouble he must stay away from the Jama Masjid area. A "case" was instituted against him. He was suspended from the government department that employed him. His name remained on the police list.

Mrs Gandhi's most celebrated prisoner was served with more subtle punishment. Jayaprakash Narayan came close to death in the care of government doctors and the country's two premier, government-owned, medical institutions, the All-India Medical Institute at Delhi and the Post-Graduate Institute at Chandigarh. Released in mid-November 1975 and brought a week later to Bombay's private Jaslok Hospital, his doctors expressed surprise at his kidney collapse not being diagnosed and treated much earlier. This dramatic deterioration contrasted sharply with his condition immediately prior to his arrest. JP had been on strenuous tours, addressed mammoth meetings in the intense heat and dust of May and June, without any adverse effects except fatigue. On his release, when facts concerning his illness became known, his condition gave rise to the chilly joke: "The British just put you in jail. But if they put you in jail now, you'll find yourself tied to

a kidney machine for the rest of your life." JP was released following a letter from his brother, Rajeshwar Prasad to the Prime
Minister, which described in detail the systematic deterioration,
month by month, in the prisoner's condition, at times bed-ridden
and unable to move without help.

Rajeshwar Prasad's letter, drafted at his request with my help
in the second week of November 1975, reads:

Madam,

You are aware that I am the brother of Shri Jayaprakash
Narayan.

I have been meeting him every month since July '75 in Chandigarh.

In July and August I found him in dubious but not serious ill
health. He had been suffering from low blood pressure, low
blood sugar, and had feelings of nausea.

In September I found that he had lost all appetite, was not
able to eat or relish any food. He had become very weak.

In October, when I met him on the 5th, he told me that he had
a severe pain in the stomach. A few days before I met him the
acuteness of the pain had subsided, but the pain was persisting,
and investigations and examinations were going on by the
doctors to find out the cause. At that time he was in the hospital.
His condition had deteriorated. He was very weak and his loss
of appetite persisted.

Subsequently in the later weeks of October our other relatives
met him. They found that he had been transferred to the hospital ward for better medical care and attendance. They found
him completely bed-ridden and on a liquid diet.

I met him again on the 7th of November. I found that he was
now able to move about in the room, but he had to be supported
during his movements, such is his weakness. He was still on a
liquid diet. And what is most alarming is that even after such
a long period, and in spite of several so-called thorough examinations and investigation, the disease has not been identified.
He is not even told what medicines are being administered to
him.

His general condition has fast deteriorated during these three
months. Swelling in the legs is still there. Two toes are bent.
There is some trouble in the eyes, apart from the fact that there

are swellings below both the eyes as big as hanging pouches.

I have very serious apprehensions that if his condition continues like this he might not survive for more than two months. This is causing us the greatest anguish. I have not discussed my anxiety with J P, nor mentioned that I would be writing to you, but I feel I must apprise you of his condition so that you can make your own assessment. Apart from the great personal tragedy that his loss would mean to our family, it is for you to decide whether it would be in the interests of the Government if JP dies in jail.
Yours truly,
Rajeshwar Prasad

Morarji Desai, aged 80, a prisoner in one of Haryana government's circuit houses, took the precaution of refusing to eat any cooked food, except what was on occasion provided by his family.

Arbitrary arrest, with the denial of appeal or trial, created the fear necessary to obedience, while censorship kept people ignorant of events and opinions adverse to government. Both were indispensable to a state of affairs where drama substituted for the real and arduous process of governing. Ministers carried out "surprise" visits to their departments to check on punctuality and much was made about getting to office on time. Orders to retire at 50 were served on "officers with a bad reputation for integrity." Government made examples, via arrest, intimidation and "tax raids," of "economic offendors." Overnight clearances of selected localities, and sterilization drives based on quotas, indifferent to age and whether or not a man was married and had any children at all, went into operation. It soon became clear that achievement not based on sound programmes was illusory and could not be sustained. In a free market economy prices would fluctuate. The low price of vegetable oil in the summer of 1975 had been the result of bumper crops of mustard seed and groundnut already in the market, while low grain prices were made possible by a good monsoon. No artificial low price level could be maintained and prices gradually took their course, with new high levels registered in a range of goods from kerosene and cooking gas to vegetables, fruit, and bus tickets. Violent uprisings, with hundreds killed and imprisoned, erupted in fury against evictions and sterilization, at Turkman Gate, Delhi, in April 1975, and the following year in Uttar Pradesh and Maharashtra. Continuing arrests, and repeated official references to the forces of disruption, made it clear that a large and politically-conscious country could not easily be reduced to submissive conformity. Government's anti-corruption measures acquired a spuriousness as the drive against economic offendors became linked with its own political opponents, and action to clean up the administration left the power structure around Mrs Gandhi intact, including those whose reputations had attracted the greatest public anger and criticism. Bansi Lal was appointed Union Defence Minister, while L.N. Mishra was enshrined for posterity on a postage stamp. At a ceremony on his 54th birth anniversary the Prime Minister called him "a shining example of bravery and courage and readiness to make the supreme sacrifice for the cause of his country." D.K. Barooah announced a statue of the late minister would be put up in the capital. Drama accompanied a scheme for the voluntary disclosure of wealth, promising tax evaders immunity from punishment or probe, and yielding government Rs 250 crores in tax revenue. The question remained that the tax department, armed with drastic powers under the emergency, could have attained its object more respectably, without showing leniency to the corrupt.

The language in use contributed to the atmosphere of bad theatre. Emergency perorations abounded in repetition and cliché. Political heterogeneity had accustomed Indians to every kind of political speech. From the flights of early Bengali oratory to the thoughtful evocations of Nehru, a tradition had been shaped. The speeches of trade unionist, district politician, student and worker, radical and conservative, had reflected a whole political development. Public speeches and political expression, now limited to the Congress-CPI combine, filled the air with verbal gunsmoke. The once dignified addresses of governors repeated it: "The tide of fascists and reactionaries has been repulsed but we must not be complacent." (Governor of Punjab, 14 August 1975.)

A joint statement issued by the Congress and CPI units in Bihar on 2 August warned people against complacency over the inactivity of reactionary conspirators. . . . They want to utilise the present economic distress of the people to instigate them in support of their diabolical venture . . . the counter revolutionaries fondly hope that the 21-point programme will fail so that they can engineer their sinister conspiracy once again.

D.K. Barooah referred to L.N. Mishra as "a symbol of our

struggle against the dark and sinister forces of fascism." This trend displayed its full psychosis at several "anti-fascist" conferences organized by the Congress and CPI. The first, held on 11 September 1975 at Town Hall, Amritsar, made much of human skulls and weapons found by the police and said fascist forces had gone underground to create chaos and destroy democracy. At the last, in Patna in December, advertised as a "world anti-fascist conference" D.K. Barooah spoke somewhat obscurely of "the dark forces of neo-imperialism and eastern racial arrogance which were combining in a sinister attempt to snuff out the light of democracy in this part of the world." Vested interests in India and abroad, he said, felt deeply hurt and frustrated by Congress policies, and had combined for a most vicious and violent onslaught on the party. Not much research was required, the Congress President declared, to spot the international forces behind this conspiracy. On 10 February 1976 in Trivandrum a session of the CPI's national council stressed vigilance against "the sinister conspiracy of imperialism and its monstrous agencies."

Mrs Gandhi's own statements sounded strangely fantasy-laden:

I am such a meek and mild person. (To Paul Saltzman of *Macleans Magazine*, Canada.)

I am a very humble person. (To Mauritius Broadcasting Corporation, 4 October 1975.)

Hundreds of thousands of poor and humble people of India will rise in revolt if any harm were done to her. (To a news conference at Bhubaneshwar, 27 September 1975.)

Had this [emergency] been a question about me as an individual I would have been least concerned, but it involved the Prime Minister of India. (Radio broadcast, 10 November 1975.)

The verdict of the Allahabad High Court did not cause any disturbance to me, nor was I tempted to take any decision or steps because of it. (27 December 1975.)

Until the age of 13 or 14 I hated people, some but not many, one or two, e.g., the police. But after 14 or 16 I cannot remember having hated anyone . . . . I am not at all concerned with things like achievement, success, failure. (*Hindustan Times* interview, 7 February 1976.)

I am not the Prime Minister because I like power. I want to

serve the people and their service is the only thing I have before me as my life's mission. (Public meeting, Durgapur, 3 March 1976.)

In January 1976 the Congress Party celebrated Mrs Gandhi's "dynamic decade" of power. The Directorate of Advertising and Visual Publicity released a book, *A Decade of Achievement 1966-75*, and the President opened a "Decade of Achievement" exhibition. Vidya Charan Shukla, Information and Broadcasting Minister, declared that more had been done during Mrs Gandhi's decade then during the last thousand years.

As against the fulsome self-congratulation of emergency language and its sharp attack on invisible antagonists, actual tragedy was met with subdued vocabulary and casual approach. Patna was flooded in the third week of August 1975. On 23 November Suman Dubey reported in the *Indian Express:*

> . . . it is hard to come by evidence of government-sponsored rehabilitation in this city. . . .Where rehabilitation is under way . . . it is mainly through the efforts of private voluntary agencies. . . .The condition of roadside dwellers, such as along Serpentine Road opposite the Circuit House, is the worst of all. With the cold of the winter settling in, all these people have for shelter are four bamboo boles supporting a thatch or piece of tin or pieces of cloth. . . .

A mine disaster of shocking magnitude at Chasnala on 27 December 1975 killed 372 workers. A warning by the Central Mining Research Station nine months earlier, that the mine was unsafe, was ignored. Rescue was delayed and the operation confused. A request for high performance American pumps was cancelled. On 11 January the UNI reported that five Indian pumps had developed "working difficulties" that day, five high capacity Polish pumps were yet to arrive, and only two Indian and two Soviet pumps were working. On 19 January when the first rescue attempt could be made, there was no sign of life in the mine. The Minister for Steel and Mines, admitting 372 deaths, told the Lok Sabha that conditions in India were better than in some countries, and everything possible would be done to improve mine safety.

The longest constitutional amendment Bill in the world revealed the emergency's true rationale. Boycotted by the Opposition, it received the emergency Parliament's sanction at the end of 1976, and established the institutions and powers of authoritarian government.

An individual's headlong will and urge to power had transformed the government and politics of India. The setting for personal rule had now been consolidated by the Constitution.

CHAPTER FOURTEEN

CONCLUSIONS

As a member of the Congress Working Committee, Mrs Gandhi made her debut into politics at the highest level. Her first responsibility admitted her to the rarefied atmosphere of policy and programme, the top level of decision-making, without exposure to the processes leading up to it or encountering in a systematic way the lower levels where practical experience of an organization is garnered through a daily brush with its sentiment and its problems. Policy and decision were seen by her as handed down. The ultimate attitude of a party dependent on the goodwill and votes of an electorate has to take note of local situations, personalities, and compulsions. The "executive suite," setting Mrs Gandhi at the uppermost layer of confabulation, without a thorough education in the levels supporting it, looked to her like an easy exercise in authority. On gaining ascendancy in her party she took, of deliberation, steps to dismantle the effectiveness of the "process," establishing, as she gained control of the machine, a single omnipotent command. This left her no possibility of learning from a complex developing organism, and her concept of leadership as "pinnacle" authority, unaccountable to any forum, perpetuated a great gulf between her and the party. No connecting links could, except as temporary devices, span the gulf, since these had to be reshuffled to prevent local seats of power from developing. The loyalty she demanded thus became an affair of change and chance. Loud and repeatedly expressed, its expression often had no meaning, a fact she was well aware of, for flattery, unless it was accompanied by subservience, was quickly detected and disposed of by her. The stripping of H.N. Bahuguna's chief ministership in Uttar Pradesh in 1976 is a classic example of Mrs Gandhi's treatment of allegiance when it came from a sturdy and popular politician with roots of his own. Rival power in the states was not permitted to surface by so much as a flicker. But even an assumption of indispensability to the Prime Minister in a more subordinate capacity was unwelcome and could be met with reprimand or suitable action. Favourites at court could not count on remaining so, hence Mrs Gandhi had no sincere inner circle to rely on. The atmosphere and intrigues of a medieval palace prevailed. Similarly, she created a situation where she could not depend on the loyalty of her senior cabinet colleagues. From these, her one-time equals, public statements or other signs of allegiance were extracted. An abject example was Y.B. Chavan's (then Minister for External Affairs) on 8 March 1975 in Sholapur, Maharashtra, when he told Congress workers he had no political ambition and no stake in the prime ministership.

Chavan had been in politics all his life. An activist in the Quit India agitation, a respected Chief Minister of Maharashtra, an able and popular Union Defence Minister during the Indo-Pakistan war in 1965, this was for him a pathetic act of submission showing how senior Congressmen of recognized ability had been humbled in obedience to the leadership cult. On 19 January 1976, unable to attend a Congress Party symposium in New Delhi to praise Mrs Gandhi's decade, Chavan took the precaution of explaining his absence by letter, setting forth in it the standard florid tribute for her "amazingly firm and far-sighted leadership." The letter ended: "Apart from the fact that you have grown to the stature of a leading world figure, what is important for me is that you have grown to become a symbol of the hopes and aspirations of millions of Indians. As one of them, I wish you many more years of achievement at the helm of the nation's affairs."

A more significant rival cut to size was Jagjivan Ram, then Union Food and Agriculture Minister, who was assigned the task of justifying the emergency in the Lok Sabha on its opening day, 21 July 1975. As government's mouthpiece, Jagjivan Ram's speech contained the compulsory homily to the Prime Minister and such stock phrases, clearly not his own, as "the nefarious plans of the [railway] strikers were dashed to the ground." Brought up in the hard school of untouchability, Jagjivan Ram had known no easy road to power, and much was expected of a man whose command of a substantial untouchable vote could have carried weight in his equation with Mrs Gandhi. Jagjivan Ram was a contender for power when the move to replace Mrs

Gandhi after the Allahabad High Court judgement began with the Congress Parliamentary Party collecting signatures supporting the election of a new leader.

These two men, playing the waiting game, missed their opportunity and evidently found it preferable, in their sixties, to continue where they were than to suffer total political eclipse or arrest. If they tried earlier to dislodge Mrs Gandhi through intra-party manoeuvres, there were definite limits on how hard they could try in circumstances where surveillance had become pervasive and routine. Once a police state was openly established, they could not try at all. The average man, of any nationality, feels fear and caution when there is reason to feel it. A picture comes vividly to mind of Chavan's arrival at the French Embassy's national day reception on 14 July 1975, accompanied by seven gunmen. Wearing bush shirts that distinguished them from the invited guests, who wore "lounge suit or national dress" as specified by the invitation, they made no attempt to hide the pistols bulging from their trouser pockets. Clustering around Chavan, their presence quickly set normal conversation at rest. Chavan, of genial and pleasant disposition, looked drawn and strained by the "protection" he was receiving. The glitter of naked power during the early months of the emergency served as a business-like warning to Mrs Gandhi's senior colleagues, and ended all political surmise and conjecture about their own possible future roles.

An extraordinary range and depth of human encounter might have served Mrs Gandhi as "education" for the political process during her father's lifetime, through the ebb and flow of Nehru's relationships, intimate and public, with individuals and the mass. Her own temperament set limits on this opportunity. No miracle of "love and affection," so eloquently described by Nehru as his cherished gift from the Indian people—a transforming personal and political experience for him—could come her way and work its mutuality. A heritage of devotion, waiting for her, changed in her hands to the public's awe and fear of her. Politics was for her, therefore, the very antithesis of the experience it had been for her father, for whom even a mass meeting was people, and one he addressed as such. Mrs Gandhi's meeting with the mass was gradually reduced to a formal encounter. Her public personality, compared at first with her father's, lost this resemblance as it took on the aura and exaggerations of The Leader. Her mass meetings were accompanied by increasingly heavier management, armed security and distance from the crowd that gave them an artificial aspect of "performance" alien to Indian politics. At one time undeterred by situations of risk, she showed less confidence as she abandoned democratic procedures and relied on her intelligence and police. A government officer referring to Mrs Gandhi's visit to Ludhiana, Punjab, some months before the emergency, said she had needed more security than Linlithgow, unpopular British Viceroy during the 1942 Quit India upheaval. In 1974 the contrast between her meetings and the vast spontaneous crowds drawn to Jayaprakash Narayan's public engagements was particularly striking. Remote from the seat and emblems of power, with nothing but his personal reputation to attract the crowd, and with authority mounted against him, JP represented an abiding urge: the desire for a leader whose life was his message. Mrs Gandhi thus missed the crux and essence of leadership in India. More and more her eminence had to be buttressed, arranged, safeguarded from natural political processes, from the moons and tides of Indian politics in particular. She could not permit any natural development within her party or the country that might unseat her. The following she commanded progressively shed its thoughtful, enlightened, discriminating sections, and was reduced either of the cynical camp-follower or the "lamp post" variety, those whom she had raised to office out of mediocrity or obscurity, and who were not troubled by independent thought or the critical faculty. Prestige and following in India had taken note of the kind and quality of human being, rather than the temporal power, if any, he wielded. The emergency, establishing a police state, and eliminating civil liberties and opposing opinion, illustrated Mrs Gandhi's total retreat behind the barrier of force. By 1975 she had become a prisoner of her own politics. She would never be able to come out from behind the barrier and feel safe with democratic processes again.

Talented and abundant political leadership has been a feature of modern India, an outgrowth of the national movement, for 30 years a training ground under Mahatma Gandhi. The Congress was the only liberation movement in Asia to successively convert itself into a political party, and to provide stable government in the post-independence era. But the leadership phenomenon has extended to the Opposition. Gifted men of the Right and Left, with a high degree of individualism, have been able to capture the Indian imagination sufficiently to show election results and form state governments. In the Indian context state leadership has constituted impressive power, backed not only by large numbers, but by the culture, language, and economics of a region. Against this canvas Mrs Gandhi stands out as the only manufactured leader, consistently built up through the media and other channels, and relentlessly imposed on the Indian mind through a campaign of emotional appeal and outcry resorting to her father's name. The campaign of manufacture was extended to her son, Sanjay, imposed on the nation in an exactly similar way but without even the slim credentials Mrs Gandhi brought to her job. Her ceaseless drive to establish herself as India's exclusive leader has revealed the fundamental anxiety and weakness in her position, driving her to measures that a genuinely mass-based, psychologically secure leader would never have needed to take.

Considered a master of political technique, Mrs Gandhi's career classically demonstrates, in fact, the failure of political functioning, and its substitution, when failure endangered her political survival, by "direct action" or outright authoritarianism. She became Prime Minister through the party's traditional method of consensus, one she fully endorsed and cooperated with at the time. She discarded consensus when it went against her in her party's choice of a presidential candidate for the country, and abandoned political ethics altogether in her support of another candidate. Unsure of her continuance as leader of the party, she used street arousal as a technique to proclaim herself the "people's" choice. Both these tactics depended for their success on moves outside her party, her cabinet and accepted political standards. Six years later, faced with the Allahabad High Court judgement and the Congress Parliamentary Party's move to replace her, she responded swiftly with the emergency, imprisoning and outlawing opposition, both within and outside her party.

The absence of disciplined political functioning shows up, too, in Mrs Gandhi's remarkable indifference to the cultivation of good comradeship and goodwill with her partymen, ordinarily of great importance to a democratic politician. At turning points, in 1969 and 1975, when her future was in the balance, she fought a bitter battle to the kill, leaving no scope for compromise, no detail to chance. At both stages, the people who had started out as her supporters—the ruling clique of the Old Congress who had raised her to power in 1966, and the radicals who had backed her in the Congress split in 1969—became baffled and astonished by her behaviour in the course of events, and finally, in self-respect unable to accept it. Indifference to party opinion is highly unusual in democratic politics where differences of opinion must be faced and accommodation sought, and where a politician's future is linked to his party's acceptance of him. Yet though Mrs Gandhi destroyed her credit with two entirely different groups, she did not on either occasion suffer the political consequences thereof.

In the light of the Supreme Court order in Balraj Madhok's case for an examination of ballots cast in the 1971 elections, the mid-term election can no longer be ruled out as a category of successful "coup" staged by Mrs Gandhi. Many who would not have considered an election fraud of any proportion conceivable in India, or any respectable leadership capable of resorting to it, have had time to think again during the years that followed, when Mrs Gandhi's uses of power did not allow ethical considerations to stand in her way. She showed herself unburdened by conscience, scruples or soul-searching. Her profound belief in her own indispensability adds weight to the argument that she could not risk getting less than a two-thirds majority at the polls, and solved this dilemma matter-of-factly and efficiently though artifice. In this way she also ensured a docile majority for any future plans. The Congress Party in Parliament that came into being with the mid-term election accepted almost without demur the constitutional changes after the emergency—Mrs Gandhi having taken the precaution of jailing its dissident members beforehand—though the party outside Parliament did not uniformly accept them. The opposition view, that fundamental constitutional changes could only be considered by a constituent assembly elected for the purpose, and not, in any case steered through a parliament that had outlived its five-year mandate, could be ignored altogether.

All of this, while it may be termed "politics" in a broad general sense, is far from accepted political behaviour in a democratic framework, and wholly alien to established principles and practices in India. The emergency climaxed her failure as a politician. Coming upon the decay of her personal and political image, her shock at the High Court judgement, and her party's series of defeats at the polls during 1974 and 1975, it rang down the curtain on the political process altogether, sweeping from sight the issues of corruption, political scandal, and economic mismanagement for which she and her party were being indicted.

There appears to be no logic in a situation where a party leader in a parliamentary system thrives regardless of opinion in the party; where she not only ignores party support but alienates it, ultimately imprisoning those who seek, through legitimate democratic channels, to elect another leader during the breathing space provided by the High Court for this purpose. Yet this form of illogic has been a consistent factor through Mrs Gandhi's career. Her sources of power have resided outside party forums, and if we are to include the 1971 elections as selectively rigged, outside the electoral process. Her emphasis has been on control of the party machine and money, and of men through it. Her expansion and use of intelligence and paramilitary forces has taken the place of ordinary administration. The art and tasks of real governing have diminished correspondingly as her individual power grew. The transition to dictatorship was not made overnight. It was the last step in a steady erosion of democratic procedures. The ground had been prepared—politically, administratively, openly and clandestinely—for the final tilt.

If Indian events provide no clue to Mrs Gandhi's behaviour, some logic must be sought outside these to explain both the manner and the success of her functioning. Since 1969 the Soviet Union had thrown its immense prestige and support behind the leadership of Mrs Gandhi. Beginning with denunciations of "rightist reactionaries" in her party who were said to be blocking radical policies, a tide of forceful official Soviet comment had buttressed, exalted, and protected Mrs Gandhi against Indian opposition to her, a vocal flourish surrounding the solid political-cultural-economic scaffolding erected by the Indo-Soviet Treaty of 1971. The Bihar Movement and Jayaprakash Narayan's leadership were savagely attacked by *Pravda*, while on 21 July 1975 *Pravda* lauded "India's new economic plans." Admiration for Mrs Gandhi was pointedly expressed by Leonid Brezhnev at the 25th congress of the Soviet Communist Party in Moscow in February 1976. Compliments travelled both ways with great regularity. On 6 April 1976 Bansi Lal, new Defence Minister, expressed "a sense of deep gratitude to the Soviet Union for appreciating our special problems and difficulties." Government denials in India's censored press were particularly significant as confirmation of events and policy. On 24 July 1975 K.R. Ganesh, Union Minister for Petroleum and Chemicals, "denied here today the presence of any Soviet experts in Delhi to help the Union Government." Ganesh said "the Rightist parties had started a whispering campaign after the proclamation of emergency that 100 Soviet experts were working in Delhi and that the Soviet Union had assured the Government of all assistance." Thus the Soviet presence as an armoured escort to Mrs Gandhi's leadership may provide a logic to her otherwise puzzling and irrational behaviour. This logic had a life of its own, unaffected by the CPI's ups and downs in prestige, power shares and ideological thrust in its relationship with the Congress, with Mrs Gandhi, and after the emergency with Sanjay Gandhi. Though the CPI noticeably lost influence, and became increasingly disillusioned with the ruling party, the Soviet ballast remained undisturbed.

Mrs Gandhi's attempts to explain why she declared an emergency, based on a charge of "conspiracy" to dislodge her and her government, unsupported by evidence or argument, transparently lacked truth and credibility, while they revealed her far from healthy or rational frame of mind. The alarm she raised over internal and external threats to the country, over the country's unity and its economic problems, had no basis in fact as a justification of emergency. No crisis but that of Mrs Gandhi's own political survival necessitated the emergency in 1975. That it was a coup for self-protection was borne out with omnibus amendments to the Constitution giving legal definition and sanction to authoritarian power, and with the fevered campaign to promote a dynastic succession, leaving no shade or shred of democracy to impede Mrs Gandhi's design.

In contrast, genuine crisis conditions have been met and resolved by Indian leadership in the past through genuine practical measures that took no toll of existing freedoms. Independence itself brought a formidable quota of crises: partition murders on a mass scale, whole transport systems paralyzed when essential supplies could not be moved, huge movements of population throwing the new nation's unity and stability into grave jeopardy, anxieties accompanying the integration of the princely states into the Union, the 1947 war in Kashmir and the continuing pressure for solution in Kashmir. There followed periods of flood, famine, and crop failure, communist insurrection in Telegana, Naga insurgency, the Chinese attack, fevers aroused by the linguistic states, problems of law and order. At no juncture had the leadership seized on any of these very real crises to shut off democratic processes and end freedom.

Nehru, who could with ease have become a dictator, utterly rejected the idea, believing that India's people, long exploited and deprived, needed growth and nurture in freedom and expression; that while dictatorship and conformity might achieve the military grandeur and destructive potential necessary for great power status, they seldom achieve the basic requirements of life and dignity faster than a free society; and that freedom, far from being a luxury for the affluent, is a fundamental human aspiration, even more necessary to those who have little else and from whom much is required in courage and endeavour. Thus the Indian people were led between 1947 and 1966 within the framework of consent into a very different dimension of life and expectation. Nothing less than a revolution took place under Nehru, with defined programmes and definite steps towards a socialist order. The base India stood on when Mrs Gandhi came to power—whether in industry and agriculture, or the confidence created by free political institutions—was the result of the Nehru years. The problems India was then facing were those arising out of change. Mrs Gandhi's style resulted not only in a very different political order, culminating in dictatorship, but in the destruction of a vital human process, without any assurance of compensating economic gain. Inheriting a flourishing enterprise, she halted it and reversed its direction.

The most unusual aspect of India's political system has been the nature and quality of its leadership, committed to serve and safeguard the liberties of a people not experienced enough yet in the exercise of freedom to defend free institutions for themselves. India's leadership before Mrs Gandhi was among the world's most sensitive, civilized, and humane. Her two predecessors treated their task of guiding the millions of an underdeveloped nation as an adventure of faith and trust, in circumstances where dictatorship would have been the cruder and more facile choice. Mrs. Gandhi's recourse to dictatorial power was a need of her own temperament, and not of any new need in the Indian situation. That she succeeded in establishing it is not surprising. The twentieth century in Europe provides ample example of nations with far better and older opportunities in education, economic development, and political experience who fell prey to totalitarianism.

That Indians, who in 1947 had their first opportunity in centuries to live as free human beings, responsible for themelves, should have so succumbed, is not strange. The tragedy of this situation was Mrs Gandhi's betrayal of a trust, and had she succeeded the destruction thereby of a heroic experiment, unique in Asia.

CHAPTER FIFTEEN

POSTSCRIPT

The Constitution of 1950 allowed the government, under conditions of emergency, to postpone elections to Parliament for a year at a time. Mrs Gandhi took advantage of this provision to postpone the election due in March 1976 for one year. In November 1976 she announced a further year's postponement. Her November decision, and its sudden reversal on 18 January 1977 when she announced an election for March, revealed once again personal temperament rather than orderly political process as characteristic of the style she had brought to Indian politics. Like her declaration of emergency, the new decision appeared to be intimately connected with her estimate of her own political fortune, and now, in addition, that of her son's.

Mrs Gandhi had declared an emergency when her party's future was at a distinct crossroads. In the preceding months the Congress had suffered stunning defeats in four out of five by-elections at the hands of the Opposition combine produced by the Bihar Movement, known as the Janta Front. These defeats had been climaxed on 12 June 1975 by the Front's victory in the Gujarat state election. While by-elections and state elections are not always pointers to major change on the national scene, the emergence for the first time of a united Opposition as victor showed a new weight in politics that could not be ignored. The Congress might be returned to power in the next election, but not since 1967 had its credit been so low. If it was returned with a greatly reduced majority, it would pave the way for Opposition governments in several states, and the breakdown of its monolithic rule at the Centre and states since 1971-72. The Bihar Movement, apart from securing the cooperation of four political parties, had been a potent force in intensifying political awareness in the countryside and organizing new sections of the population against the Congress. It had also stir-red the conscience of Congressmen and driven high office-holders in the party and the government to forthright criticism. By June 1975 the cracks in the Congress were plain to see, but it was plainer still that Mrs Gandhi had a fight ahead of her to retain control of it. For those now grouping against her she represented the autocratic structure that would have to be dismantled if the Congress were to recover the confidence of its own rank and file, as well as mass sympathy and backing. The Allahabad High Court judgement invalidating her 1971 elections to Parliament for two violations of the election law gave the Congress a quiet opportunity to replace her without any tinder being lit over the event or appeals to loyalty and emotion being launched. The citadel of power she had built did not permit a normal open debate about a change in leadership. But Chandersekhar, Mohan Dharia, Krishna Kant, Ram Dhan, and others had already made their views public and had become the focus of admiring attention. This was reinforced by the wall of unspoken resentment her style of leadership had brought into being. The astute and ambitious among her rivals in the party bided their time for the denouement that now seemed inevitable.

Mrs Gandhi's characteristic recourse to "spontaneous" rallies arranged at her residence, this time to condemn the High Court judgement and uphold her as the people's choice, and her effort to stir and inflame feeling in the capital, was drawing little response. The routine had staled. Small, straggling groups, rounded up with difficulty from Delhi and its environs, sat polite, patient, and bored in the enervating heat, listening to the now familiar claim to unique sacrifice, ancestry, and position. The signs, for any temperament not comfortable with the democratic process and the change it now seemed certain to bring, were ominous. Against an impending possibility of checkmate Mrs Gandhi declared an emergency and launched a police state, with one gesture disposing of her opponents in and outside her party and immobilizing the gathering opposition to the Congress. What were the factors, nineteen months later, that influenced her to risk an election?

The element of risk now seemed small, as far as a Congress win was concerned, for it had held the stage without competition for those nineteen months. During that period Mrs Gandhi had disciplined the dissidents in her party through arrest or its threat. She had successfully introduced, and systematically pushed the idea of dynastic rule, a thing she would have found difficult, if not

impossible to do in normal times. The Opposition was severely
handicapped by nineteen months out of the public gaze, with no
chance to make its views heard, while the government, with its
monopoly of public meetings, demonstrations, and media control,
had been able to keep up a steady barrage of accusation and
condemnation in extreme language against it. Some Opposition
leaders were crippled with illness in long confinement. The Chairman
of the Socialist Party, George Fernandes, was not granted release
to stand for election, and had to do so from jail. For thousands of
party workers, release from jail would mean first of all the urgent
rehabilitation of their families, often reduced to severe hardship
with the sole wage-earner in prison. For the Opposition as a
whole the process of reassembling, collecting funds, and preparing
for an election would be painful. The censored press—its independent editors dismissed or silenced— had daily assured Mrs Gandhi
of her popularity. It is certain she believed the election would
be a formal affair renewing her mandate.

There were other hopeful signs for a ruling party victory. The
emergency had benefited by two good harvests when grain had
been abundant and its price comparatively stable. With about 80
per cent of the average Indian budget spent on foodgrains, inflation in the basic needs had been kept in check. High inflation
in the West at this time had provided Indian exports with a noticeably improved market, and these had fetched better prices,
adding substantially to India's foreign currency reserves, as had
government's belated measures against smuggling and tax evasion.

As against these advantages, the prices of many goods had risen
and there were signs of shortage. Protest had remained alive, confirmed by expanded police vigilance and continuing arrests. The
law courts had tried to act as a brake upon the government's arbitrary behaviour and to uphold prisoners' rights. In Delhi and
Muzzafarnagar (U.P.) there had been large-scale and bloody riots
against forced sterilization and premptory eviction. And vigorous
objection to the constitutional amendment package giving the
Prime Minister virtually unlimited powers had erupted when the
government modified the ban on public meetings to permit a
degree of debate on the amendments. The outcry against the
amendments, not confined to the intelligentsia and the cities, was
heard in the countryside. The Indian villager had come to rely on
the court system for redress of wrongs. Courts took time but he

could expect justice from them. Under the new dispensation, the powers of the courts to deal with land and other specific categories of cases was to be reduced or eliminated. For land cases, government tribunals were to be appointed. Small landowers and the landless feared that local vested interests and government bosses would end all impartial decision-making.

A combination of these plus and minus factors may have decided Mrs Gandhi to go to the polls while she had complete control of the situation and before affairs, in the shape of man or nature, took an uncontrollable turn.

But the election appears to have been necessary for another reason. Mrs Gandhi had used the emergency to bury the scandal surrounding her son's business ventures and to raise him to an exalted status surrounded by the obeisance due to a hereditary heir apparent. Though he had no official position or political experience, and was not even a primary member of the party, Sanjay was hailed as the leader and inspiration (even though he was not official president) of the Youth Congress. A concerted drive was launched to swell the organization's membership to provide him with a following personally loyal and beholden to him, and to empower it with independence of authority and action. Mrs Gandhi introduced the new perspective at the annual session of the Congress in Gauhati (Assam) in December 1976 when she praised the exemplary role of the Youth Congress and spoke of its importance for the country's future. Sanjay had, since the emergency, been a force to reckon with in political and administrative decisions in Delhi and in the states, and in December 1975 he had been escorted with fanfare into the party limelight at the Komagata Maru annual session at Chandigarh, but even earlier there were strong indications that Mrs Gandhi had succession in mind. On 19 September 1975 in a speech to educators she had denied allegations of vast powers in her hands and said that nowhere in the world had the head of government less power than she had. "Every decision," she said, "has to go through a number of levels." In the same speech she continued. "But I may not be alive. What happens then? What is the next rank? Who is going to carry the fight forward?" In normal democratic procedure who would this be but the next democratically chosen leader and his cabinet? Why, with less power than any head of government in the world, did Mrs Gandhi then raise the question of what may happen after her?

The rise and projection of Sanjay, in the face of his reputation and the bitter resentment against his arrogant use of power during the emergency, reveal a curious yet classic flaw in his mother's otherwise tough political armour, without which it is conceivable that Mrs Gandhi's experiment in dictatorship might have survived an election, or at least not ended in her own humiliating defeat at the polls. Her refusal to acknowledge the facts about Sanjay's behaviour and transactions had been an emotional blind spot. She now seized the moment to consolidate his future so that if she died within the next five or six years, his power base was secure. The 1971 Parliament, a body largely subservient to her individual authority, had secured her own power base. The 1977 Parliament would ensure Sanjay's if it brought in a majority of his handpicked supporters.

As soon as censorship was suspended for the election, compaigning permitted, and the fear guaranteeing obedience and silence lifted, it was obvious this strategy could not be employed. A political avalanche in support of the Janata Party had overtaken opinion, with huge crowds walking miles to listen in pindrop silence to Mrs Gandhi's recent prisoners. Another impending development fast followed, with a break in the Congress led by Jagjivan Ram, his formation of Congress for Democracy, and its electoral alliance with the Janata Party. Jagjivan Ram gave as his reason for silence thus far that, had he made his intention clear any earlier, the election would not have taken place and he would probably never have been heard of again—reasons the public considered valid, judging by the enthusiasm and support his breakaway received and his own election to Parliament. In these circumstances further erosion in the Congress could not be risked, with elements in the party known to be antagonistic to Sanjay's domination. The original list, with heavy weightage to Youth Congress names, had to be abandoned, and a majority of the old candidates brought back.

Yet Sanjay's rise had been made possible by the police state, and it could have been consolidated within those credentials. He himself, according to her statement in a post-election party meeting, had advised his mother against an election. Was it necessary to risk an election for this purpose?

The answer may lie in the complexity of human personality. India's leader, from 1966 to 1977, had been a woman whose childhood, education, and family tradition had provided her with unusual opportunities for training in democratic ideals, yet whose own temperament had never felt entirely comfortable with this inheritance. The stages of her career as Prime Minister made it plain she was not a democrat by belief or instinct. She firmly believed in her own indispensability. Concessions, compromise, and discussion signified weakness to her, and opposition jarred and angered her. She needed the constant assurance of acceptance and loyalty to feel secure. Psychologically she seemed incapable of settling down into the routine of conducting the business of government, doing the homework practical decisions required, or understanding that in a democratic country the leader is fallible and dispensable, besides being mortal. She had watched democracy and indispensability successfully at work in her father's lifetime, and had assumed the combination would be hers by right of birth. When it did not appear to be so, she looked for reasons outside the pale of fact or logic. As a child she had imagined herself a Joan of Arc, a liberator of her people with the forces of the foreign power ranged against her. As an adult she continued to see herself as a martyr. Though, as Nehru's daughter, she had from the start an assured and prestigious place in the party, and became the choice of its senior leaders for its highest post, yet she imagined vested interests obstructing and threatening her, and used the agreement to seize and retain absolute control. She saw enemies in the normal democratic process and frequently claimed she was in physical danger from the Opposition. She gave extreme labels—"fascist" and "reactionary"—to her critics, and to a genuine mass movement, Gandhian in method and programme, led by a nationally revered figure. Finally she assumed dictatorial powers under the cloak of an "emergency" on unproven accusations of conspiracy against herself and her government.

Democracy was not Mrs Gandhi's style, but it remained an insistent craving. In a world where leadership had to be one of two kinds, coercive or persuasive, she could not resolve her dilemma and fell between the two, debasing democratic values and destroying the system while repeatedly avowing her dedication to it. The confusion gave her pronouncements during the emergency a ring of unbalance. With tens of thousands of citizens jailed without charges or trial, and her critics outlawed and silenced, she could calmly and convincedly repeat, "I am a democrat." The repetition carried that element of yearning we often have for what we ourselves are not, and cannot be.

Why should democracy have been a craving in such a character at all? It was part of India's British connection. It had been the heart and soul of India's struggle for freedom, recalling much older values in the soil. It had been fundamental to her father's philosophy, and the letter and spirit of his government. The modern Indian imagination could not easily set democracy aside. It was a spectre that haunted Mrs Gandhi. She longed for a democratic image and never admitted to having any other. It was an image an election could only strengthen and brighten, and a continuing emergency could only tarnish. She did not doubt that its outcome would be favourable to her party and to herself. But it might also achieve the deeply desired establishment of Sanjay as her successor.

India's sixth national election to Parliament was transformed by the events of the emergency to a referendum on a single issue: Would Indians give the Congress Party a mandate to continue the form of dictatorship established by Mrs Gandhi in June 1975, or would they choose to return to a rule of law and the restoration of civil liberties? Of an electorate of 320 million, roughly 60 per cent voted a new party to power, reducing the Congress for the first time since independence, to a minority. Significantly, Mrs Gandhi and her son, along with the ministers who had represented unpopular policies—V.C. Shukla (Information and Broadcasting), H.R. Gokhale (Law), Bansi Lal (Defence)—went down to shattering defeat at the polls. George Fernandes, who had to contest from prison, won by one of the largest majorities of any candidate.

The election made history for other reasons. The Janata Party which defeated the Congress was inspired and led by the most unusual figure in Indian politics since Mahatma Gandhi. Jayaprakash Narayan's return to national prominence as leader of the Bihar Movement in 1974 had the profound impact it did because it restored the breath of idealism to the political controversy and revived echoes of an age of grand striving still fresh in Indian memory. Long regarded as an impractical idealist and visionary, it was his supremely practical accomplishment to unite the Opposition and guide it to victory on the issue that the masses need both bread and freedom and there is no separating the two.

The election revived two political processes stunted by Mrs Gandhi's style and techniques of governing party and country: the natural development of the post-Nehru leadership within the Congress, and the natural development of an opposition as a growing chellenge to the Congress. The myth of indispensability was quietly disposed of at the polls and a path opened for a new, perhaps unknown leadership of the Congress. With the vote in favour of the Congress concentrated in the south, its centre of power, for the first time since its birth, might shift to the south. The expanding political awareness of the electorate had first made itself felt with significant Opposition victories in 1967. It was reflected in the Opposition's by-election victories in early 1975, while the 1977 elections reflected the new preference in the mass vote. The *Indian Express* editorial of 22 March 1977, entitled "Finest Hour," called attention to this mass awareness, not a small, tidy, city elite, when it wrote:

> The average Indian voter has demonstrated his maturity in exercising his franchise and has taught a lesson to rulers who might be inclined to take him for 'granted as a passive and pliable pawn in the game of power politics. Indian democracy will never again be the same after the traumatic experience of the last two years. No future government, however large its majority in Parliament, can afford to assume that it can drive a coach and four through the Constitution and the laws, make inroads on the liberties of the people and hope to escape nemesis from an outraged people. It is significant that the people's vote went against Mrs. Gandhi despite all her warnings that her defeat would mean plunging the country into chaos. . . .

The election's immediate achievement was the restoration of a legitimate political process, more important in the long run than the question of whether the coalition it had brought to power would survive. Indians no longer faced the terrors and uncertainties of arbitrary power or the prospect of dynastic rule. The electorate's rejection of the dictatorship Nehru's daughter had established, and of her leadership, was a vindication of Nehru's own passionate conviction that his countrymen must live and grow in freedom.

INDEX